MICHIGAN

GETTING STARTED GARDEN GUIDE

Grow the Best Flowers, Shrubs, Trees, Vines & Groundcovers

First published in 2013 by Cool Springs Press, an imprint of the Quayside Publishing Group, 400 First Avenue North, Suite 400, Minneapolis, MN 55401

Cool Springs Press titles are also available at discounts in bulk quantity for industrial or sales-promotional use. For details write to Special Sales Manager at Cool Springs Press, 400 First Avenue North, Suite 400, Minneapolis, MN 55401 USA. To find out more about our books, visit us online at www.coolspringspress.com.

Library of Congress Cataloging-in-Publication Data

Myers, Melinda.
  Michigan getting started garden guide : grow the best flowers, shrubs, trees, vines & groundcovers / Melinda Myers.
      p. cm.
  Includes bibliographical references and index.
  ISBN 978-1-59186-569-8
  1. Gardening--Michigan. I. Title.

SB453.2.M5M94 2013
635.09774--dc23

2013021175

Acquisitions Editor: Billie Brownell
Design Manager: Brad Springer
Layout: Danielle Smith

Printed in China
10 9 8 7 6 5 4 3 2 1

MICHIGAN

GETTING STARTED GARDEN GUIDE

Grow the Best Flowers, Shrubs, Trees, Vines & Groundcovers

Melinda Myers

COOL
SPRINGS
PRESS
Home and Garden Experts™

MINNEAPOLIS, MINNESOTA

DEDICATION AND ACKNOWLEDGMENTS

This book is dedicated to Pete. Thanks for joining me on life's journey. I am looking forward to all the new adventures that lie ahead.

A huge "thank you" to my editor Billie Brownell. You have been patient beyond belief, supportive, and kept me moving forward.

Thanks to the Michigan gardeners who have invited me into your gardens and to your gardening events. Your generosity is endless and your enthusiasm feeds my gardening passion and love for what I do.

A special thanks to all the University and Extension specialists, horticulture educators, horticulturists, master gardeners, greening volunteers, and professionals in related fields, as well as my friends and mentors in the media and garden writers, who have so willingly shared their enthusiasm, knowledge, experience, and perception to help me make this book and my career a great experience. Your insights are invaluable and make a difference in every garden you touch and to every gardener or professional you meet.

To my former, current, and future students in the traditional classroom, garden setting, botanical gardens, and lectures—thanks for your wide-eyed exuberance and varied perspectives that help keep my gardening, advice, and books fresh and relevant.

I want to thank my family and friends for their patience, understanding and support. Writing allows me to share what I have learned along the way but the process can be taxing, especially on those in my life. Pete, thanks for being my cheerleader, motivator, and partner. Nevada, Maya, and Sammy, thanks for helping me sing, dance, play, and laugh throughout this process.

Thanks also to Diana and Dawn of my team. Your talents and dedication help us continue to expand our efforts so we can inspire and educate more gardeners. And to Mark for helping Pete and me create a new space for additional educational opportunities to pass along to all of you.

And thanks to Tracy Stanley and all the staff at Cool Springs Press and Quayside Publishing for the opportunity to write this and other gardening books.

CONTENTS

WELCOME TO GARDENING

IN MICHIGAN

The diverse climate and long history of gardening, agriculture, and horticulture make Michigan a great place to live, work, and garden.

This horticulture paradise is one of the top states for gross sales of horticulture crops in the United States. A look at the orchards, vineyards, farms, and nurseries reveals why. You'll find cherries, apples, blueberries, other fruits, all kinds of vegetables, and Christmas trees are grown here. You can supplement the edibles you grow at one of the many farmers markets, CSA (Community Supported Agriculture) farms, or pick-your-own locations.

And a great resource both for professional and home gardeners is Michigan State University. It was founded in 1855 as the Agriculture College of the State of Michigan and maintains its outstanding reputation for research in agriculture and horticulture. The Extension service, the outreach arm of this land grant college, produces useful publications to help horticulture professionals, home gardeners, and children be successful in their horticulture and gardening endeavors. I was lucky enough to feature several of their research, demonstration, and, of course, the children's gardens on my PBS show *Great Lakes Gardener.* We also showcased W. J. Beal Botanical Garden, the oldest continuously run university botanical garden in the United States. This outdoor laboratory is filled with plant collections, demonstration plots, and ongoing research with an emphasis on the Great Lakes region.

And speaking of the Great Lakes, these bodies of water greatly influence the gardening climate. They buffer the climatic extremes of winter and moderate summer temperatures, especially along their shorelines. Spring can be frost-free but cooler while fall frost arrives later lakeside. The most recent USDA hardiness zone map shows the southern lakeshore area as a zone 6b and that in the Upper Peninsula as zone 4a. But I know many of us are slow to embrace the new hardiness zones as winters and summers can vary greatly from year to year. In fact, the old saying goes, "if you don't like the weather, wait five minutes and it will change."

Snow cover influences gardening success and can also vary from year to year and throughout the state. The blanket of snow in the UP allows daring gardeners to push the limits. I have seen several good-looking Japanese maples, and a few other cold-sensitive plants, thriving in Marquette and Escanaba despite the cold winter extremes.

Civic Pride

These extremes have not stopped gardeners from making a difference in their land-scapes and communities. The Garden Club of Michigan was founded in 1911. As industrial growth was quickly expanding, fifty women from more than nine Michigan cities came together to promote the value and love of gardening.

Soon after, many of the wealthy industrialists enlisted the help of landscape archi-tects like Jens Jensen to design the landscaping of their states. Some of these are now parks or public gardens. And of course Michigan gardeners joined the "Food Fights for Freedom" by planting over 20,000 Victory Gardens in 1944.

The love of gardening and passion for sharing garden knowledge continued. In 1978 Michigan State University brought the Master Gardener program to the state. These University-trained volunteers donate their time, knowledge, and energy to help-ing home gardeners and children learn more, improve their skills, and increase their enjoyment of gardening.

Along with master gardeners, University Extension agents, garden writers, garden center staff, and other horticulture professionals continue the long tradition of garden-ing in Michigan.

Massed impatiens are spectacular in this border planting.

Using This Book

Michigan Getting Started Garden Guide is designed to help you make the connection with nature and achieve some gardening success of your own. I wrote the book with you, the gardener, in mind. I tried to include answers to the questions gardeners are always asking me.

I mostly selected plants that are easy to find here and are often used in gardens and yards. Trust me, there are many more I would like to add, but this should give you a good start. And for those that are looking for something a bit different, I did add a few excellent but lesser-used plants. You may also notice I omitted some common landscape plants that are considered invasive. I wanted to provide some alternatives that would be good for you, your landscape, and the environment.

The information included in the pages of this volume should help you grow a healthy and attractive landscape. I divided this book into chapters by plant categories. These include annuals, bulbs, groundcovers, lawns, ornamental grasses, perennials, shrubs, trees, and vines. I mixed our native plants in with the non-native plants in the appropriate category. I thought that arrangement would make the book easier to use for planning your landscape. You may be surprised to learn how many of our common garden plants are natives.

Each chapter includes an introduction with general information unique to that group of plants. Read the chapter introductions before turning to the plant entries. Every plant entry within the chapter features a plant profile for quick reference. And take a look at James Fizzell's *Month-by-Month Gardening in Michigan* and my *Midwest Gardeners Handbook* for more gardening information for your garden. Not only do they provide additional details on managing individual plants and your landscape in our climate, but they make excellent companions to this book.

Getting the Most Out of Your Garden

This book is just a starting point. Use the basic information I have provided along with your own experience to increase your gardening success. Start keeping a garden journal to record your experiences. It doesn't have to be fancy. It's just a place to record your gardening successes and failures. Yes, failures. I've learned as much from them as my successes. Record significant weather events. The impact of droughts, floods, and extreme heat and cold can show up years later. Buy a weather calendar or almanac and let the meteorologists keep track of some of the climate data for you.

Thomas Jefferson, a horticulturist as well as our third president, inspired me to keep a garden journal. I read that he kept a garden journal for 50 years, entering the name, date, and source of every plant he purchased; how it grew; and when and why it was removed. I have not mastered his discipline, but as my memory fades, I am getting more motivated.

With all that said, the most important thing is to relax and have fun. If a plant dies (and it happens to all of us), look at this as an opportunity to try something new. If you put a plant in the wrong spot, move it to a new location. Gardening should be enjoyable, not a weekly chore. And when you get discouraged, think about what Thomas Jefferson said: "Though an old man, I am but a young gardener."

The Garden Environment
Weather and Rainfall

We base our plant selection and care on average weather conditions and expected extremes. Then, weather exceptions like droughts, floods, plant-damaging late spring snowstorms, and too many others to list come along.

In the more than thirty years I have been gardening, I have yet to experience "normal" weather. There always seems to be some type of weather extreme to keep gardeners and horticulturists challenged and humble. An overview of our average weather conditions, however, may help you better plan and care for your garden.

Let's start with frost dates. On the back of every seed packet and throughout this book you will read, "Start seeds XX number of weeks prior to the last spring frost." That date varies from May 6 along the shores of Lake Michigan in Grand Haven to July 9 at Champion in the Upper Peninsula. Look for the average number of frost-free dates on the maps provided on page 220. Now, count the days between the last spring frost and the first fall frost. That will give you the number of growing days for your region. The frost-free season varies from as few as 40 in parts of the Upper Pennisula and as many as 165 along the southern shores of Lake Michigan. These are average frost dates based on one hundred years of data, but they can vary greatly from year to year. Soil temperature and the frost tolerance of each plant along with this data should determine your planting date. Average growing temperatures and seasonal extremes will influence plant growth and development. Some plants need warm temperatures to thrive and flower. Others become stressed or stop flowering in hot weather. Winter temperature extremes are among the major factors that influence winter survival. The U.S. Department of Agriculture hardiness zones are based on the *average annual minimum* temperatures. These zones were recently adjusted to reflect more recent changes in our climate. Find your growing zone on the USDA Cold Hardiness Map on page 21.

Rainfall is also important for growing healthy plants. Most plants need an average of 1 inch of water each week. Plants need more water during the hot, dry days of summer and less during cooler periods. The type of plants grown and the care you provide influences the amount and frequency of watering. Some plants, like yucca and coneflowers, are more drought tolerant and can go longer between watering. Others, like astilbe and hostas, need moist soil and will scorch if the soil dries. Select more drought-tolerant plants if you are unable to water during dry periods. Mulching will also reduce the need to water by keeping the soil cool and moist.

Select plants that tolerate your landscape's climate to increase survival and minimize maintenance. But what about those gardeners who like to push plants to the extremes? Well, we can't change the weather, but we can modify it by creating microclimates or modifying our gardening practices.

The Explorer series is an especially hardy rose bred to withstand more cold than other rose varieties. This tree form is underplanted witih petunias, lobelia, and scaevola.

Modifying the Climate

Microclimates are small areas that have slightly different growing conditions from the surrounding areas. Large bodies of water and nearby vegetation can affect microclimates, even altering frost dates and moderating temperatures. Did you ever notice that gardens near large bodies of water are the last to freeze in the fall? On the other hand, cold air sinks, creating frost pockets in valleys and other low areas. Woodlands and shelterbelts can block the northwest winter winds and reduce winter

These 'Hans Anrud' and 'Peer Gynt' tulips look great in a border planting mixed wiith lungwort, bleeding heart, hellebores, and lady's mantle.

damage to cold-sensitive plants. These areas can also shade the landscape, keeping temperatures cooler.

Use the following ideas to create microclimates. Plant windbreaks or install decorative fencing to block damaging winter winds. Grow heat-loving plants near brick buildings and walls. Even a flat warming stone in the perennial garden can add warmth for a nearby plant. Use an outdoor thermometer to track the temperatures in different parts of your garden. Record this information for future use.

Mulch can also be used effectively. Organic mulch used on the soil keeps roots cooler in the summer and warmer in the winter and minimizes soil temperature fluctuations that can stress plants. Winter mulches can be used to protect the aboveground portion of the plant. Roses, rhododendrons, and other tender plants are frequently mulched for winter protection. Apply weed-free straw, marsh hay, or evergreen branches once the ground lightly freezes. The purpose is to keep the soil temperature consistent throughout the winter. This prevents early sprouting that often occurs during our frequent, but short, midwinter thaws. Mulching also prevents the drying of stems and evergreen leaves. The mulch blocks winter wind and sun to reduce moisture loss. Those of you in more northern areas have access to the best winter mulch—a reliable snow cover. Even as you tire of shoveling snow in the winter, remember that all that white stuff is protecting your plants.

Maybe it's not the cold winter that limits your gardening, but rather the short growing season. You can easily lengthen the growing season by several weeks or even a month or more. Gardeners traditionally use cold frames to get a jump on the growing season. These structures require talent to build and room to store, and they also need venting and watering. I never seem to have the time to do all that. Season-extending fabrics like ReeMay and other spun-bonded fabrics can make this task easier. Plant annuals or frost-sensitive perennials outside several weeks earlier than normal and loosely cover the planting bed with a season-extending fabric. The covers keep the plants warm and protect them from spring frost. Air, light, and water can all pass through the fabric, so it doesn't need to be removed for watering or ventilation. Remove the covering once the danger of frost has passed. You can also use these fabrics, bed sheets, or other material to protect plants from the first fall frost. Cover plants in the late afternoon or early evening when there is a threat of frost. Remove the frost protection in the morning. The season-extending fabric can be left in place day and night if the meteorologists predict several days of cold, frosty weather. I find the first fall frost is often followed by two weeks of sunny, warm weather. Providing frost protection will give you a few more weeks of enjoyment before our long winter arrives.

Soil

Soil is the foundation of our landscape. Not many gardeners enjoy spending the time, energy, or money it can take to build this foundation. I have to admit it's more fun to show someone a new plant than to show off my properly prepared soil. But it's a good idea to have and follow the recipe for productive soil.

The Basics

Let's start by looking at our soils. I'm going to greatly simplify this discussion with some broad generalities. I hope the soil scientists out there will forgive me.

Soil is composed of mineral material, organic matter, water, and air. The mineral matter comes from the weathering of bedrock. Michigan's native soils vary from clay to sand, rocky glacial deposits, and good agricultural soils. Most of us are not lucky enough to start with good garden soil. Construction, roads, and pollution have greatly changed our soils. In fact, some plant and soil scientists don't call this soil, but rather "disturbed materials." When buildings are constructed, the topsoil is scraped off the lot and removed. Once the basements are dug, much of the clay, sand, or gravel subsoil is spread over the lot. Some of the building materials, many of them made from limestone, accidentally get mixed into this "soil." An inch or two of topsoil is spread, sod is laid—and it's left, waiting for you to landscape. This conglomeration is usually poorly drained, very alkaline or acidic, and hard on most plants. Fortunately, many municipalities and customers are requiring builders to stockpile the topsoil for reapplication to the site.

Landscaping on less-than-ideal soil is challenging but not impossible. Start by checking the soil drainage. Dig a hole 12 inches deep and fill it with water. Allow the water to drain and fill the hole again. If it takes more than one hour to drain the second time, you need to amend the soil. Soils that drain too quickly, sandy and rocky types, need amending to increase the soil's ability to hold water. Add 2 to 4 inches of organic matter to the top 6 to 12 inches of garden soil to improve drainage and increase water-holding capacity. Till the compost, peat moss, aged manure, or other organic matter into the soil prior to planting.

Do *not* add sand to clay soil. You need an inch of sand for every inch of soil you are trying to amend. If you add less than that, you will end up with concrete. Do not add lime to improve the drainage of alkaline soil. Lime improves drainage, but it also raises the soil pH. That increases problems with nutrient deficiencies in alkaline soil. Gypsum works only in soils high in sodium, so it's not really effective here either.

Gardeners growing plants in poorly drained, disturbed sites have a bigger challenge. These soils will take years to repair. Many gardeners give up and bring in additional

This somewhat formal design uses plants of differing color, height, and form to create an interesting pattern.

topsoil. Make sure the topsoil you buy is better than that you already have. Purchase a blended or garden mix. Many garden centers and nurseries sell small quantities of topsoil. For large quantities, contact a company that specializes in topsoil. Friends, relatives, or a landscape professional may be able to recommend a reliable firm.

A 2-inch layer of good topsoil spread over disturbed material will not help much; water drains through the good soil and stops when it hits the bad material. A better solution is to create planting beds throughout the landscape. Large, raised planting beds and berms at least 12 inches high will give plants a good place to start growing. All the time and energy spent in preparation will pay off in healthy plants, less maintenance, and years of enjoyment.

Testing the Soil

Now that you have improved the soil drainage and structure, you need to develop a fertilization program. That starts with a soil test. Contact your University Extension Office listed in the phone book or online at www.csrees.usda.gov/Extension. Extension personnel can provide you with the necessary forms and information for soil testing, or contact a state-certified soil-testing laboratory.

The soil test report tells you how much and what type of fertilizer to use for the type of plant you are growing. It also tells you the soil pH and what, if anything, should be done to adjust it.

Amending Soil pH

Soil pH affects nutrient availability. Soils can be alkaline with a pH above 7.0, causing iron and manganese deficiencies in our plants. The nutrients *are* in the soil; they are just not available to be used by the plants. That creates problems for acid-loving plants, such as rhododendrons, red maples, and white oaks. It is very difficult to lower the soil pH. Incorporating elemental sulfur and organic matter can slightly lower it. Using acidifying fertilizers, chelated iron and manganese, and organic mulch will help. But all of these methods can take years to lower the pH and have a minimal impact. It is much easier on you and the plant to grow plant species that are adapted to high-pH soils.

Acidic soils have a pH less than 7.0. Most plants grow best in slightly acidic soils. But when the pH drops too low, phosphorus, calcium, and magnesium are bound to acidic soils and are unavailable to the plants. Many gardeners add lime to raise the soil pH. Follow soil test recommendations carefully. It takes years to correct improperly limed soils. Never add lime to alkaline soils.

Selecting a Fertilizer

Your soil-test report will tell you what types of fertilizer to add. The main nutrients are nitrogen, phosphorus, and potassium. The percentage of each of these nutrients contained in a fertilizer is represented by the three numbers on a bag of fertilizer. For example, an analysis of 15-10-5 fertilizer has 15 percent nitrogen, 10 percent phosphorus, and 5 percent potassium.

Nitrogen stimulates leaf and stem growth. It is used in relatively large amounts by the plants. This mobile element moves through the soil quickly. You can use slow-release forms to provide plants with small amounts of nitrogen over a longer period of time. These products also reduce the risk of fertilizer burn. Excess nitrogen encourages leafy growth and discourages flowering. It also leaches through the soil, harming our lakes, streams, and groundwater.

Phosphorus is the middle number on the bag. Phosphorus stimulates root development and flowering. This nutrient is used in smaller amounts by the plants and moves very slowly through the soil. Excess phosphorus can interfere with the uptake of other nutrients and damage our lakes and streams.

Potassium is used in even smaller amounts by plants. It is essential in many plant processes and helps the plants prepare for winter.

Urban soils tend to be high in phosphorus and potassium. That comes from years of using complete fertilizers, like 10-10-10 and 12-12-12. Excessive amounts of one nutrient can interfere with the uptake of other nutrients. You can't remove the excess nutrients, but you can stop adding to the problem by following your soil test recommendations.

Michigan has joined other Great Lakes states and implemented regulations and bans on the use of phosphorous fertilizer. You must have a soil test to show a deficiency or be starting a new lawn to use phosphorous-containing lawn fertilizers, plus you are not to fertilize frozen or saturated soils. Always sweep fertilizer, chemicals, and plant material off your walks and drives to further preserve water quality.

And if soil test results aren't available, consider using slow-release low nitrogen fertilizers when a nutrient boost is needed. They are less likely to burn your plants and leach through the soil. All this will save you money, improve plant growth, and help our environment.

Think About Design

Now that we've taken care of the soil we can start talking design. Select plants that serve the desired function and tolerate, or preferably thrive in, the growing conditions. Note the height and width of each plant and make sure it will still fit into the location once it reaches its mature size.

Use straight lines and plant in rows for a more formal design. Create curved beds, plant in masses, and incorporate mixed borders for a more informal look. See my book *Can't Miss Small Space Gardening* for help drawing a landscape plan, whether your property is large or small.

Select colors that help create the feel and look you want for your landscape. Warm colors of red, orange, and yellow make large areas appear smaller, add a feeling of warmth, and attract attention. Cool colors of blue, green, and violet make small areas appear larger and give a cool, peaceful feeling to the area. Use contrasting colors to create a focal point and complementary colors for continuity and blending. And remember it takes more cool-color flowers to offset a few bright orange, red, or yellow blossoms.

Allium mixes in well with tiger eyes, sumac, and willow amsonia.

Repeat colors throughout the landscape through color echoing. For example, a red flower in one area can be echoed by the red foliage of a plant in another section and the red brick on the home. Color echoing increases the impact of the plants while creating a sense of unity throughout the yard.

Texture is another element that can help unify the garden or add contrast for greater impact. Fine-textured plants have dissected or grass-like foliage and airy or spike-like flowers, such as ornamental grasses. Bold-textured plants have broad leaves with round flowers, like sunflowers. Repeat textures throughout the landscape to tie the garden or parts of the landscape together. Mix a few bold-textured plants in with the fine-textured plants to give the garden some punch.

And use a variety of plants to create year-round color and interest. Colorful bark, interesting form, and persistent fruit and seedheads can brighten a winter landscape and help bring in the colorful birds. Make sure something is blooming spring, summer, and fall or providing colorful foliage or interesting texture in the landscape.

Grooming and Pruning

Deadheading and pruning can help control growth, increase flowering, and reduce pest problems. Some plants require a lot of work and others perform fine on their own. Some cultivars require less maintenance and have fewer problems than the species. Select the plants and their cultivars that best fit your growing conditions and maintenance schedule.

Pest Management

Once your plants are growing, some unwelcome visitors may enter the landscape. These pests come in the form of weeds, diseases, insects, and plant-devouring wildlife. A healthy plant is your best defense against pests. Even with proper planting and care, you may need to intercede to help plants through difficult times.

Weed Control

You will simplify your life by eliminating existing weeds before planting. They can be physically removed, solarized with a clear plastic covering, or smothered with paper and organic mulch. You can also use a total vegetation killer; just be sure to read and follow label directions and wait the required time before planting.

Mulch the soil with shredded leaves, evergreen needles, woodchips, or other organic mulch after planting. This step will prevent many weed seeds from sprouting. Any that do creep through will be easy to pull. Plus these mulches conserve moisture, moderate soil temperature and improve the soil as they decompose.

What could be nicer than relaxing in your garden at the end of a summer's day?

Dealing with Diseases

Leaf spots, stem rots, mildew, and blights are just a few of the diseases found on plants. Growing the right plant in the right location will reduce the risk of infection. Proper soil preparation will help reduce rot problems. Remove infected leaves as soon as they appear. Fall cleanup will reduce disease infection the following season. Most disease problems develop in response to the weather. You will have problems some years and not others. Plants are usually more tolerant of these problems than the gardener. Contact the University Extension Service, certified arborists, or other landscape professionals for help in identifying and controlling these problems.

Managing Insects

As you battle the insects, remember that less than 3 percent of all the insects throughout the world are classified as pests. Many more are beneficial and desirable to have in your garden. Keep in mind insecticides also kill the caterpillars that turn into beautiful butterflies and aphid-eating ladybugs. Try some environmental (and often fun) control techniques before reaching for the spray can. Always read and follow label directions carefully before using any pesticide.

A strong blast of water is often enough to keep plant damaging aphids and mites under control. Use several applications of an eco-friendly product like insecticidal soap if you need to step up control. Or wait for lady beetles, green lacewings, and other good guys to come in and clean up the problem. Working in concert with nature greatly reduces your workload and increases the long-term success.

Slugs are slimy creatures that eat holes in the leaves of hostas and other garden plants. They feed at night, so you will notice the damage before you see the slugs. Slugs love cool, dark, damp locations and multiply quickly in wet weather. Stale beer poured in a shallow dish or half-empty beer bottle laid on its side makes a great slug trap. Commercial slug baits are also available, but most have toxic materials and should be used with care around children, pets, and wildlife. New slug-control products with the active ingredient iron phosphate are effective at killing slugs, but not harmful to birds and wildlife.

Animals in the Garden

Wildlife can be a nice addition to the landscape—until the animals start eating all the plants. Start by eliminating hiding and nesting areas, such as brush piles. Fences, scare tactics, and repellents may provide some control. Vary the tactics for better results. And work with your neighbors—make sure one of you isn't feeding the wildlife while the other is trying to eliminate it from the neighborhood.

Next Year's Garden

If all these methods fail, there is always next year. Someone passed along to me a great definition of a green-thumb gardener: the green thumb gardener is someone who grows a lot of plants, kills a few without mentioning it to others, and keeps on planting! So take heart. If you've lost a few plants, you're on your way to a green thumb.

How to Use *Michigan Getting Started Garden Guide*

Each entry in this guide provides you with information about a plant's particular characteristics, habits, and basic requirements for active growth, as well as my personal experience and knowledge of the plant. I include the information you need to help you realize each plant's potential. Only when a plant performs at its best can one appreciate it fully. You will find such pertinent information as mature height and spread, bloom period and colors, sun and soil preferences, water requirements, fertilizing needs, pruning and care, and pest information.

Sun Preferences

Symbols represent the range of sunlight suitable for each plant. Full sun means eight hours or more, including midday. Part sun means six to eight hours, but not midday. Part shade means four or six hours, preferably in the morning. Shade means less than four hours of sun. Some plants can be grown in more than one range of sun, so you will sometimes see more than one sun symbol.

Full Sun   Part Sun   Part Shade   Shade

Additional Benefits

Many plants offer benefits that further enhance their value. The following symbols indicate some of the more important additional benefits:

 Native

 Fall color

 Resists drought

 Attracts beneficial insects like bees, butterflies, and predaceous insects that eat the bad bugs

 Attracts hummingbirds

Companion Planting and Design

For most of the entries, I provide ways to use the plants in your landscape, as well as suggestions for companion plants to help you create pleasing and successful combinations—and inspire original compositions of your own. This is where I find much enjoyment from gardening.

Try These

These sections describe those specific cultivars or varieties that I think you will want to try. Some I have grown in my garden, for others I have monitored their performance in other gardens, and some are just too cool to resist. Give them a try . . . or perhaps you'll find your own personal favorite.

Cold Hardiness Zones

Plants are hardy throughout the state unless otherwise noted. Keep in mind there may be hardier or less hardy cultivars within a particular group of plants.

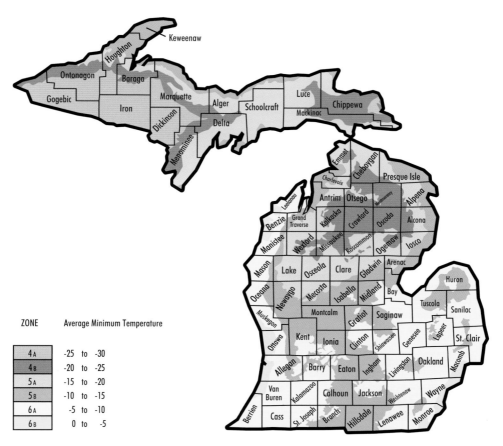

ZONE	Average Minimum Temperature
4 A	-25 to -30
4 B	-20 to -25
5 A	-15 to -20
5 B	-10 to -15
6 A	-5 to -10
6 B	0 to -5

USDA Plant Hardiness Zone Map, 2012. Agricultural Research Service, U.S. Department of Agriculture. Accessed from http://planthardiness.ars.usda.gov.

ANNUALS

FOR MICHIGAN

G row them in a pot, in the ground, intermingled with your vegetables, or tucked in amongst your perennials. Use annuals to brighten the landscape from spring through fall. Include traditional favorites and try some of the new varieties to add some pizzazz to your landscape and make gardening with annuals even more fun.

Botanically speaking, annuals are plants that complete their life cycle (from seed to producing seeds) and die in a single season. Horticulturally speaking, they can be true annuals or perennials that can't survive the rigors of our winters and must be replanted each year. Some gardeners extend their growing season and plant life by moving a few plants indoors for winter. Cuttings can be taken, whole plants can be moved indoors, or some are stored in a cool dark location in a somewhat dormant state. We'll discuss that more in the plant profiles.

Cockscomb has many forms. This is Celosia argentea var. cristata 'Ballet Yellow'.

Starting and Selecting Annuals

Annuals can be started from seeds or purchased as transplants. Some annuals, like zinnias and marigolds, can be planted directly outside in the garden. Others, like geraniums, take a long time to mature and blossom. These should be started as seeds indoors for best results. Starting your own plants from seeds takes extra work but gives you a greater selection of new and different plant varieties. Many gardeners prefer to buy transplants from their local garden center, greenhouse, or nursery. The extra expense provides the advantage of ready-to-plant and soon-to-bloom annuals. Select transplants with full-sized green leaves and stout stems. Avoid insect- and disease-infected plants. And this is a case where bigger isn't necessarily better. Smaller plants that aren't rootbound will suffer less transplant shock than larger-blooming, rootbound transplants.

Getting Annuals Off to a Good Start

Prepare your plants for the garden before you put them in the ground. Plants moving from the shelter of the greenhouse or your home need a little help preparing for the great outdoors. This process is called "hardening off." Move the plants outdoors into partial shade. Gradually allow the soil to go a bit drier between watering and stop fertilizing. At the same time, gradually increase the amount of light the plants receive each day. In two weeks, the plants will be ready to move to their permanent location. Many garden centers do this job for us. Ask if you're not sure.

Properly prepare the soil as described in the general introduction. The extra effort invested now will pay off with healthier better blooming annuals all season long. Carefully slide the plants out of the container. Gently massage the roots before planting, to encourage them to grow out of the rootball and into the surrounding soil. Place the plant in the ground at the same level it was growing in the container.

Fan flower is a lovely complement to this brick path.

Water your new planting thoroughly, moistening the top 6 inches of soil. This will encourage deep, more drought-tolerant roots. Check new plantings several times per week. The small rootball growing in the soil-less mix will dry out quickly. Once established, plants need about one inch of water each week.

Water established plants thoroughly whenever the top few inches of soil are moist but crumbly. During dry periods, you will usually provide the needed water once a week to plants growing in clay soil and half the weekly rate twice a week to plants in sandy soil. You may need to water more often during hot weather and less frequently when temperatures are cool. Mulch the soil with a layer of shredded leaves or evergreen needles to conserve moisture so you'll be watering less often, reducing weeds to save you some weeding, and improving the soil for future gardens.

Fertilize according to soil test recommendations. If this is not available, use three pounds or less per one hundred square feet of a low-nitrogen slow-release fertilizer in spring. For more details on fertilization, see "The Garden Environment."

Creating an attractive annual garden involves planning, proper planting, and a little follow-up care. Here are a few of my favorite tried-and-true annuals to get you started.

Ageratum

Ageratum houstonianum

Botanical Pronunciation
a-jer-AY-tum hoos-tone-ee-AY-num

Other Name Floss flower

Bloom Period and Seasonal Color
Spring through frost blooms in blue, lavender, white, and pink

Mature Height × Spread
6 to 15 inches × 12 inches

Gardeners have been enjoying the longevity of this neat and tidy edging plant for many years. The compact types form tight mounds covered with flowers all season long. These are often sold as blue, white, or pink ageratums. Selecting a named cultivar will help ensure you get the size, flowering, and growth habit desired. Planted in large numbers, these annuals will provide a mass of color. The blue cultivars are often combined with red and white annuals for a patriotic display. The taller types are looser and more open. They are great for cutting and work well as fillers in perennial gardens or as part of an informal flower border. Add ageratums to the landscape to help attract butterflies to your yard.

When, Where, and How to Plant
Purchase ageratums as transplants or start from seeds indoors. Start seeds indoors in mid-March. Sprinkle the fine ageratum seeds on the surface of moist, sterile, seed starter mix. Gently tamp the seeds for good soil contact, but do not cover them—they need light to germinate. Keep the soil about 70 to 75 degrees Fahrenheit, and moist. Seeds will sprout in five to ten days. Transplant hardened-off seedlings outdoors after all danger of frost is past. Grow in full sun or partial shade with moist, well-drained soil. Space compact plants 6 inches apart and taller cultivars up to 9 inches apart.

Growing Tips
If placed properly, ageratums require little maintenance. Make sure the soil is slightly dry before watering. Too much water can lead to root rot. Excess fertilization can encourage leggy growth and discourage flowers.

Regional Advice and Care
Occasional deadheading keeps the plants blooming throughout the season and improves the appearance of white cultivars as the flowers fade. Cut back leggy plants halfway to encourage more attractive growth. Powdery mildew may be a problem; avoid it by growing plants in a sunny area and properly spaced for good air circulation.

Companion Planting and Design
Ageratums make great additions to flower gardens, containers, rock gardens, or shrub borders. They combine well with dusty miller, salvia, geraniums, and marigolds. I tuck a few of the taller ones in with allium, blue oat grass, Russian sage, and other perennials. They blend in with the perennials and help fill any voids or cover mistakes in the perennial garden.

Try These
'Blue Horizon' grows 18 × 12 inches, looks good in adverse weather, and has nice long stems for cutting. 'Leilani Blue' grows 14 to 16 × 10 to 12 inches. Both have big fluffy flowers that do not need deadheading. The Hawaii series is compact (6 inches) and readily available. The Artist series is a Proven Winner selected for its uniform growth (7 to 9 inches tall) and weather resistance. 'Blue Danube' also has uniform growth, and 'Swing Pink' is a compact (6 to 8 inches), pink-flowering cultivar.

Alyssum

Lobularia maritima

Botanical Pronunciation
lob-yew-LAR-ee-ah mah-RIT-ih-mah

Other Name Sweet alyssum

Bloom Period and Seasonal Color
Spring through frost blooms in white, pink,
lavender, and apricot

Mature Height × Spread
4 to 8 inches × 10 to 15 inches

Sweet alyssum is a longtime favorite of gardeners. Its lovely fragrance makes a nice addition to any landscape. Alyssum is one of those annuals that may reseed in your garden as long as you don't weed it out when preparing the soil. I must admit there was a period I did not plant alyssum—too common for a horticulturist's garden. But one day when helping a friend carry and plant flats of alyssum, I was reminded what I was missing. Now I include a few plants in with perennials where they reseed and always have a border of parsley and alyssum at the edge of my vegetable garden. The butterflies are also glad I decided to add one of their favorites in my garden.

When, Where, and How to Plant
Purchase alyssum as a transplant or start seeds indoors in mid-March. Sprinkle seeds on moist, sterile seed starter mix. Gently tamp the seeds for good seed-soil contact, but do not cover them. Keep the soil at 70 degrees Fahrenheit, and moist. They sprout in about eight days. Overwatering and deep planting can lead to damping-off of seedlings. Reduce that risk by using a sterile mix and clean containers. Seeds can be sown directly outdoors after the last hard frost. These plants will bloom much later than those started indoors. Hardened-off transplants can be planted outdoors after all danger of frost is past. Plant alyssum transplants 6 to 8 inches apart for complete and quick cover.

Growing Tips
Plants need little care when grown in moist, well-drained soil. Extreme heat may cause the plants, especially purple ones, to stop flowering. Clip back leggy plants, water as needed, but don't fertilize. Plants will begin flowering as soon as temperatures cool.

Regional Advice and Care
Alyssum is low maintenance, free flowering, and basically pest free. Alyssum is at its peak in cool weather and will even tolerate a light frost, giving you a good fall show.

Companion Planting and Design
Try direct-seeding alyssum around spring-flowering bulbs. The alyssum will cover declining foliage and fill empty spaces. Use it as an edging plant in your annual flower beds or rose gardens. It mixes well with other container plants, spilling over the edge. Alyssum can also be used to provide some color while softening the look of steppers and planting walls.

Try These
Plants are often sold simply as white, pink, or purple alyssum. Snow Princess® is a billowy, more heat-tolerant white alyssum that spreads up to 24 inches. Blushing Princess™ is similar in habit but has blush lavender flowers. Frosty Knight™'s variegated foliage will make you take a second look and it is heat tolerant, growing 18 to 24 inches wide. 'Snow Crystals' is a low grower with larger flowers and good heat tolerance. 'Easter Bonnet' cultivars are compact, uniform in size, and come in pink, violet, or mixed colors.

Angelonia

Angelonia angustifolia

Botanical Pronunciation
an-jel-OH-nee-ah an-gus-tih-FOE-lee-ah

Other Name Summer snapdragon

Bloom Period and Seasonal Color
Spring through frost—in white, pink, blue, and bicolor

Mature Height × Spread
12 to 24 inches × 9 to 18 inches

Include angelonia in your containers, annual gardens, and tuck a few in amongst your perennials. I was sold on these plants when I observed them used *en masse* at the Ball Horticultural Trial Gardens. Garden art set amongst a bed of white 'Angelmist' looked as if it were floating on clouds. A close look at the flowers will reveal the source of its common name, summer snapdragon. Though they look somewhat alike, their growing requirements are quite different. Angelonia thrives in the heat of the summer and is drought tolerant once established, while snapdragons prefer moist soil and most fade as the temperatures rise. Pick a few blossoms to include in vases indoors and take a whiff. Some gardeners say the foliage smells like apples.

When, Where, and How to Plant
You can sow seeds indoors late March. Plant in clean containers filled with seed-starting mix or well-drained potting mix. Keep the growing media warm, 68 to 70 degrees Fahrenheit, and moist. Seeds sprout in less than a week and should then be moved under artificial lights. Plants are available at most garden centers. Move hardened-off transplants into the garden once the soil has warmed and danger of frost has passed. Space plants 9 to 12 inches apart in full sun location with moist well-drained soil.

Growing Tips
Water new plantings enough to keep the roots and surrounding soil moist. Once established, water thoroughly and only when the top few inches of soil

are crumbling and starting to dry. These plants will tolerate hot dry conditions. Fertilize according to soil test recommendations or apply a slow-release fertilizer at the start for the season.

Regional Advice and Care
There're no serious problems and minimal care is required. Avoid overwatering that can lead to root rot. No deadheading is needed and the compact varieties do not need pinching or pruning. You can cut taller varieties back midseason if you need and want to encourage more compact growth. Flowers will return in about two weeks.

Companion Planting and Design
Their upright habit makes angelonia an excellent vertical accent (thriller) for containers. I prefer to use it as a filler in planters and gardens. The narrow leaves and dainty flowers contrast nicely with bolder textured plants and provide a sense of depth in the garden. I like to combine pink cultivars with Persian shield (*Strobilanthus*). The pink flowers of the angelonia echo the pink accents on the Persian shield foliage. The silver leaves of dusty miller are a nice foil for this plant.

Try These
Angelface® series sports larger flowers, has good heat tolerance, grows upright 18 to 24 inches tall with good branching. The Serena™ series is more compact at 10 to 14 inches, and Angelmist™ series grows 14 to 24 × 10 to 14 inches. 'Serenita' is drought and heat tolerant in colors of rose, lavender, purple, and white.

Begonia

Begonia semperflorens

Botanical Pronunciation
bah-GO-nyah sem-per-FLOOR-enz

Other Name Wax begonia

Bloom Period and Seasonal Color
Summer to frost blooms in white, red, rose, and pink

Mature Height × Spread
6 to 12 inches × 6 to 12 inches

egonia is a standard plant for park, municipal, business, and home landscapes. This durable choice provides attractive foliage and a season of bloom with minimal care. Most gardeners buy transplants since the tiny seeds (2 million per ounce) take more than four months to develop into flowering plants. Some gardeners extend their growing season and save a few plants for next year's garden. Simply take cuttings and start new plants or move potted plants indoors for the winter. Wax begonia leaves are glossy and come in green or bronze. The bronze-leafed cultivars tend to be more sun tolerant. Individual flowers are small and can be single or double. Though the blooms are diminutive in size, they are large in number providing an impressive display.

When, Where, and How to Plant
Place hardened-off transplants outside in late May or early June, after all danger of frost is past. Begonias can grow in a wide range of light. They prefer partial shade but will tolerate full sun if the soil is kept moist. Adding organic matter to most of our soils will increase the health and vigor of the plants. Wax begonia transplants can be purchased in flats or 3- to 4-inch pots. Space small cultivars about 6 to 8 inches apart. Larger cultivars can be planted 8 to 12 inches apart. Proper spacing will help prevent diseases.

Growing Tips
Make sure the soil is moist but not overly wet. Avoid overhead watering and remove diseased plant parts as they appear to help minimize problems. Avoid excess nitrogen fertilizer that can increase the risk of disease and decrease flowering.

Regional Advice and Care
Begonia's small flowers give you a great display without regular deadheading. Wax begonias occasionally suffer from powdery mildew, botrytis blight, leaf spots, and stem rots. Good soil preparation and proper spacing of the plants can help prevent these problems. Remove diseased flowers and leaves as soon as they appear. I find deadheading during wet weather helps reduce botrytis blight and leaf spot diseases.

Companion Planting and Design
Begonias look great when used as an edging plant, *en masse* in a flower bed, or as an annual ground cover. Try using them in containers and hanging baskets. They perform well in many of the new vertical wall planters.

Try These
Dragon Wing™ has extra large leaves and flowers and grows equally well in sun and shade. The 14- to 18-inch plant is covered with red flowers all season. 'Whopper Red with Bronze Leaf' has a similar habit with bronze leaves, 'Sparks Will Fly' sports tangerine blooms and bronze foliage on 10- to 24-inch mounds; *B. boliviensis* 'Million Kisses Honeymoon' is a trailing begonia with large yellow flowers; *B. boliviensis* 'Santa Cruz Sunset' is a vigorous trailer with 5-inch-wide scarlet flowers. It was voted Most Popular by gardeners and received an American Garden Award Grand Prize.

Cleome

Cleome hassleriana

Botanical Pronunciation
klee-OH-mee hass-ler-ee-AY-nah

Other Name Spider cleome

Bloom Period and Seasonal Color
Summer through fall blooms in white, pink, rose, or purple

Mature Height × Spread
Up to 6 feet × 1 to 2 feet

This unique large annual was grown in the Victorian-era cottage gardens, then found a new home in park and boulevard plantings. Recent introductions have increased its use in home gardens by allowing even those with small spaces to enjoy their beauty. The common name, spider cleome, aptly describes the flower. The long stamens extend beyond the petals, giving the plant a light, airy appearance. The long, thin seedpods are also attractive and add to its "spidery" look. The former botanical name, *Cleome spinosa*, describes the small spines on the base of the leaves. Keep these in mind when placing and weeding around the plants. Cleome attracts butterflies and hummingbirds and makes a great cut flower. Its fragrance is often described as musky or skunk-like on warm nights.

When, Where, and How to Plant
Start seeds indoors about six weeks before the last frost. Seeds can be purchased or collected from existing, non-hybrid, plants. Place collected seeds in the freezer for one week before planting. Provide seeds with light and warm (80 degrees Fahrenheit) temperatures for germination. Transplants are usually sold in 3- or 4-inch pots. Purchased or homegrown transplants should be hardened off and then planted outdoors after all danger of frost is past. They grow in a variety of soils and full sun to part shade. These are big plants that need lots of space. Allow at least 2 feet between plants. Cleomes often reseed. Just move or weed out unwanted seedlings.

Growing Tips
Although they are very tolerant of heat and drought, they will also benefit from ample moisture. Water thoroughly whenever the top few inches of soil begin to dry.

Regional Advice and Care
Cleomes require very little maintenance. You may have to weed out a few unwanted plants the following year. They are self-supporting (no staking required), but they do tend to slouch with age. Staking or nearby plantings can provide support if you want to contain the plants or prefer a more stiff and formal appearance.

Companion Planting and Design
This tall plant is an excellent backdrop to flower borders or a striking centerpiece in an island bed. Its large size and color can add punch to undeveloped landscapes. Use them to fill voids left between properly spaced young shrubs or empty spaces left for future plantings. As the shrubs fill in, you will eventually need none of these large annuals as fillers.

Try These
Senorita Rosalita® 3 to 5 feet tall, full and branching with lavender-pink flowers, will not reseed. Spirit® series is 2 to 4 feet tall sporting lavender, white and pink blooms. The Sparkler series is smaller, 3 to 4 feet tall; plants are uniform in size, have a long bloom period, and tolerate extreme heat and sun. 'Sparkler Blush' has 4- to 6-inch flowers in pink with a flush of white, and 'Sparkler Rose' has similar rosy red flowers.

Cockscomb

Celosia species

Botanical Pronunciation
sell-OH-see-ah

Other Name Celosia

Bloom Period and Seasonal Color
Summer through fall blooms in red, yellow, gold, orange, and pink

Mature Height × Spread
6 to 30 inches × 6 to 18 inches

Bright, bold, and tough, cockscomb is a good choice for hot, dry areas. It provides a bold splash of color outdoors in the garden or indoors in a vase. The flowers can be crested like a rooster's comb (Cristata group) or plumed (Plumosa group) like a feather, or short, narrow, and barley-like (Spicata group). The crested types remind me of brains though others say colorful coral sounds much more attractive. The cresting is the result of fasciation. This abnormal cell growth produces flattened stems and a proliferation of flower buds. All flower types come in warm colors of red, yellow, gold, orange, and pink with green, red, or bronze leaves. In fact the genus name *Celosia* means "burned" in Greek and refers to the flower color.

When, Where, and How to Plant
Start seeds indoors eight weeks prior to the last spring frost. The seeds need light, moisture, and 70 to 75 degree Fahrenheit temperatures to germinate. Cockscomb can be seeded directly outdoors, although plants started outdoors will bloom much later. Lightly cover the seeds and keep them moist. Move hardened-off transplants outdoors after all danger of frost is past. Wait until the soil and air are warm to avoid stunted plant growth. Cockscomb performs best in full sun and well-drained soil. Space small cultivars 6 to 8 inches apart and, larger ones 12 to 15 inches apart.

Growing Tips
Water new transplants often enough to keep the soil moist. Once established, you will only need to water when the top few inches of soil are dry.

Regional Advice and Care
Properly placed, celosias are low maintenance. Poorly drained soil can result in stem rot; wet weather can result in leaf spot. Mites may be a problem in hot, dry weather. A strong blast of water from the garden hose or insecticidal soap is often enough to keep mites under control. Occasionally deadhead or harvest flowers to keep the plants blooming all season long. Mist the dense blooms with water to dislodge stowaway insects before bringing indoors.

Companion Planting and Design
A mass planting of cockscomb makes a bold statement in any landscape. Try using the short, crested types as edging. Use the taller types of plume, crested, or wheat celosia in the middle or the back of the flower border. Celosia's drought tolerance makes it a good candidate for containers. Add these to your cutting garden; they are long lasting in a vase and the flower color intensifies when they are dried.

Try These
Celosia caracus 'Intenz' has bright purple wheat-type blooms on 1 to 2 foot plants. Gold Medal winners 'New Look Red' and 'New Look Yellow' are low maintenance 12- to 18-inch plants covered all season with plume type blooms. 'Prestige Scarlet' has small red-crested flowers atop 12- to 15-inch-tall plants. *Celosia spicata* 'Flamingo' series are tall plants with barley-like flower spikes.

Coleus

Solenostemon scutellarioides

Botanical Pronunciation
sol-en-oh-STEM-on skoot-el-lar-ee-OY-deez

Other Name Painted nettle

Bloom Period and Seasonal Color
Season-long foliage in combinations of green, chartreuse, yellow, buff, salmon, orange, red, purple, and brown

Mature Height × Spread
6 to 24 inches × 12 inches

Many of you may know coleus as a houseplant first and a bedding plant second. That's the case for me. An easy-to-grow indoor plant, coleus is equally at home in the garden. The Victorians used this popular plant both ways. Coleus spent the summers outdoors with other annuals and moved indoors for winter. Pinched, groomed, and watered throughout the winter, the original plant and any offspring were moved back outdoors the following summer. This annual is grown for its colorful foliage, not its flowers. Breeding efforts have resulted in a wide variety of leaf shapes, colors, and variegation. Minimal flowering and self-branching types are also available. These features result in less maintenance and a better-looking plant. And the new warmer colors and sun-loving cultivars add to its appeal.

When, Where, and How to Plant
Purchase coleus as transplants or start from seeds and cuttings. Start seeds indoors eight weeks before the final spring frost. Seeds need light, moisture, and 70-degree Fahrenheit temperatures to germinate. Start plants from cuttings of non-patented plants. Allow at least four weeks for cuttings to develop a sustainable root system before planting them outdoors. Coleus is very frost sensitive, so wait until late May or early June when all danger of frost is past before placing hardened-off transplants outdoors. Coleus prefers moist soil with lots of organic matter and performs best in partial shade. It will tolerate full shade and sun. Heavy shade causes thin and leggy plants, while full sun may cause leaves to fade and even scorch. Buy coleus as bedding plants in flats or small, 3- to 4-inch pots. Space plants 10 to 12 inches apart.

Growing Tips
Water whenever the top few inches of soil are crumbly and moist. Mulching will help keep the roots cool and moist.

Regional Advice and Care
Remove flowers as soon as they appear to encourage new branches to form, giving you a fuller, more compact plant. The self-branching types of coleus produce only a few flowers and require very little pruning. Slugs may be a problem on coleus grown in the shade. Coleus will die with the first fall frost. So take cuttings or move plants indoors if you want to continue enjoying them throughout the winter. Grow as a houseplant in a bright location and water thoroughly when soil is slightly moist.

Companion Planting and Design
Try coleus in flower beds or containers. Planted *en masse* they put on quite a show. I like to back their colorful foliage with solid green plants such as hosta or single-color flowers that echo one of the colors found in the coleus leaves.

Try These
Look for self-branching cultivars that do not require pinching. 'Wasabi' with chartreuse and ColorBlaze® Marooned™ with burgundy leaves that hold color in sun and shade are large plants growing 24 inches or more, 'Fishnet Stockings' prefers shade and has chartreuse leaves with purple veins.

Cosmos

Cosmos species

Botanical Pronunciation
KOZ-mose

Bloom Period and Seasonal Color
Summer until frost blooms in yellow, orange, red, white, pink, rose, and purple

Mature Height × Spread
12 to 72 inches × 12 to 24 inches

Neat and tidy, loose and wild, or somewhere in between: all these descriptions fit cosmos. *Cosmos sulphureus* is neat and tidy producing single and double yellow, orange, or orange-red flowers throughout summer. *Cosmos bipinnatus* is somewhat looser and informal. These tall plants are covered with finer-textured leaves and large single flowers of pink, white, red, or purple creating an airy feel in the garden. Grow shorter cultivars like 'Sonata' (12 to 18 inches) for the same texture on smaller plants. And watch for butterflies to visit and cut a few blooms to enjoy in a vase indoors. Once you plant cosmos, you will be rewarded with seedlings the following year. And watch for surprises as the seedlings from hybrids may not look like the parent plant.

When, Where, and How to Plant
Start seeds indoors four weeks before the last spring frost. Seeds need moist, warm, 70-degree Fahrenheit, starting mix to germinate. Cosmos seeds can be planted directly outside. Plant seeds or transplants after the last spring frost. Seeds should germinate in five to ten days. Cosmos can also be purchased as bedding plants in flats. Move hardened-off transplants outdoors after all danger of frost is past. Cosmos does best in full sun and well-drained soil, although it will tolerate hot, dry conditions once established. Thin seedlings to and space transplants 12 inches apart.

Growing Tips
Minimal care is needed to keep the plants producing beautiful flowers. Keep seedlings and recent transplants slightly moist. Water established plants whenever the top few inches of soil start to dry. Avoid overfertilizing since too much nitrogen will give you tall, leafy plants that tend to fall over.

Regional Advice and Care
Pinch back tall cultivars of *Cosmos bipinnatus* early in the season to promote fuller, sturdier plants. If sited correctly, these plants are fairly pest free. You may occasionally see aphids and Japanese beetles feeding on these plants. Natural predators and a strong blast of water should control the aphids and knocking the beetles in a can of soapy water is a good eco-friendly control. Wilt and aster yellows can be damaging. Remove infested plants as soon as they are found.

Companion Planting and Design
Add these plants to the garden, and you will be sure to attract butterflies. Taller cultivars of *Cosmos bipinnatus* can become floppy and are best used as fillers or background plants where the surrounding plants can provide support. Both species blend with a wide range of annuals and perennials.

Try These
Cosmos bipinnatus 'Sea Shells' grows 36 inches tall and has fluted flowers of white, pink, and crimson that resemble a shell. *Cosmos bipinnatus* 'Rubenza' flowers open dark ruby red maturing to deep rose. *Cosmos sulphureus* 'Cosmic Orange' is a 2000 AAS winner with bright orange flowers on 12-inch plants. Chocolate cosmos (*Cosmos atrosanguineus*) is prized for its velvety maroon-chocolate flowers and chocolate fragrance.

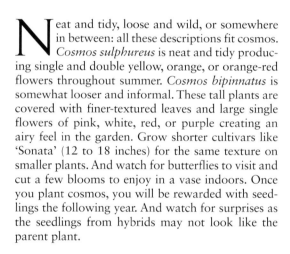

Dusty Miller

Senecio cineraria

Botanical Pronunciation
sen-EE-see-oh sin-er-AIR-ee-ah

Bloom Period and Seasonal Color
Season-long foliage in silver-white

Mature Height × Spread
6 to 15 inches × 6 to 15 inches

The silvery gray foliage of dusty miller provides a nice contrast in the flower garden. The leaves can be slightly lobed or deeply divided and lacy, depending on the cultivar. It is often used as an edging plant in rose gardens and annual gardens. The light-colored leaves stand out in the night landscape and make a nice foil for dark colored flowers. Include a few in the garden where they can be enjoyed even after the first fall frost. Some gardeners have managed to keep plants over winter. A little winter mulch, a protected site, and cooperation from nature results in two, three, even *four* seasons of enjoyment. The plants may not be pretty, but the accomplishment is great for any northern gardener.

When, Where, and How to Plant

Start seeds indoors about ten weeks before the last spring frost. Use a well-drained, sterile seed starting mix. Spread the seeds on the surface of the potting mix and water. Keep the planting mix moist, not wet, and at 75 degrees Fahrenheit. Use clean containers and sterile potting mix to avoid damping off disease. Place hardened-off transplants outdoors after all danger of a hard frost has passed. Dusty miller prefers well-drained soil. It will tolerate light shade but *not* wet feet. Space plants 8 to 10 inches apart.

Growing Tips

This is a low-maintenance, easy-to-grow plant when it is in the right spot. Avoid stem and root rots with well-drained soil and proper watering. Water the soil thoroughly and allow it to dry slightly before watering again.

Regional Advice and Care

Trim back unruly plants to keep them full and compact. Many newer cultivars have been bred to maintain a compact growth habit without shearing. Watch for small, cream or yellow, butterfly-attracting flowers that may appear late in the fall or on older plants. Clip off the flowering stems to keep the plant neat and tidy or leave them for the butterflies.

Companion Planting and Design

Combine dusty miller with other annuals in containers. Use the silver foliage as an eye-catching contrast behind dark blue or deep purple flowers. Or use the silvery foliage to provide visual relief or continuity in a multicolored flowerbed. Dusty miller is often used as an edging plant. Use it with care. I have seen its bold features create an out-of-place formal edge when it was used in an informal garden.

Try These

'Silver Queen', 'Silver Dust', and 'Silver Lace' are all compact, 6- to 8-inch-tall plants with lacy foliage. 'Silver Lace' has the most finely divided leaves. 'Cirrus' is slightly taller, with rounded, only slightly lobed leaves. 'Hoar Frost' has finely cut leaves on 12-inch plants. 'Snow Storm' has strap-like leaves that are more tufted in appearance. 'New Look' and 'Diamond' have very white foliage making them an excellent choice for nightscaping.

Fan Flower

Scaevola aemula

Botanical Pronunciation
skay-VO-lah EYE-mew-lah

Other Name Creeping scaevola

Bloom Period and Seasonal Color
Summer-long blooms of blue, violet, white, or mauve

Mature Height and Spread
Up to 8 inches × 36 inches

The blue unique shaped flowers and low maintenance qualities have quickly increased the popularity of this annual. A native of Australia, it tolerates the hot, dry, and humid summers we often experience. The summer-long bloom is easy to maintain with minimal care. Allow this trailing beauty to spill over and soften the edge of a container or raised bed. Or use it as an annual groundcover weaving around and under other plants. You'll find it easy to mix this colorful yet subtle annual into just about any garden or container. The name *Scaevola* is from the Latin word *scaevus*, for "on the left side." This refers to the flowers with their petals arranged to one side much like a fan. Thus the common name fan flower.

When, Where, and How to Plant
Fan flowers are sold as seed or as bedding plants, usually in 3- or 4-inch pots. Start seeds indoors six to eight weeks before the last spring frost. Grow in sterile seed starter mix that is moist and 66 to 75 degrees Fahrenheit. Or take cuttings in late spring from patent-free plants overwintered indoors. Plant hardened-off transplants in the garden after the danger of frost has passed. Grow in full to part sun with moist, well-drained to dry soils. Use several plants in a container or space 20 to 24 inches apart in the garden.

Growing Tips
Fan flower is heat, drought, and salt tolerant. Water new plantings to keep the soil moist but not soggy. Allow the top few inches of soil to dry before watering established plants in the garden. Check container gardens daily and water as needed. Proper fertilization will encourage summer-long bloom.

Regional Advice and Care
These plants are basically pest free. Avoid poorly drained soils and overwatering. Take 4- to 6-inch cuttings in late summer or move healthy plants indoors to extend your enjoyment into the winter. Remove any flowers and buds and root cuttings in a moist well-drained potting mix. Keep the potting mix moist the first few weeks. Once rooted move to a sunny window and water thoroughly whenever the potting mix begins to dry.

Companion Planting and Design
Use it in containers or hanging baskets mixed with silver foliage trailers such as lotus vine and licorice plants. These and *Dichondra* 'Silver Falls' make nice partners when growing fan flower as an annual groundcover. Then round out the combination with lantana for added color and butterfly appeal. The blue flowers and green leaves make fan flower a great floral base for the large silvery leaves of cardoon.

Try These
The Proven Winner 'Blue Wonder' is probably the most readily available cultivar. It has blue flowers from planting until frost. 'Whirlwind White' performs just about as well as 'Blue Wonder' but with white flowers. New Wonder® has purple blooms; Bombay® series comes in white, pink, or blue flowers.

Flowering Tobacco

Nicotiana alata

Botanical Pronunciation
nih-koe-shee-AY-nah ah-LAY-tah

Other Name Nicotiana

Bloom Period and Seasonal Color
Summer until frost blooms in white, red, pink, lavender, green, and yellow

Mature Height × Spread
10 inches to 5 feet × 6 to 24 inches

Include the free-flowering *Nicotiana* in containers and gardens for a season long floral display. The flower clusters are held above the leaves, creating a colorful display that moves with the breeze. And their star-shaped flowers with long throats are perfect blooms for attracting hummingbirds. Their ability to draw butterflies into the garden has given them the nickname of butterfly plant. Flowering tobacco is easy to grow. Many flowering tobacco plants are fragrant in the evening, which is another big plus. Include a few plants near the garage or front door for a fragrant welcome home. Don't forget to cut a few to enjoy indoors. Flowering tobacco plants will reseed themselves in your garden. Seedlings tend to be taller, wider, and more fragrant than their hybrid parent.

When, Where, and How to Plant
Start seeds indoors about eight weeks before the last spring frost. Flowering tobacco seeds need light, moisture, and 70-degree temperatures to germinate. Sprinkle the seeds on the surface of the starting mix. Lightly tamp and water. Flowering tobacco is sold as a bedding plant in flats also. Move hardened-off transplants outdoors after all danger of frost is past. They prefer moist, well-drained soil but will tolerate an occasional dry spell. Space transplants 8 to 12 inches apart depending on the cultivar; larger cultivars need a little more space.

Growing Tips
Once it is established, it tolerates dry periods, but even properly watered plants may appear wilted in hot afternoon sun. Before you water, wait until the temperature cools to see if the plants recover.

Regional Advice and Care
Though free-flowering all season long, occasional deadheading will help keep the display fresh and full. Healthy plants tolerate the few diseases and insects that can attack. Watch for Colorado potato beetles. These insects eat holes in the leaves, and large populations of them can be quite damaging. Handpicking is usually sufficient.

Companion Planting and Design
Shorter cultivars can be planted *en masse* as bedding plants or used in containers. Larger cultivars serve as specimen or background plants. Even these larger cultivars can be effectively used in container plantings. Try adding a few flowering tobacco plants to your perennial garden. Their informal growth habit and smaller flowers help them fit right in.

Try These
'Perfume Deep Purple' is a 2006 All American Selection winner. The deep purple, highly scented (evening only) flowers atop 20-inch plants. 'Whisper' is 3 feet tall with slightly nodding blooms in shades of pink. The flowers provide fragrance in the evening garden. 'Avalon Bright Pink' is a 2001 AAS winner. The bright pink flowers top the 10-inch plants. The low maintenance plants are heat and drought tolerant and provide season-long bloom. *Nicotiana sylvestris* is a big plant that produces fragrant white flowers. The plant grows 5 feet tall and does not need staking. *Nicotiana langsdorfii* 'Cream Splash' is a distinctive variety with lime green blooms.

Fuchsia

Fuchsia hybrids

Botanical Pronunciation
FEWK-see-ah

Other Name Lady's eardrops

Bloom Period and Seasonal Color
Summer until frost blooms in pink, red, purple, and white

Mature Height × Spread
8 to 36 inches × 12 to 24 inches

How many of us have given or received a hanging fuchsia basket for Mother's Day? Fuchsias are traditional favorites for shade-tolerant hanging baskets. These unique flowering plants put on quite the show on a patio, porch, or shepherd's crook in that shady spot in the landscape. Consider mixing them with other shade-tolerant plants for a different look. The single, semidouble, and double pendulous flowers are quite ornamental, leading to the other common name—lady's eardrops (earrings). Place one of these beauties near your hummingbird feeder to help attract these colorful flyers. I like to use the upright types in containers and in-ground gardens. The tubular flowers are a bit less ornate but just as attractive to gardeners, butterflies, and hummingbirds.

When, Where, and How to Plant
Fuchsias are available as hanging baskets or in 3- to 4-inch pots. They can also be started from cuttings and seed (from specialized catalogs). Take cuttings from overwintered patent-free plants in early spring, root, pot in a well-drained planting mix, and harden off. Move hardened-off plants outdoors after all danger of frost is past. Grow fuchsias in shady locations with moist soil. Avoid hot sun and windy locations. Plant the upright types in the ground spaced 12 inches apart.

Growing Tips
Fuchsias require moist soil. Mulch will help maintain moisture and water in-ground plants when the soil is crumbly and slightly moist. Check the soil in hanging baskets and containers once or twice daily during hot weather. Water containers thoroughly, allowing the excess to run out the drainage holes. Fertilize planters at the start of the season with a slow-release fertilizer or frequently throughout the summer with any flowering plant fertilizer according to the label.

Regional Advice and Care
Remove faded flowers to keep the plants blooming all summer. Fuchsias will stop flowering during hot weather and restart once the weather cools. Fuchsias can be overwintered indoors. Take cuttings and root or bring the whole plant indoors and grow like a houseplant. Or store in a cool dark place, watering about once a month. Bring dormant fuchsias out of storage in late February, prune them back to old wood, and grow them as houseplants. They have no serious pests, but control aphids during hot dry weather.

Companion Planting and Design
Try mixing fuchsias with other shade-tolerant plants like ferns, begonias, and sweet potato vine. Use tree-trained fuchsias as specimen or patio plants. Upright forms can be used in containers or as bedding plants. Use micro-fuchsias and mini-fuchsias in tabletop planters.

Try These
'Thalia' and 'Gartenmeister' are the most available upright types with tubular, orange-red flowers. *F. triphylla* 'Firecracker' is an upright variety with red-veined variegated cream-and-green foliage and long tubular salmon flowers.

Geranium

Pelargonium × hortorum

Botanical Pronunciation
pel-ar-GO-nee-um ex hor-TOR-um

Other Name Zonal geranium

Bloom Period and Seasonal Color
Summer until frost blooms in red, pink, rose, violet, salmon, and white

Mature Height × Spread
12 to 20 inches × 12 inches

The geranium has long been popular in both home and public gardens. Geraniums form a mound of decorative foliage at the base. The leaves are rounded with scalloped or toothed edges and may be solid green or variegated. Either type may have a zone (a ring around the middle of the leaf) of bronze-green or red. The showy flowers are held above the leaves and can be single, semidouble, or double. There are new geranium cultivars introduced every year. The trailing geranium used in hanging baskets is the ivy geranium (*Pelargonium peltatum*). This plant has waxy leaves and performs best in full sun and cool conditions. Grow it in an east-facing location or other area where it is sheltered from the hot afternoon sun.

When, Where, and How to Plant

Sow seeds twelve to sixteen weeks prior to the last spring frost. Seeds need a moist, 70- to 75-degree Fahrenheit starting mix to germinate. Or start plants from cuttings taken from patent-free plants in spring. Geraniums are available in 3- or 4-inch pots. Plant hardened-off transplants outdoors after all danger of frost is past. Geraniums prefer full sun with moist, well-drained soil. Space plants 8 to 12 inches apart.

Growing Tips

Mulch to keep roots cool and moist and the plants at peak performance. Water established plants thoroughly whenever the top few inches of soil are crumbly and moist. Check the soil moisture in planters at least daily. Fertilize planters with a slow-release fertilizer at the start of the season or frequently with any flowering plant fertilizer according to label directions.

Regional Advice and Care

Deadhead to keep the plants blooming and looking their best. Though easy to grow, geraniums have several problems. Bacterial leaf spot, stem rot, and botrytis blight are some of the more common diseases. Avoid these problems by purchasing disease-free plants, planting them in well-drained soil, and watering properly. Remove damaged leaves as soon as they appear. Geraniums can be wintered indoors as houseplants or in a somewhat dormant state. This is the least successful but most space efficient method.

Companion Planting and Design

Geraniums work well in containers and hanging baskets. A mass planting of geraniums will provide a season-long floral display. Try interplanting other annuals like heliotrope for a little different look. Consider adding scented geraniums (*Pelargonium* species). They come in a variety of shapes, textures, and fragrances. Place these plants where you will brush against them for a fragrant surprise.

Try These

The Black Magic series flowers contrast nicely with the chocolate color leaves. The pink with dark rose centered flowers makes 'Freckles' a favorite. 'Pinto Premium White to Rose' is the 2013 AAS Winner; its white petals mature to rose-pink. *P. peltatum* Great Balls of Fire series is a double flowering ivy geranium bred for heat tolerance in red, rose, white, and other colors.

Heliotrope

Heliotropium arborescens

Botanical Pronunciation
hee-lee-oh-TRO-pee-um ar-bor-RES-senz

Other Common Name Cherry pie plant

Bloom Period and Seasonal Color
Summer until frost in violet-blue, light blue, and white

Mature Height × Spread
12 to 18 inches × 12 to 15 inches

A favorite of the Victorian era gardeners, this fragrant annual has been finding its way back into our gardens. It originally arrived here via covered wagon but now is available as seed through garden catalogs and transplants at some garden centers. The dark green leaves are slightly hairy, creating a nice backdrop for the large flower clusters. I have heard the fragrance described as somewhat like vanilla, baby powder, or licorice. I tend to smell the last. The hummingbirds and butterflies also find the flowers attractive. Some gardeners move the plants indoors for the winter. Used for perfumes and scenting bath water, you won't want to miss the lovely fragrance. Place it near the patio, window, or entryway where it can be enjoyed.

When, Where, and How to Plant
Heliotrope is available as seed through garden catalogs and as bedding plants in 3- or 4- and even 6-inch containers. Start seeds indoors ten to twelve weeks before the last spring frost. Grow in a moist, sterile potting mix kept at 61 to 68 degrees Fahrenheit. Be patient; it takes three weeks for the seeds to germinate. Plants can also be started from cuttings in early spring. Move hardened-off transplants outdoors after the danger of frost. Grow in full to part sun in moist well-drained soil. Space plants 12 inches apart in the garden.

Growing Tips
Water established plants thoroughly whenever the top few inches of soil are crumbly and moist. Check container gardens every day and water when the top few inches start to dry. Water thoroughly so the excess

runs out the bottom of the pot. Incorporate a slow-release fertilizer into the container soil at the beginning of the season or use a liquid flowering plant fertilizer throughout the summer. Read and follow label directions. For in-ground plantings; follow fertilization recommendations in the chapter introduction. Mulch the soil to conserve moisture and suppress weeds.

Regional Advice and Care
Heliotrope are fairly pest free. Purchase healthy, pest-free plants to avoid problems. Monitor plants for mealybugs, spider mites, aphids, and whiteflies and control as needed. If problems arise, use insecticidal soap to keep these insect populations at a tolerable level. Some gardeners overwinter these as houseplants.

Companion Planting and Design
Use heliotrope in containers or combine it with common annuals for an updated looked. I like to mix the purple heliotrope with other lesser used annuals such as Persian shield (*Strobilanthes*). I was inspired by a planting at an arboretum that combined heliotrope with osteospermum. Add a few edibles such as ornamental peppers, 'Purple Ruffles' basil, and 'Tricolor' sage.

Try These
'Marine' is 18 inches tall, topped with deep violet flowers, and the most readily available. 'Atlantis' has maintained a strong vanilla scent despite years of hybridizing. Look for the white cultivars of 'Alba' or 'White Lady'. 'Light Eyes' has lavender flowers with a lighter center.

Impatiens

Impatiens walleriana

Botanical Pronunciation
im-PAY-shenz wall-err-ee-AY-nah

Other Name Busy Lizzie

Bloom Period and Seasonal Color
Summer until frost blooms in white, red, pink, orange, and purple

Mature Height × Spread
6 to 18 inches × 12 to 24 inches

Impatiens provide a sea of color for the shade garden. That's why it's such a popular annual. With its mound of green leaves covered with 1- to 2-inch-diameter single or double blooms, this free-flowering plant will reward you with color from summer through frost. And with minimal care. And don't worry if you lack the shade. The new SunPatiens® really do thrive in full sun. I grew them in pots on stone pillars surrounded by blacktop. They looked great despite record heat and the difficult growing conditions. Next time you walk through a wetland, notice our native impatiens, jewelweed. Known botanically as *Impatiens capensis* and *Impatiens pallida*, it grows to 5 feet, producing yellow and orange flowers.

When, Where, and How to Plant

Start impatiens from seeds twelve weeks before the last spring frost. Seeds need light, moisture, and 70-degree Fahrenheit temperatures to germinate. Be patient; it takes two to three weeks for the seeds to sprout. Impatiens is subject to damping-off disease. Use a sterile starting mix and clean containers and don't overwater. Impatiens is available as a bedding plant in flats, 3-inch containers, or as a hanging basket. Hardened-off transplants can be moved outdoors in late May or early June after all danger of frost is past. They are very sensitive to frost. Even the traditional impatiens can take some sun when they are grown in moist, organic soil. Space small cultivars 8 inches apart and larger cultivars 12 inches apart.

Growing Tips

Mulch the soil to keep the roots cool and moist. Water thoroughly and often enough to keep the soil moist but not waterlogged. The more water and fertilizer you provide, the bigger the plants grow. Dwarf plants won't stay small if you give them extra water and nutrients.

Regional Advice and Care

These easy-care annuals are free flowering and won't need deadheading. Pinch back leggy or tired plants. Leaf spot diseases and slugs can sometimes be a problem. Impatiens will die with the first fall frost. Remove and replace them, or live with the void left by the frost-killed plants. You can winter impatiens indoors as houseplants but watch for spider mites. Spray plants with a strong blast of water. If needed, use the most eco-friendly product labeled for this pest.

Companion Planting and Design

Impatiens makes an impressive flowering groundcover under trees and shrubs. In containers and planters, it brightens a shady spot on the deck or patio. Mix individual plants with ferns and hostas to add season-long color to the perennial shade garden.

Try These

The Fiesta and Fiesta Ole series grow 14 inches tall with double flowers that look like miniature roses. The Fusion series has uniquely shaped flowers of yellow, peach, coral, and apricot. New Guinea impatiens Celebration series sports larger flowers and has good heat tolerance.

Lantana

Lantana camara

Botanical Pronunciation
lan-TAN-ah kah-MAR-ah

Bloom Period and Seasonal Color
Summer until frost—in red, peach, purple, pink, orange white, yellow, and often bicolor

Mature Height × Spread
12 to 20 inches × 12 to 15inches

Add color to your garden with lantana and the hummingbirds and butterflies the flowers attract. These heat- and drought-tolerant plants are small shrubs in their native habitat and the South. But here in the North we grow them as annuals. The foliage has a distinct fragrance—some may say smell—when crushed that helps identify this plant when it's not blooming. Handle carefully as some gardeners report a minor skin irritation when in contact with the leaves. The flowers are a collection of small individual flowers. The flowers in the cluster can be the same color or a mix of several colors. Enthusiastic gardeners can train individual plants into small trees. Use the lantana trees as a focal point or to dress up the patio, deck, or balcony.

When, Where, and How to Plants
Purchase transplants in 3-, 4-, or 6-inch containers from your local garden center. Plants can be started from 4-inch cuttings taken from patent-free plants. Remove the lowest leaves and any flowers or flower buds. Stick the cutting in a moist well-drained potting mix. Once rooted, move plant to a sunny window and water as needed. Plant hardened-off transplants outdoors when the soil is warm and danger of frost has passed. Grow lantana in full sun with well-drained soils. Space transplants 12 to 15 inches apart, according to the label, in the garden.

Growing Tips
Water new plantings to keep the soil moist. Slowly extend the periods between watering. Established

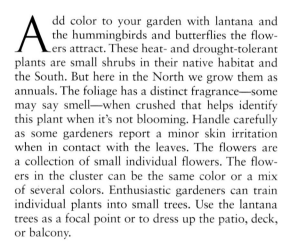

plants are very heat and drought tolerant. Water thoroughly as the top few inches of soil start to dry for best performance. Overwatering and poorly drained soils can lead to root rot. Deadhead for better bloom and remove any berries that form. These are poisonous and can slow or stop flowering. To train lantana into a small tree, secure a single stem on a stake. Allow only the top branches to fully develop. You'll want to overwinter specimens for years of enjoyment.

Regional Advice and Care
Some gardeners move plants indoors to enjoy in the winter. Move plants to a sunny window and grow as a houseplant. This includes those trained into small trees. Other gardeners take cuttings and grow them on to enjoy indoors.

Companion Planting and Design
Plant a bed of lantana and intersperse 'Toffee Twist' sedge for a surprise vertical accent. Or combine it with other drought-tolerant annuals like fan flower and dichondra to grow in front of shrubs for added summer color. I used a 'New Gold' lantana with a 'Blackie' sweet potato vine and a gold-fruited tomato for a colorful and edible container.

Try These
Luscious® Citrus Blend is a combination of all the popular hot colors of tobacco red, flaming oranges, and a brilliant yellow. Simply Beautiful® Landmark series has vibrant colors and strong vigor, so plants quickly fill in and flower. 'Confetti' has a mix of yellow, pink, and magenta flowers.

Licorice Vine

Helichrysum petiolare

Botanical Pronunciation
hel-ih-KRY-sum pet-ee-oh-LAR-ee

Other Name Licorice plant

Bloom Period and Seasonal Color
Colorful silver foliage all season

Mature Height × Spread
Up to 2 feet long

Include this vine in your container plantings, in hanging baskets, or as a groundcover mixed with colorful annuals. The silvery foliage is a nice foil for dark flowers and provides contract with glossy green leaves of neighboring plants. Licorice vine is native to South Africa and tolerant of heat and drought. You may find a few holes in the leaves. Don't worry about the damage. The plant produces enough leaves to share with this hungry visitor. Plus if you let them stay, you will soon be rewarded with beautiful swallowtail butterflies. If you can't stand the plant damage then move the caterpillars to a nearby parsley plant. The caterpillars will get the food they need and you will still get to enjoy the butterflies.

When, Where, and How to Plant
Plants can be purchased as bedding plants in 3- or 4-inch pots. They can also be started from cuttings from patent-free plants in early spring. Root cuttings in a well-drained potting mix. Move rooted cuttings to small containers filled with potting mix and grow in a sunny window or under artificial lights. Seeds of certain cultivars are available and can be started indoors. Sow seeds twelve to fourteen weeks before the last spring frost. Grow in a moist sterile starting mix at 60 degrees Fahrenheit. Hardened-off transplants can be moved outdoors after the danger of frost has passed. Grow licorice vine in full to part sun and well-drained soils. Place one or two plants in mixed containers and space those growing in-ground 12 inches apart.

Growing Tips
Established plants prefer drier soil. Water thoroughly whenever the top few inches of soil begin to dry. Check container plantings daily and water thoroughly when needed. Avoid excess fertilization, which can lead to leggy growth and increase the risk of disease.

Regional Advice and Care
Licorice plants are low maintenance and relatively pest free. An occasional caterpillar may feed on the leaves. But try to tolerate the damage—the adult butterfly is a real beauty you'll want in the garden. Leaf spot and rust can be a problem in wet soils and overfertilized gardens.

Companion Planting and Design
Licorice vine is nice as a trailer for containers and an annual ground cover in the garden. I like to combine this silver foliage plant with trailing petunias, verbena, and fan flower. These also make good annual ground-hugging plant combinations in the annual garden.

Try These
'Petite Licorice' and 'Silver Mist' are compact varieties. 'Variegatum' has gray-and-cream variegated leaves; 'Roundabout' is a miniature version of it. 'Limelight' has the same hairy leaves, but they are lime green. 'Icicles' has long narrow leaves and is more upright in habit. *Dichondra* 'Silver Falls' is another attractive silver foliage trailer often used in place of licorice vine in pots or as a groundcover. It has round silver leaves that hug the container.

Lisianthus

Eustoma grandiflorum

Botanical Pronunciation
yoo-STOE-muh gran-dif-FLOR-um

Other Name Prairie gentian

Bloom Period and Seasonal Color
Summer until frost single, double, or bicolor flowers of white, pink, red, lavender to blue, and yellow

Mature Height × Spread
6 to 30 inches tall × 6 to 12 inches

Native to the prairies and fields of northern Mexico to Colorado and Nebraska, this delicate beauty is heat and drought tolerant. Add it to your containers, gardens, and flower arrangements. The cut flowers last up to ten days in a vase. The flowers and blue green foliage resemble our native gentians. Lisianthus fits in well in both formal and informal gardens. Tuck a few in the perennial garden to fill in voids or mix with other flowers in the annual garden. The taller varieties have limited branching and look their best when staked or supported by nearby plants. Fortunately, newer dwarf and self-branching cultivars are being introduced, reducing the maintenance needs. Lisianthus flowers best and suffers fewer disease problems in warm, dry seasons.

When, Where, and How to Plant
Lisianthus is truly a biennial treated as an annual in our gardens. It is slow to germinate and grow into a flowering plant. Start seeds indoors in late December or early January. Sow seeds in moist sterile starter mix at 55 to 60 degrees Fahrenheit. Grow under artificial lights and provide proper spacing to avoid diseases. Or purchase transplants sold as bedding plants in flats or in 3-, 4-, or 6-inch pots. Grow in full sun to partial shade in moist, well-drained to dry soils. Space small cultivars 6 inches apart and, larger cultivars 9 to 12 inches apart.

Growing Tips
Avoid overwatering, which can lead to root rot. Water established plants thoroughly whenever the top few inches of soil start to dry, but don't water

leaves and flowers. This can lead to leaf spot and botrytis blight. Follow soil test recommendation or the fertilizer recommendations at the beginning of this chapter.

Regional Advice and Care
Stake taller varieties or plant with sturdy neighbors that can provide needed support. Minimal deadheading is needed for these long-lasting flowers. Deadhead during wet weather to reduce the risk of botrytis blight. Removing diseased flowers or spotted leaves as soon as they appear, along with drier weather, will usually keep this disease under control. Avoid excess fertilizer that can increase the risk of disease and decrease flowering.

Companion Planting and Design
The airy texture of baby's breath and sweet alyssum makes for a nice container or garden combination. Tuck a few of the taller cultivars in with perennials for added color. They look nice with blue fescue, blue oat grass, and alliums. Lisianthus can be pricey and difficult to find, but it's well worth the effort. Use a few in containers, as a specimen or combined with more traditional plants to extend your planting budget.

Try These
The All America Selections winners 'Forever Blue' and its white counterpart 'Forever White' are 12 inches tall and are freely branched cultivars. They are heat and drought tolerant and suited to container and garden culture. The Echo series has double flowers on 18-inch plants.

Lobelia

Lobelia erinus

Botanical Pronunciation
lo-BEE-lee-ah air-EYE-nus

Bloom Period and Seasonal Color
Summer to fall blooms in white, blue, rose, and purple

Mature Height × Spread
4 to 8 inches × 6 to 18 inches

Lobelia has traditionally been used in containers or as an edging plant. Cultivars can be upright, forming 4- to 8-inch mounds. The trailing types can spread as much as 18 inches. This makes them good candidates for containers or to cascade over boulders and garden walls. The fine-textured leaves and delicate flowers add a softening touch to any garden. I like to use it as a filler plant since it often stalls out during the heat of our summers. Use heat-tolerant cultivars liberally or plant in cool locations where it will flourish all summer long. Edging lobelia is a relative of our native red cardinal flower, *Lobelia cardinalis*, and giant blue lobelia, *Lobelia siphilitica*. Both are large upright perennials suited to moist perennial and natural gardens.

When, Where, and How to Plant
Buy lobelias as bedding plants in flats or small containers from your local garden centers. Or start your own plants from seed ten to twelve weeks prior to the last spring frost. Seeds need light, moisture, and 70-degree Fahrenheit temperatures to germinate. Plant hardened-off transplants outdoors after all danger of frost has passed. Lobelia prefers full sun, cool temperatures, and moist, well-drained soil. Plant lobelia in partial shade to keep the roots cool and moist for season long bloom. An east location will provide sufficient light while avoiding the heat from the afternoon sun. Space plants about 6 inches apart.

Growing Tips
Keep the soil moist but not wet. Mulch the soil to keep roots cool and moist. Fertilize according to soil test results or apply a slow-release low-nitrogen fertilizer to provide season long nutrients without damaging heat stalled plants.

Regional Advice and Care
Lobelias grow and flower best in cool weather. They often stop growing and flowering in hot weather. Once cool weather returns so will growth and flowers. Continue to water as needed but stop fertilizing when plants stall from the heat. Lightly prune lobelias after the first flush of flowers to encourage new growth. Leggy plants can be pruned back halfway.

Companion Planting and Design
Lobelias can provide splashes of color throughout the landscape. They mix well with annuals planted in the ground or in containers. Their delicate texture makes them easy to blend with perennials in the garden. Design container plantings to take advantage of their color and texture. I combined 'Hot Springs' white with blue plumbago. The fleck of blue in the white lobelia flowers complemented the plumbago. Use more heat-tolerant lobelia cultivars when growing these as bedding and edging plants.

Try These
Techno® series is a trailer and tolerates are summers well. The 6- to 8-inch tall Laguna series and compact 'Hot Springs' are also heat tolerant and come in colors of white, lavender, blue, and rose, often with a contrasting eye and throat. 'Crystal Palace' is a compact type with dark blue flowers and bronze foliage.

Madagascar Periwinkle

Catharanthus roseus

Botanical Pronunciation
kath-ar-AN-thus ROSE-ee-us

Bloom Period and Seasonal Color
Summer to fall blooms in white, pink, rose, red, and rose-purple

Mature Height × Spread
8 to 18 inches × 8 to 17 inches

Though Madagascar periwinkle, or rose periwinkle, has the same neat, tidy, and mounded appearance as impatiens; they tolerate much different growing conditions. This sturdy plant will thrive and keep flowering in some of the toughest garden conditions. Heat, drought, and pollution won't stop the blooms, which are framed by glossy green leaves. Flowers are solid or have a colorful eye. Whether grown in a container or mixed in with other annuals, it is sure to attract the attention of visitors and butterflies. Move a few Madagascar periwinkles indoors to extend the garden season. They often bloom when grown in a southern window or under artificial lights. Bring existing plants indoors before frost or take cuttings and start new plants to enjoy indoors for the winter.

When, Where, and How to Plant
Madagascar periwinkles are available as bedding plants or in 3- to 4-inch pots. Or start seeds ten to twelve weeks prior to the last spring frost. Seeds need moist, warm conditions to germinate. Keep the starting mix at a temperature of 70 degrees Fahrenheit. It takes fifteen to twenty days for the seeds to germinate. Madagascar periwinkle can also be rooted from cuttings of patent-free plants in the spring. Hardened-off transplants can be placed outdoors after all danger of frost is passed. Though it prefers moist, well-drained soil, established plants can tolerate heat and drought but not wet soils. Space the plants 8 to 12 inches apart.

Growing Tips
Madagascar periwinkle requires very little care. Water established plants thoroughly whenever the top few inches of soil start to dry. Plants will rot in poorly drained soils or waterlogged soils. Follow soil test recommendations, or those in the chapter introduction, for fertilizing.

Regional Advice and Care
These plants need very little grooming to maintain their attractive appearance. Leaf spot disease and slugs may be problems during wet weather. Remove disease-infested leaves and control slugs with beer traps or the less toxic iron phosphate baits.

Companion Planting and Design
Madagascar periwinkle makes a nice flowering annual groundcover or container plant. They can be planted alone or mixed with other plants. Combine the bicolor Madagascar periwinkles with dusty miller or white alyssum. Or mix with ornamental peppers, tri-color sage, and alyssum. Try using this plant when you want the look of impatiens in hot, sunny areas.

Try These
Cora series sports larger flowers and the Mediterranean series is a trailing variety. 'Jaio Dark Red', 'Jaio Scarlet Eye', and Jams 'N Jellies Blackberry are AAS winners. The first of these has dark red flowers with a white center and grows 15 inches tall. The second is similar in size, but the flowers are more rosy-red with a white center. Jams 'N Jellies Blackberry has deep purple, almost black, petals with white throat.

Marigold

Tagetes species

Botanical Pronunciation
tah-JEE-deez

Other Name French or African marigold

Bloom Period and Seasonal Color
Summer through fall blooms in yellow, orange, gold, bronze, and creamy white

Mature Height × Spread
6 to 36 inches × 6 to 15 inches

Marigolds are one of the easiest annuals to grow. With very little care, you will be rewarded with season-long blooms. Perhaps you or your child started a plant in school for Mother's Day. The French and African marigolds are the most popular. Both produce a colorful display. Their round flowers and warm colors command attention in any landscape. The French marigold, *Tagetes patula*, is a compact plant, 6 to 18 inches tall. The flowers can be single or double and up to 2 inches across. The heat-tolerant African marigold, *Tagetes erecta*, is usually taller, 10 to 36 inches, with large 2- to 5-inch flowers. Triploids are a cross between the French and African marigolds. They are more heat-tolerant than the French and will keep flowering in hot weather.

When, Where, and How to Plant

Start seeds indoors about four weeks before the last spring frost. Keep the starting mix moist and at a temperature of 70 degrees Fahrenheit. Seedlings will appear in about five to seven days. You can start seeds outdoors in the garden after the last spring frost. Sow marigolds directly in a properly prepared planting bed. Lightly cover the seed with soil and keep it moist until the seeds germinate. Or purchase transplants from the garden center in flats. Plant hardened-off transplants outdoors after all danger of frost is past. Space transplants 6 to 18 inches apart.

Growing Tips

Marigolds are relatively low maintenance. Though drought tolerant, they will perform best in moist, well-drained soil. Water thoroughly whenever the top few inches of soil are crumbly but still moist. Use mulch to keep the roots cool and moist. Excess fertilization can result in all leaves and few to no flowers. Follow soil test recommendation and avoid fertilizing heat-stressed plants.

Regional Advice and Care

Remove faded flowers to encourage branching and continual blooms. French marigolds will stop flowering during hot weather (heat stall), but once temperatures cool, they will resume blooming. Don't fertilize but continue to water heat stalled marigolds as needed. African marigolds are more heat tolerant, although the flowers won't look as nice in extreme heat. Despite their reputation, rabbits and woodchucks will eat marigolds. Although usually problem-free, marigolds can be damaged by slugs, spider mites, aphids, and aster yellows disease. Remove aster yellows infested plants as soon as they are discovered.

Companion Planting and Design

Marigolds work well throughout the garden and in containers. Plant yellow marigolds with 'Victoria' blue salvia. The contrasting colors and flower forms are quite striking in the garden. I like to use 'Purple Ruffles' basil with marigolds. Use one of the yellow or golden marigolds with maroon-tipped flowers to echo the purple in the basil leaves.

Try These

The Signet marigold, *Tagetes tenuifolia*, is a compact plant with fern-like leaves. It produces small single flowers all season. 'Lemon Gem' has a lemony fragrance and small edible flowers.

Moneywort

Lysimachia nummularia

Botanical Pronunciation
Lye-sih-MAK-ee-ah num-yew-LAR-ee-ah

Other Name Creeping Jenny

Bloom Period and Seasonal Color
June blooms in yellow

Mature Height × Spread
2 to 4 inches × spreading

You will find this perennial sold alongside annuals, groundcovers, and perennials at the garden center. This fast grower will quickly cascade over the container edge or cover the ground. I considered putting this plant in the groundcover chapter, but there is some concern of invasiveness. The plants don't appear to spread by seed but, rather, cuttings, which does help to limit the threat. Avoid using this as groundcover in landscapes near natural wetlands and springs. The adaptability and fine texture of moneywort make this a useful container plant. The bright green or chartreuse leaves are round like coins and cascade over the edge of the container. My moneywort often overwinters in containers left outside. These are incorporated into new container gardens saving me money to spend on new plants.

When, Where, and How to Plant

Plant seeds in early spring. Or purchase plants in cell packs, 3- or 4-inch pots. You can also dig and use divisions from in-ground plantings for your containers. Moneywort will tolerate a wide range of conditions from sun to shade and wet to well-drained. It prefers shade with moist to wet organic soil. Plants grown in full sun need to be kept moist. Space plants 15 to 18 inches apart.

Growing Tips

Check containers daily and water as needed. Mulch plantings to conserve moisture and reduce weeds. Minimal fertilization is needed. Applying a low-nitrogen slow-release fertilizer at the start of the season will usually provide all the nutrients this and the other plants in the container need all season.

Regional Advice and Care

Overwinter moneywort outdoors for use in next year's garden. Sink inexpensive weatherproof pots in a vacant part of the garden in fall. Or set weatherproof pots in an unheated garage for winter. Water whenever the soil is thawed and moist. I've had good success setting my plastic pots among other plants I overwinter aboveground on my patio. I surround planters with annual containers or bagged leaves and cover with snow. They do quite well. Moneywort sawfly can devour lots of the leaves in early summer. Handpick when these worm-like insects are found. Fortunately, healthy plants will tolerate their feeding.

Companion Planting and Design

Include moneywort in spring and fall container gardens. Use 'Bright Lights' Swiss chard as a vertical accent, surround with hardy and edible pansies and allow golden moneywort to spill over the edge. Golden moneywort and 'Silver Falls' dichondra pair up nicely when used as "spillers" in container gardens. Or pot up a few hostas and gold leaf moneywort for shady areas. The chartreuse leaves will make the green hosta leaves stand out.

Try These

'Goldilocks' seems to be the most common yellow leafed cultivar. You may still find yellow-leafed form, *Lysimachia nummularia* 'Aurea'. Both develop the best foliage color when grown in full sun or light shade. The leaves tend to be more chartreuse in shade.

Moss Rose

Portulaca grandiflora

Botanical Pronunciation
por-tew-LAH-kah gran-dih-FLOOR-ah

Other Name Rose moss

Bloom Period and Seasonal Color
Summer through fall blooms in white, yellow, orange, red, rose, and lavender

Mature Height × Spread
4 to 8 inches × 6 inches

Moss rose is a great choice for hot, dry locations and busy gardeners. These plants thrive, and flower, in areas where most annuals would be lucky to survive. Their narrow, fleshy leaves give them a moss-like appearance. The flowers can be single or double. The double ones resemble a rose, thus its name. The botanical name *Portulaca* comes from Latin and means "to carry milk," referring to the milky sap. And as you probably guessed, *grandiflora* means "large flower." Use moss rose in containers, rock gardens and flower beds that can be enjoyed during the day. The flowers close late in the day, so there won't be much of a display to see in the evening. Use this unique response to light to interest children in gardening.

When, Where, and How to Plant
Start moss rose seeds indoors six weeks before the last frost. Sprinkle the seeds on the planting mix surface (don't plant deeply) and water them in. Keep the mix slightly moist and at 70 degrees Fahrenheit. Seeds can also be planted directly outdoors after the danger of frost is past. Prepare the planting bed, sow seeds on the surface of the soil, and water them in. Or purchase bedding plants. Place hardened-off transplants outdoors after the last spring frost. Space transplants 6 to 12 inches apart. Plant moss rose in areas with full sun and well-drained soil. Once you have grown moss rose, you will be rewarded with seedlings the following season. These can be dug and moved to other planting locations.

Growing Tips
If placed properly, moss rose is low maintenance. Keep the roots of young transplants slightly moist. Once established, allow the top few inches of soil to dry slightly before watering. Avoid overwatering, which leads to root and stem rot problems. Minimal fertilization is needed.

Regional Advice and Care
Moss rose is fairly free flowering with no real pest problems. Occasional deadheading can improve the overall appearance.

Companion Planting and Design
Moss roses thrive in hot, dry conditions, making them perfect for rock gardens, hanging baskets, containers, and other hot spots in the landscape. They can be used as a groundcover or edging plant. Try direct-seeding moss rose near early-fading perennials and spring bulbs. As these perennials die back, the moss rose will fill in the void.

Try These
Many of the new cultivars have been bred to stay open later in the day or during cloudy weather. The flowers of 'Afternoon Delight', 'Sundance Mix', and the 'Sundial' series will stay open for most of the day. The 'Calypso' series is probably the most readily available double-flowering moss rose. It comes in a variety of colors. 'Margarita Rosita', the 2004 AAS winner, has rose-colored semidouble flowers. A cultivar of a close relative, *Portulaca molokiniensis* 'Maraca' is grown for the foliage. The tightly spaced leaves curl around the stem creating an interesting texture.

Nasturtium

Tropaeolum majus

Botanical Pronunciation
tro-pay-OH-lum MAY-jus

Other Name Indian cress

Bloom Period and Seasonal Color
Summer to frost blooms in yellow, orange, red, and white

Mature Height × Spread
12 inches × 12 to 14 inches

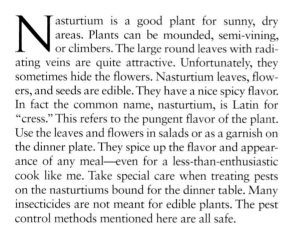

Nasturtium is a good plant for sunny, dry areas. Plants can be mounded, semi-vining, or climbers. The large round leaves with radiating veins are quite attractive. Unfortunately, they sometimes hide the flowers. Nasturtium leaves, flowers, and seeds are edible. They have a nice spicy flavor. In fact the common name, nasturtium, is Latin for "cress." This refers to the pungent flavor of the plant. Use the leaves and flowers in salads or as a garnish on the dinner plate. They spice up the flavor and appearance of any meal—even for a less-than-enthusiastic cook like me. Take special care when treating pests on the nasturtiums bound for the dinner table. Many insecticides are not meant for edible plants. The pest control methods mentioned here are all safe.

When, Where, and How to Plant
You may be able to find transplants in flats or 3-inch pots at garden centers or farmers markets. Or plant nasturtium seeds directly outdoors in the garden after the last spring frost. Sow seeds in a prepared planting bed. Or start seeds indoors four to six weeks before the last spring frost. Consider using biodegradable pots to reduce transplant shock. Plant them ¼ inch deep in any sterile starter mix, and keep the mix at a temperature of 65 to 70 degrees Fahrenheit. Move hardened-off transplants outdoors after the last spring frost. Grow nasturtiums in full sun in a well-drained location spaced 8 to 12 inches apart.

Growing Tips
The old saying, "be nasty to your nasturtiums" is true. Excess nitrogen results in lots of large leaves and no flowers. Overwatering can lead to disease problems.

Regional Advice and Care
Established plants need little care. In extreme heat, they may stop flowering, but once the weather cools, blooming will resume. Aphids are the most serious pests. A strong blast of water or several weekly sprays of insecticidal soap will take care of these insects. Watch for mites, cabbage worms, and thrips. Handpick or apply *Bacillus thuringiensis* (*Bt*) to control cabbage worms. The aphid treatment will also keep mites and thrips under control. Leaf spot disease can be a problem; avoid overwatering and wet foliage.

Companion Planting and Design
Plant nasturtiums where you can enjoy the hummingbirds and butterflies that come to nectar on the plants. It is a good choice for rock gardens, containers, and other difficult sites. The low-growing types make attractive edging plants and groundcovers. Seed nasturtiums in the garden next to early-fading perennials. As the perennials die back, the nasturtiums will fill in the empty spot.

Try These
'Alaska' and 'Amazon Jewel' have green leaves with creamy speckles and yellow, orange, or red flowers. 'Whirleybird' is a spurless cultivar with single and semidouble flowers that face up for a good floral display. The annual canary vine *Tropaeolum peregrinum* reaches heights of 8 feet. The small yellow flowers are fringed like a bird's wing.

Pansy

Viola wittrockiana

Botanical Pronunciation
vy-OH-lah ex wit-rok-ee-AY-na

Other Name Viola

Bloom Period and Seasonal Color
Spring to early summer and fall blooms in white, blue, purple, yellow, dark red, rose, apricot, and brown

Mature Height × Spread
4 to 8 inches × 9 to 12 inches

Pansies make excellent spring and fall bedding plants in containers or the garden. They are an old-time favorite experiencing a renewed interest and expanded role in the landscape. The newer cold-hardy cultivars give us at least two seasons of interest from one planting. Plant these in fall for a colorful end to the season. When spring arrives, the pansies are already in place providing a welcome bit of color. Their flowers can be used for fragrant cuttings or pressed for crafts. They also provide needed nectar for the early- and late-season butterflies. Use a few of these edible flowers in your salads, as a garnish, or frozen in ice cubes and served in a glass of sparkling water.

When, Where, and How to Plant

Start seeds indoors in January. Place them in moist media and chill in the refrigerator for one week. Seeds need moist, dark, 65-degree Fahrenheit conditions to germinate. Lower the growing temperature to 50 degrees Fahrenheit once the seeds sprout. Or plant seeds outdoors in summer for a fall display. Purchase pansies as bedding plants in flats, 3- to 4-inch pots, or planted containers. Plant hardened-off transplants outdoors in April, as soon as the soil is dry enough to work, or in fall. Pansies prefer full sun but perform best in cool temperatures. Grow pansies in full sun or partial shade in moist, well-drained soil. Space plants 6 inches apart in the garden, although they can be planted closer in containers.

Growing Tips

Mulch to keep the soil cool and moist when trying to grow pansies through our hot summers. Water thoroughly whenever the top few inches of soil are moist and crumbly. Fertilize as you do your other annuals.

Regional Advice and Care

They are pretty free flowering, but deadheading pansies will maximum their blooms. Select a heat-tolerant cultivar when using pansies for season-long interest. Even those may stop blooming during hot weather. Remove faded flowers and keep the soil moist but do not fertilize. Unkempt plants can be pruned back. Once temperatures cool, flowering will resume. Pansies are generally pest free. Slugs and fungal leaf spots may be problems in wet weather.

Companion Planting and Design

Pansies work well in planters alone or mixed with annual or perennial plants. Use them as a ground-cover around spring-flowering bulbs. This doubles your flower display and helps mask the fading bulb foliage. Plant one of the trailing pansies in a pumpkin for a fun seasonal display.

Try These

Cool Wave and WonderFall™ series are trailing varieties that can be planted 12 inches apart. These and the non-trailing 'Icicle' and 'Sub Zero' pansies survive the rigors of our winters. 'Imperial', 'Maxim', 'Springtime', and 'Universal' are heat-tolerant cultivars. Johnny-jump-up, *Viola tricolor*, a close relative, produces small flowers with "faces" made of blue, gold, and deep violet and reseeds readily.

Pentas

Pentas lanceolata

Botanical Pronunciation
PEN-tas lan-see-oh-LAY-tah

Other Name Star cluster

Bloom Period and Seasonal Color
Summer until frost with white, pink, rose, or lilac flowers

Mature Height × Spread
Up to 18 inches × up to 18 inches

I always include a few of these long blooming annuals in my garden. I tuck a few in containers, add a couple to my perennial garden, and often use them next to my entranceway. I like the bold accent of the reds and the more subtle accents the pink flowers provide. You have probably seen these plants in books and magazines featuring butterflies. They are a popular plant for butterfly gardens since they are a favorite nectar source. Hummingbirds can also be seen feeding on the red and dark pink cultivars. The leaves are deeply veined and slightly hairy. They make a nice backdrop for the long-lasting and self-cleaning clusters of star-shaped flowers. Plant plenty since you will want to pick a few for garden-fresh flower arrangements.

When, Where, and How to Plant
You can purchase plants or start from seed. Pentas are usually sold in 3- or 4-inch pots and have become more readily available in the last few years. Or order seeds from garden catalogs to start your own plants. Sow seeds indoors about eight to ten weeks before the last spring frost. Use clean containers and a sterile starter mix. Keep it moist and 60 to 65 degrees Fahrenheit for best results. Move hardened-off transplants outdoors after the danger of frost has passed. Grow pentas in full sun with moist, well-drained soils. They will tolerate light shade but flower best in full sun. Space plants 10 to 12 inches apart.

Growing Tips
Keep the soil around new transplants slightly moist. Water established plants thoroughly whenever the top few inches of soil are starting to dry. Check containers daily and water thoroughly as needed. Mulch around plants in the garden to conserve moisture and suppress weeds. Incorporate a slow-release low-nitrogen fertilizer into the soil or container mix at planting. This is usually enough for the season.

Regional Advice and Care
These annuals will flower all summer long with little or no deadheading. Though generally pest free, you may have problems with mites and aphids during hot dry seasons. A strong blast of water or several applications of insecticidal soap will reduce their populations to a tolerable level.

Companion Planting and Design
Use them alone or with other plants in containers. They are a bit pricey, so I like to scatter my investment throughout the landscape, using them much like perennials. And plant them where you can enjoy the hummingbirds and butterflies that visit. Mix pentas with annual and perennial grasses. They combine nicely with perennials, lisianthus, rudbeckia, and salvia.

Try These
Availability may dictate your selection. The 'Butterfly' series has white or deep pink, deep rose, or red with white-eyed flowers. Northern Lights® is more tolerant of our often cool summer and cooler fall temperatures. I like the dark pinks and reds in my garden. The New Look series is compact plants with red, pink, violet, or white flowers.

Petunia

Petunia hybrid

Botanical Pronunciation
peh-TOON-yah

Bloom Period and Seasonal Color
Summer through frost blooms in pink, red, violet, lavender, yellow, salmon, and white

Mature Height × Spread
6 to 18 inches × 6 to 36 inches

I remember helping my mother deadhead the cascading petunias in our front planters. The sticky stems and my youth made this seem like torture. Fortunately, many of the new petunias have minimized the need to deadhead. Enjoy their fragrance and the butterflies and hummingbirds they attract. The grandiflora petunias are covered with large flowers and still require some deadheading. The multifloras are free-flowering and weather resistant. They are covered with medium-sized blooms that need little deadheading. Calibrachoa, sold as Million Bells and Superbells, looks like a small-scale petunia. This fast growing compact plant is self-cleaning and works great alone or mixed with other plants in hanging baskets and containers. And if this isn't convincing, drive into Marquette on U.S. Highway 41 for a glimpse of petunia pandemonium.

When, Where, and How to Plant
Start petunias from seeds indoors ten weeks prior to the last spring frost. Petunias need moisture, light, and 70 degree Fahrenheit temperatures to germinate. Or buy petunias in flats, small containers, or hanging baskets. Place hardened-off transplants outdoors after the danger of frost is past. Grow petunias in full sun to part shade and well-drained soil. In full shade, the plants get leggy and fail to flower. Plant miniatures 6 inches apart, bedding types 10 to 12 inches apart, and the trailing types up to 24 inches apart when used as a groundcover.

Growing Tips
Water established petunias thoroughly whenever the top 3 to 4 inches are moist and crumbly. Use a watering wand or soaker hose to avoid wet leaves and flowers that will be more subject to disease.

Regional Advice and Care
Remove faded flowers and clip back leggy stems to keep the plants full and flowering. The amount of grooming needed depends on the cultivar selected. The grandifloras usually need deadheading and suffer rain damage more readily than the others. Stem rot can be a problem with any petunia grown in poorly drained soil. Botrytis blight can cause flowers and leaves to brown, but regular deadheading and removal of infected plant parts is effective as a control. Flea beetles and aphids can also infest petunias, as well as tobacco mosaic virus, spread by aphids.

Companion Planting and Design
Use petunias in containers and hanging baskets or as edging and bedding plants. Trailing types work well in containers, hanging baskets, and even as groundcovers weaving throughout nearby plantings.

Try These
The trailing Pretty Much Picasso® has green edged pink flowers. The 2003 AAS winner 'Merlin Blue Morn' unique flowers transition from a velvety blue edge to the white center and seem to glow at dusk. 'Trellis Pink' is vigorous and upright growing petunia suited to trellising in a container. Supertunia® Vista Silverberry is a vigorous, mounding blooming machine that never gets leggy. The popular Wave™ petunias are vigorous multifloras that grow 36 inches long and flower all season long.

Salvia

Salvia splendens

Botanical Pronunciation
SAL-vee-ah SPLEN-denz

Other Name Scarlet sage

Bloom Period and Seasonal Color
Summer until frost blooms in red, salmon, pink, blue, lavender, and white

Mature Height × Spread
8 to 30 inches × 8 to 12 inches

Nothing grabs your attention like red salvia. The intense color and large flower spikes make it stand out in the landscape. Both hummingbirds and butterflies nectar on the flowers and goldfinches enjoy the seeds. Use it as a focal point to accent a hard-to-find entrance or landscape feature. Salvia is often used to provide the red in patriotic red, white, and blue gardens. They combine well with most of the commonly grown annuals. It's a great annual for the garden or flower arrangement. I like its close relative mealycup sage, *Salvia farinacea*. Its narrower flower spike makes it easy to blend with annuals, perennials, and various gardening styles. This long bloomer needs little deadheading, and the flowers are great for fresh and dried arrangements.

When, Where, and How to Plant

Start salvia from seeds indoors about six to eight weeks before the last spring frost. Sow seeds on a sterile starter medium and water. Do not cover since these seeds need light to germinate. Avoid problems with damping off by using a sterile mix, clean containers, and by not overwatering. Or buy salvias as bedding plants in flats or in 3- to 4-inch pots from the garden center. Plant hardened-off transplants outdoors after all danger of frost is past. Salvia prefers full sun with moist, well-drained soil, and cool temperatures. Light shade often intensifies the flower color without compromising the vigor. Space smaller cultivars 8 inches apart and larger cultivars 10 to 12 inches apart.

Growing Tips

Mulch the soil around salvias to keep the roots cool and moist. Water established plants thoroughly whenever the top few inches of soil are moist but crumbly.

Regional Advice and Care

Deadhead to encourage branching and continual blooming. Salvias may suffer from downy and powdery mildew. Plants in full sun and properly spaced are less vulnerable. Avoid overhead watering and remove infected plant parts to reduce the spread of these diseases.

Companion Planting and Design

Salvias grow well in containers or as edging, bedding, or background plants. Red salvia is an attention getter in the garden, although the intense red can be overpowering. Temper this by planting red salvia in front of evergreens or mixed with dusty miller. Or try growing 'Lady in Red'. The red flowers on this compact plant are more open and less overpowering. I find it blends better with perennials and less formal landscapes.

Try These

The Vista series displays dense flower spikes on compact 10- to 12-inch plants. *Salvia farinacea* 'Victoria' grows 18 inches producing narrow violet-blue flower spikes while 'Strata' has bicolor flowers. *Salvia coccinea* 'Coral Nymph' has delicate coral flowers that seem to float above the foliage. Blue and Black *Salvia guaranitica* has bold foliage and blue flowers with dark blue, almost black, sepals and is a hummingbird magnet.

Snapdragon

Antirrhinum majus

Botanical Pronunciation
an-ter-REE-num MAY-jus

Bloom Period and Seasonal Color
Summer to frost blooms in white, yellow, bronze, purple, pink, and red

Mature Height × Spread
6 to 48 inches × 6 to 24 inches

Snapdragons are an old-time favorite with new cultivars providing a modern update. They perform best in cool weather making them great additions to spring and fall gardens. These stately plants hold spikes of colorful flowers over whorls of narrow green leaves. The snapdragon is an impressive flower outdoors in the garden or inside in a flower vase. Harvest the flowers when the bottom third of the blossoms are open, the middle portion is just starting to show color, and the top third is in bud. This will give you the longest floral display in your arrangement and encourage the plants to produce more blooms. And don't forget to put your nose in close and you may be rewarded with a light fragrance.

When, Where, and How to Plant

Start snapdragons from seeds indoors about ten weeks before the last spring frost. Seeds need light, moisture, and a temperature of 70 degrees Fahrenheit to germinate. Snapdragons can be direct-seeded outdoors in the spring as soon as the soil is workable. Plants are available from garden centers as bedding plants and in small containers. Hardened-off transplants will tolerate light frost but should be protected from hard freezes. Plant them in an area with moist, well-drained soil. Space small cultivars 6 inches apart, medium cultivars 8 to 10 inches apart, and tall cultivars at least 12 inches apart.

Growing Tips

Water established plants thoroughly and often enough to keep the top few inches of moist but not wet. Mulch the soil surface to help keep the roots cool and moist. Don't fertilize the plants during hot or dry weather, when the plants stop blooming, or show signs of stress.

Regional Advice and Care

Deadhead regularly. Remove faded flowers before too many seedpods form on the flower stem. Taller cultivars may need staking or nearby sturdy plants for support. Snapdragons may stop blooming in extremely hot weather. Prune leggy plants back and wait for an impressive fall display. A few snapdragon plants will reseed, or an occasional plant will survive a mild winter. Aphids and mites may cause leaves to curl, yellow, and eventually brown. The fungal disease rust may also cause problems.

Companion Planting and Design

Use dwarf cultivars as a groundcover, in a container, or as an edging plant. Tall cultivars make great background plants where it is easier to hide the stakes. And include in the children's garden and make the flowers "talk." Remove a single blossom from the stem. Gently squeeze the sides and watch the flower open and shut.

Try These

'Candy Showers' is a trailing variety in deep purple, orange, red, rose, or yellow. Many newer snapdragons have open flowers for a showier flower display. 'Monaco' and 'Potomac' produce long flowers stems good for bouquets on tall plants The Floral Carpet series and the improved Floral Showers series are dwarfs, 6 to 8 inches tall.

Spike

Cordyline species

Botanical Pronunciation
kor-dih-LYE-nee

Other Name Dracaena

Bloom Period and Seasonal Color
Season-long green foliage

Mature Height × Spread
24 inches × 15 inches

Spike plants are a favorite of containers and have long been used as the "thriller" (vertical accent). Many enthusiastic gardeners winter their plants indoors for quite a few years. Strong friends help move them indoors each winter where it grows in front of a sunny window with moist soil. Each spring they move the plant outdoors to the summer garden. I take the easy way out, enjoying my spikes until the cold weather kills them or the snow flies. Then I recycle them in the compost pile and start with new plants the next spring. And if you are tired of spike, please read on. There are lots of new colorful cultivars and combinations that can add life to this very popular plant.

When, Where, and How to Plant
Plant spikes outdoors after all danger of frost is past. Planted containers can be moved indoors or outdoors, depending on weather. Spikes prefer full to partial sun and moist, well-drained soil. Avoid wet soil and heavy shade where the plants are more likely to develop root rot and leaf spot disease. Spikes are available from garden centers in 2- or 3-inch pots. Usually a single spike is planted in the middle of the container. Space plants 12 to 15 inches apart when planted *en masse* to provide a new look for this plant.

Growing Tips
Spikes are very low-maintenance plants. They will thrive in properly maintained planters. Check the soil moisture in containers at least once a day. Water containers thoroughly, allowing excess water to run out the drainage holes. Apply a low-nitrogen slow-release fertilizer to plantings in spring. This usually provides all the nutrients the plants need for the season.

Regional Advice and Care
Spikes are fairly pest free and tolerate temperatures in the 40s. Avoid excess moisture that can lead to root rot and leaf spot. Brown leaf tips occur in very dry soil and from the fluoride in the water. Keep soil slightly moist to correct the problem.

Companion Planting and Design
The traditional container planting includes a spike in the middle surrounded by a couple of geraniums, a few dusty millers, alyssum, and vinca vine. I have also seen spikes planted *en masse* in the center of an island bed for an impressive show. Other gardeners use individual spikes throughout their annual plantings, creating a scattering of vertical interest. Consider using alternatives such as ornamental grass, bronze fennel, or vines trained on container size supports.

Try These
Look for some of the more colorful spike cultivars. Festival® Raspberry, 'Electric Pink', and 'Pink Passion' have colorful red foliage. Include 'Festival® Burgundy', 'Bauer's', 'Burgundy Spire', or 'Cabernett' for a purple vertical accent. Centerpiece™ has green, cream, and pink leaves. Centerpiece™ Mocha Latte has cream and chocolate streaked green leaves and 'Torbay Dazzler' sports green leaves with cream variegation along the margins.

Sunflower

Helianthus annuus

Botanical Pronunciation
hee-lee-AN-thus AN-yew-us

Bloom Period and Seasonal Color
Summer blooms until frost in yellow, white, and bronze with a yellow, brown, purple, or crimson center

Mature Height × Spread
15 inches to 15 feet × 12 to 24 inches

The sunflower, native to North America, is a longtime garden favorite. The large flowers add color to the garden, and the seeds attract hungry birds, squirrels, and children. The large seeds make planting easy, and sunflower's large size gives it great kid appeal. Add to their delight by planting sunflowers in a circle to make a playhouse or fun pattern to create a maze. Plant squash, beans, or morning glories between the sunflowers. These climbers will use the sunflowers as a trellis, forming walls of the playhouse. But don't relegate these flowers to the vegetable or kid's garden. Breeding programs have resulted in a variety of flower sizes, colors, and plant heights that make excellent cut flowers that readily blend into the garden.

When, Where, and How to Plant
Start from seeds outside after all danger of frost is past. Space seeds 6 inches apart and ½ inch deep in properly prepared soil. Thin seedlings when they are 3 inches tall, leaving 18 to 24 inches between plants. Sunflowers can be started indoors four to six weeks before the last spring frost. Plant seeds in a starter mix, keeping it moist and at about 70 degrees Fahrenheit. Seedlings should appear in ten to fourteen days. Transplants are sometimes sold in 3-, 4-, or 6-inch pots in spring. Plant hardened-off transplants outdoors after last frost date. Grow sunflowers in full sun with well-drained soil. Space transplants in the garden at least 24 inches apart and closer for dwarf varieties.

Growing Tips
Water established plants thoroughly whenever the top few inches of soil are moist and crumbly. Fertilize according to soil test results.

Regional Advice and Care
Proper spacing will help reduce problems with leaf spot and powdery mildew—both unsightly but not life-threatening diseases. Mask the problem by growing slightly shorter plants in front of diseased leaves. Aphids may cause minor damage. Cover seedheads with cheesecloth or netting to protect the harvest from squirrels and birds. Remove the flower with 1 to 2 feet of stem attached when the back of the flower is brown. Hang it upside down until dry and brown.

Companion Planting and Design
Dwarf sunflowers combine nicely with amaranth, ornamental grasses, and asters. Or use them in a fall display with mums, corn stalks, and pumpkins as a fall decoration. Many garden centers sell blooming dwarf plants in large pots for the fall garden.

Try These
'Mammoth', 'Russian', and 'Russian Giant' can reach 12 to 15 feet. The AAS winner 'Ring of Fire' produces 5-inch flowers with chocolate-brown centers surrounded by a ring of red and then gold petals on 4- to 5-foot plants. 'Chianti' is 4 to 5 feet tall, multi-branched purple stems and flowers with deep red petals, 'Solar Flare' is 5 to 6 feet tall has dark black center surrounded by gold-tipped red petals.

Sweet Potato Vine

Ipomoea batatas

Botanical Pronunciation
eye-poe-MEE-ah bah-TAH-tass

Bloom Period and Seasonal Color
Colorful lime green, purple, or variegated green, cream and pink foliage all season long

Mature Height × Spread
Branches up to 3 feet in length

The popular sweet potato vine is a cultivar of the edible sweet potato and cousin to the morning glory. The heart-shaped or lobed foliage makes a nice trailing plant for containers and groundcovers in the annual garden. First-time growers beware—one plant goes a long way. The vigorous vine will quickly fill out and engulf its neighbors. Use one sweet potato vine per pot, a less vigorous cultivar, or an equally assertive planting partner for best results. Some gardeners have overwintered the plants indoors. Some store the tuberous root for winter and start it indoors in spring with their cannas and calla lilies. The plants survived but didn't look their best that second year. Other gardeners had much better results using cuttings.

When, Where, and How to Plant
Sweet potato vines are available from garden centers in 3- and 4-inch pots. Some gardeners start new plants from cuttings from patent-free plants. Move hardened-off transplants into the garden after the danger of frost has past. Grow sweet potato vines in full or part sun with moist, well-drained soil. One sweet potato vine per container is usually enough. Space plants 24 inches apart when grown in the garden as a groundcover.

Growing Tips
Water established plants thoroughly whenever the top few inches of soil are crumbly and moist. Fertilize according to soil test recommendations or as recommended in the chapter introduction. Container gardens need a bit more attention. Check planters daily and water thoroughly whenever the top few inches of soil start to dry. Incorporate a slow-release fertilizer at the time of planting or use a water-soluble fertilizer throughout the season.

Regional Advice and Care
Sweet potato vines are low maintenance and relatively pest free. Some gardeners overwinter the plants. Take cuttings in late summer and root in a well-drained potting mix. Grow the root cutting in a sunny window, keeping the soil moist. Or, store the tuberous roots for winter. Dig them after a light frost. Clean and store them in a cool dark location. Start indoors in late winter. Take cuttings from the shoots that grow out of the tuberous roots. I am often asked "Are they edible?" Yes, but not as tasty as those bred for the vegetable garden.

Companion Planting and Design
Use the colorful foliage to complement or highlight other plants. The blue flowers of fan flower and colorful Wave™ petunias look nice against the leaves of 'Marguerite' or 'Blackie'. Canna, bananas, and palms look great when combined with these vigorous growers.

Try These
'Marguerite' is the most common and very vigorous with chartreuse heart-shaped leaves. 'Blackie' has dark purple leaves that appear black. The lobed leaves combine well with light-colored flowers and foliage. Plants in the Sweet Caroline® series are compact growing with good heat tolerance. Those in the Illusion® series have deeply incised leaves and good heat tolerance.

Verbena

Verbena hybrids

Botanical Pronunciation
ver-BEE-nah

Other Name Garden verbena

Bloom Period and Seasonal Color
Summer through frost blooms in white, lavender, purple, blue, pink, red, and apricot

Mature Height × Spread
Up to 15 inches × up to 20 inches

With all the cultivars and related species available, there is bound to be a verbena that is right for your garden. There are upright and spreading types with various shaped leaves. The flower clusters come in a variety of colors and are quite showy. There are several related annual, biennial, and perennial verbenas. The self-seeding Brazilian verbena, *Verbena bonariensis*, forms purple blooms at the tip of a 4- to 6-foot stiff stem. With small leaves near the bases, it makes a nice grow-through plant the hummingbirds and butterflies love. The perennial *Verbena canadensis* is a ground-hugging plant that blooms from late May till frost. Though the parent plant may die in a cold winter, they leave plenty of seeds for next year's garden.

When, Where, and How to Plant
Start verbena seeds indoors twelve weeks prior to the last spring frost. Chill the seeds for seven days before seeding. Plant in a well-drained sterile starter mix and maintain a temperature of 70 degrees Fahrenheit. Use sterile potting mix and clean containers and keep the starter mix slightly dry to avoid damping-off disease. Plant hardened-off transplants outdoors after the last spring frost. Grow verbena in full sun with well-drained soil. Space upright-type plants 12 inches apart and spreading types 18 inches apart.

Growing Tips
Some verbena cultivars will stop blooming during hot, dry spells. Mulch the soil to keep the roots cool and moist. Provide adequate water, and once the weather cools, the flowers will return. Avoid fertilizing during hot dry spells.

Regional Advice and Care
Remove faded flowers to encourage branching and continual blooms. Verbenas are also subject to powdery mildew. Proper spacing and a full sun location will help reduce the risk of this disease.

Companion Planting and Design
Try a few of the spreading types in hanging baskets or used as annual groundcovers mixed with *Helichrysum* (licorice vine), lotus vine, or *Dichondra* 'Silver Falls'. Use them in flower, rock, and butterfly gardens. Try this combination in a container or small flowerbed. 'Toffee Twist' sedge as a vertical accent, All American Selection winner 'Peaches and Cream' or other coral-flowered verbena, and 'Silver Falls' dichondra. Mix Brazilian verbena with ornamental grasses and other flowers. This often happens by accident as this plant reseeds throughout the garden. Brazilian verbena flowers dance above the grass, providing color all season long. Mixing it into the garden also hides the foliage that can become unsightly from mildew. I let my perennial verbena crawl throughout my garden. Stray plants can be relocated to another area or to a friend's garden.

Try These
The Lanai® series is early blooming with good resistance to heat and powdery mildew Superbena®'s come in a variety of colors. These trailing plants are heat and drought tolerant and do not need deadheading.

Zinnia

Zinnia elegans

Botanical Pronunciation
ZIN-ee-ah EL-eh-ganz

Bloom Period and Seasonal Color
Summer to frost blooms in white, yellow, green, red, orange, apricot, rose, red, and violet

Mature Height × Spread
6 to 36 inches × 18 to 24 inches

This eye-catching annual, in the garden or flower vase, is a longtime favorite of northern gardeners. Easy to start from seed indoors or right in the garden, they will quickly reach flowering size. This makes them a good choice for those with a limited plant budget and fun for gardeners of all ages. Their heat and drought tolerance is great for busy, waterwise and container gardeners. The color and movement that hummingbirds and butterflies provide while nectaring on the flowers add to their appeal. Don't let past problems with leaf spot and mildew scare you away. Many of the newer cultivars are more tolerant and even resistant to these diseases. Check out the many colors, various flower types, and plant heights available.

When, Where, and How to Plant

Start zinnias from seeds indoors about six weeks before the last spring frost. Plant the seeds in a sterile starter mix keeping it moist at 70 degrees Fahrenheit. Direct seed zinnias in the garden after all danger of frost is past. Prepare the soil and plant seeds 3 to 6 inches apart. Thin to final spacing once the seeds are 3 inches tall. Plant hardened-off transplants outdoors at the same time. Grow them in full-sun areas with well-drained soil. Plant bedding plants at the same depth they were growing in the containers. Space small cultivars 6 to 8 inches apart and the larger cultivars at least 12 inches apart.

Growing Tips

Water established plants thoroughly whenever the top few inches of soil are moist but crumbly for best performance. Established plants, however, are drought tolerant. Avoid water on the leaves to minimum the risk of disease and excess nitrogen fertilizer that can inhibit flowering.

Regional Advice and Care

Proper plant selection, siting, and spacing are critical to the health and appearance of zinnias. Select leaf spot and mildew resistant cultivars whenever possible. Remove faded flowers to encourage branching and continual blooms.

Companion Planting and Design

Zinnias are perfect plants for hot, dry locations. They work well with cockscomb, dusty miller, and annual fountain grass. Single zinnias are not as bold as the doubles but are easier to blend with other flowers. I often use the narrow-leafed zinnias, *Zinnia haageana*, to fill voids in perennial gardens. They also combine nicely with 'Purple Ruffles' basil and the purple alternanthera. Tall zinnias make nice background plants, and they all perform well in containers.

Try These

'Zahara' series is an AAS winner with good mildew resistance; 'Zowie! Yellow Flame' AAS winner has bicolor petals of scarlet and yellow. 'Profusion Cherry', 'Profusion Orange', and 'Profusion White' were selected as All-America Selections Gold-Medal winners for their low maintenance and disease resistance. They still outperform most cultivars. The cactus-flowered zinnia has twisted petals and resembles the cactus-flowered dahlia. The dahlia-flowered zinnia has large double flowers with cupped petals that give it a more rounded appearance.

BULBS
FOR MICHIGAN

After surviving the cold and snow of winter, the gardening season never seems long enough. Extend your garden's bloom time by incorporating spring-flowering bulbs into your landscape. But don't stop there. Try including some of the hardy and nonhardy summer- and fall-blooming bulbs. They can add color and interest to your annual, perennial, and container gardens.

Jumpstart your spring garden with a few of the very early blooming minor bulbs like snowdrops, winter aconite, glory-of-the-snow, and Siberian squill. These early bloomers can tolerate the cold temperatures we seem to get each spring after our early spring plants start blooming.

For the purposes of this book, I am using the term "bulb" to include plants grown from true bulbs, rhizomes, corms, tubers, and tuberous roots. Hardy bulbs can be left in the ground year-round. Nonhardy, sometimes called tender or tropical bulbs, are planted outdoors each spring. You can remove them from the ground and store them indoors over the winter. I'll cover the basics on planting and care in the individual plant profiles.

For the Best Bulb Display Possible

Order bulbs from catalogues, online, or from your local garden center. Shop early for the best selection. Purchase firm, blemish-free bulbs. Avoid those with nicks, cuts, or soft areas. Store bulbs in a cool, dark place in a perforated plastic or mesh bag until it is time to plant.

Most bulbs prefer moist, well-drained soil during their growing season and a bit drier soil when they're

Dahlias and ageratum make a beautiful formal bed.

dormant in summer. Work several inches of organic matter into the top 12 inches of soil before planting to improve the drainage in heavy clay soil and increases the water-holding capacity of sandy soil. Fertilize bulb plantings according to soil test recommendations. In general, bulbs receive enough nutrients from your regular garden fertilization program. Most garden soils do not need phosphorus, so skip the bonemeal and super phosphate. Plus, bonemeal tends to attract rodents that like to feast on our bulbs. Instead, use a low-nitrogen slow-release fertilizer at planting if nutrients are needed.

Vividly colored tulips paired with violas offer a lovely spring show.

Plant most hardy bulbs in the fall when temperatures are consistently cool, starting in early October. You can plant bulbs until the ground freezes. In general, plant bulbs at a depth of two or three times the vertical diameter of the bulb. Space them at least three to four times the width of the bulb. Water the newly planted bulbs. Avoid planting bulbs near your home's foundation, especially the south side, near a dryer vent, or close to other artificial heat sources. Bulbs planted in these spots tend to sprout early and are subject to cold damage. Reduce the risk of premature sprouting by applying a layer of evergreen boughs over bulb plantings after the ground freezes.

You can add, if needed, a low-nitrogen fertilizer to established bulb gardens in the early spring as the leaves appear. Don't forget to water if we have a dry spring. Remove faded flowers but leave the leaves intact so they can produce the needed energy for the plants to return and flower next year. If you need to move existing bulbs, mark their location for a fall transplant. The next best time is as the leaves start to fade, though every gardener has broken the rules and still had some success.

Each fall it seems like the squirrels and chipmunks dig bulbs faster than you can plant. Come spring the rabbits and deer eat the flowers on whatever the other animals left behind. Scare tactics, barriers, and repellents can help keep the wildlife at bay. If all this sounds like too much work, select bulbs that animals do not eat. Hyacinths, daffodils, allium, fritillaria, snowflake, camassia, and Spanish bluebells are larger bulbs that the animals seem to ignore. Include some animal resistant minor bulbs such as grape hyacinths, squills, winter aconite, snowdrop, autumn crocus, glory-of-the-snow, and *Crocus tommasinianus*. Not a bad list, and the many newer, more unique cultivars will allow you to add plenty of variety to your garden when using these.

Allium

Allium species

Botanical Pronunciation
AL-lee-um

Other Name Flowering onion

Bloom Period and Seasonal Color
Early, mid-, or late summer blooms in white, purple, blue, pink, or yellow

Mature Height × Spread
6 to 60 inches × 6 to 15 inches

Eye-catching alliums are guaranteed to get your garden a second look not only from passers-by, but also from the birds, bees, and butterflies looking for a place to feed. Plus, rabbits and deer tend to leave them alone. Include an assortment of alliums in your landscape for summer-long enjoyment. Select alliums that are hardy to your area and provide the look you want in your yard. The best known is the giant onion (*Allium giganteum*). The 5- to 6-inch-diameter purple flower head tops a 3- to 4-foot-tall plant. These like other alliums are great in fresh or dried flower arrangements. The wonderful foliage adds texture and slight onion fragrance to the garden all season long.

When, Where, and How to Plant
Plant allium bulbs in fall. This is also a good time to divide or move existing plantings. Most alliums prefer full sun to light shade and well-drained soil. Many are drought tolerant. Ornamental onion is often sold as a perennial at specialized garden centers. Plant the bulbs at a depth of 2 to 3 times their diameter, but no deeper than 6 inches. Bulb spacing varies with the species.

Growing Tips
Winter mulch allium plantings with evergreen boughs after the soil surface freezes. Mulching helps more tender alliums make it through our difficult winters and reduces the risk of early sprouting that can result in frost-damaged foliage. Mask frost-damaged foliage of the early bloomers with other plants, while highlighting allium's showy flowers.

Regional Advice and Care
Bulb rot is a common problem in cool, damp soil. You can't control the rain, but you can adjust your watering schedule. Water thoroughly and only when the top few inches begin to dry. Frost-damaged tips won't hurt the plant.

Companion Planting and Design
Use smaller alliums in rock gardens. Some species will reseed and naturalize. Most alliums look good mixed with perennials. The giant onion, *Allium giganteum*, is a good background plant, although I find the large flower head can be difficult to blend. Try surrounding this bold element with finer textured plants like threadleaf coreopsis or ornamental grasses. Or use an equally bold-textured plant like a yucca to create contrast in form.

Try These
Ornamental onion (*Allium senescens* 'Glaucum' or *Allium montanum* 'Glaucum') is only 6 inches tall. The attractive, slightly twisted, gray-green foliage is effective all season. The late summer lilac or mauve flowers are 1 inch in diameter. Turkestan onion, *Allium karataviense*, is a bit larger, 10 inches, with 4- to 6-inch lilac flowers gracing wide blue-green leaves that remind me of hosta. 'Summer Beauty' and the newer, more compact and prolific blooming 'Summer Peek-a-Boo'™ alliums' 2-inch lavender pink flowers add color to the summer garden. Drumstick chives (*Allium sphaerocephalon*) is a 2- to 3-foot-tall plant with many 2-inch-diameter purple blooms that mix nicely with ornamental grasses.

Calla Lily

Zantedeschia aethiopica

Botanical Pronunciation
zan-the-DES-kee-ah ay-thee-OP-ih-kah

Other Name Arum lily

Bloom Period and Seasonal Color
Late spring through early summer blooms in white

Mature Height × Spread
2 to 3 feet × 2 feet

Calla lilies are a favorite cut flower and garden plant. These long-lasting blooms are commonly sold by florists and used in bridal bouquets and funeral arrangements. The showy trumpet shaped part of the flower is called a *spathe*. The stemlike structure in the center is a *spadix*. Their fragrance is an added benefit. In the garden, calla flowers and leaves of those with spotted foliage can brighten up a shady location. Their arrowhead-shaped leaves make a dramatic statement whether the plant is in a container, in a flower garden, or near a water garden. Extend their colorful display by including close relatives such as *Zantedeschia albo-marginata* (white flowers) and *Zantedeschia elliottiana* (yellow flowers) that have white spots on the leaves.

When, Where, and How to Plant
Plant rhizomes indoors in mid-March for an earlier outdoor flower display. Grow them in a container with well-draining potting mix. Cover rhizomes with 3 inches of soil. Water sparingly until growth appears, then increase watering and fertilize. In the garden, plant rhizomes 4 inches deep and 18 inches apart. Move hardened-off transplants outdoors after the danger of frost has passed. Plant calla lilies in partial to full shade. They will tolerate full sun if the soil is kept moist. Calla lilies prefer moist, organic soil. Plants are available from garden centers in 3-, 4-, or 6-inch pots. Plant container-grown calla lilies at the same level they were growing in the pot.

Growing Tips
Keep the top few inches of soil moist. Container plantings will need to be checked daily and watered thoroughly as needed. Normal flower garden fertilization is sufficient for these plants. Or add a slow-release fertilizer to the garden soil or container potting mix at planting for a full season of fertilization in one application.

Regional Advice and Care
Calla lilies are fairly low-maintenance. Remove faded flowers for a tidier appearance. Leaf spot fungal disease may be a problem in wet years. Remove infected leaves to control this problem. Dig up calla rhizomes in the fall after the first light frost. Allow the rhizomes to dry. Store them in peat moss or perlite at a temperature of 50 degrees Fahrenheit.

Companion Planting and Design
Calla lilies will grow in shallow pools or ponds, and they look nice when planted in or near water gardens. They work well in containers alone, or try using them in perennial and annual gardens. Once a calla lily has finished flowering, its leaves provide continued interest in the garden. Try mixing them with caladiums, arums, ferns, and sedges.

Try These
'Flame' has a yellow spathe that fades to mango-orange with white spotted leaves. 'Green Goddess' has a greenish spathe with a white throat and works well in flower arrangements. 'Little Gem' is fragrant and dwarf, 12 to 18 inches tall. Calla lily 'Crowborough' produces large, 4-inch flowers and is more sun tolerant.

Canna

Canna × generalis

Botanical Pronunciation
KAN-ah × jen-er-AL-is

Other Name Canna lily

Bloom Period and Seasonal Color
Midsummer through frost blooms in orange, yellow, white, red, and pink

Mature Height × Spread
1 to 6 feet × 18 to 24 inches

A favorite of the Victorian gardener, these bold beauties have graced many a boulevard and park flowerbed in our region. Their large green, bronze, or variegated leaves are topped with big, brightly colored flowers. It only takes a few plants to make a statement. Many new cultivars are being introduced, making these a favorite flower of gardeners across the country. Use the bold foliage and colorful flowers of this non-hardy bulb to create a tropical summer retreat in your northern garden. Or include a few in your water gardens. The taller varieties create a nice screen in the landscape or backdrop and vertical accent in flowerbeds. Use them in containers alone or mixed with other sun loving annuals and edibles.

When, Where, and How to Plant
Plant rhizomes directly outdoors after the last spring frost. Set them 3 to 4 inches deep and 1½ to 2 feet apart. Start canna rhizomes indoors in mid-March for earlier outdoor bloom. Cut rhizomes into pieces with at least 2 or 3 eyes (buds) per section. Start them in a shallow flat or plant directly in a 4- or 6-inch pot filled with a well-drained potting mix. Cannas can also be purchased as transplants in 4- to 6-inch pots. Plant hardened-off transplants outdoors in well-drained soil after all danger of frost is past.

Growing Tips
Cannas do not need staking. Water thoroughly when the top few inches of soil are crumbly but slightly moist. Fertilize according to soil test recommendations or apply a low-nitrogen slow-release fertilizer in the garden or container at the start of the season.

Regional Advice and Care
Cannas are low-maintenance plants except for Japanese beetles. You can tolerate the damage, knock the beetles into a cup of soapy water, or use an eco-friendly insecticide labeled for this use. Remove faded flowers to maintain a neat appearance and encourage continuous blooming. Dig up rhizomes in the fall after a light frost. Cut off the stems, leaving several inches above the rhizomes. Remove any loose soil and allow them to sit for several hours. Pack the rhizomes in peat moss or sawdust and store them in a cool, 45- to 50-degree location. Divide rhizomes in the spring before planting.

Companion Planting and Design
Use smaller cultivars as bedding plants. Larger cultivars make nice background plants or focal points. Both work in containers. Mix with spider cleome, bronze fennel, or ornamental grass to soften their bold texture. You can also grow cannas in containers submerged in water gardens.

Try These
'Tropicanna' cannas have colorful foliage and yellow, orange, or red flowers. They look good throughout the season, in or out of bloom. 'Constitution' has light pink flowers and purple-gray leaves that blends easily with neighboring plants. 'Tropical Rose' and 'South Pacific Scarlet' are both All-America Selections Award winners and can be started from seed.

Crocus

Crocus vernus

Botanical Pronunciation
KROW-kus

Other Name Dutch crocus

Bloom Period and Seasonal Color
Early spring blooms in white, purple, striped, and yellow

Mature Height × Spread
4 to 6 inches × 4 to 6 inches

Crocus is one of the first flowers to greet you in the spring. It's an easy-to-grow plant that can add weeks of enjoyment to your garden. The small plants hold their flowers above the narrow, grass-like leaves. Its early bloom period and variety of color make crocus one of the most commonly grown spring-flowering bulbs. For many, it's the signal the garden season is on its way. End the season as you started it. Plant autumn crocus (*Colchicum*), a close relative, for a fall display in Zones 4 to 5. Plant corms by late August. This plant produces leaves in early spring, which die back to the ground in six to eight weeks. In September, you will be pleasantly surprised when the flowers appear without leaves.

When, Where, and How to Plant
Plant crocus corms in the fall. They prefer well-drained soil but seem to tolerate all our soils. Place corms 3 inches deep and 4 inches apart. Plant them in groups of at least 15 to 20 for an eye-catching display.

Growing Tips
Avoid overwatering that can lead to root rot. Fertilize according to soil test recommendation or as directed in the beginning of the chapter. Note the white stripe down the middle of the leaves. This identification tip will help prevent you from "weeding out" the grass-like crocus leaves.

Regional Advice and Care
Crocuses are low-maintenance plants except for the animals. Squirrels and chipmunks will dig, move, and eat crocus corms. Rabbits love to nibble on the flowers and buds. Try repellents, scare tactics, and barriers or better yet plant the squirrel-resistant *Crocus tommasinianus* described below. Crocus flowers will close on cloudy days or in heavy shade. Corm rot is a problem in poorly drained soil.

Companion Planting and Design
Crocuses make an impressive spring display when planted *en masse* under trees, naturalized in the lawn, or throughout perennial and rock gardens. A well-manicured lawn is not the place to naturalize crocuses. You need to let the crocus foliage grow after the flowers fade. That means you must delay cutting your grass or cut it as high as possible at the start of the mowing season. Plant autumn crocus among groundcovers for a fall floral surprise. They also work well in annual, perennial, and rock gardens.

Try These
I almost gave up on crocus until I discovered *Crocus tommasinianus*. The squirrels really do leave them alone. *Colchicum* 'Waterlily' has wonderful double lilac-pink blooms on leafless stems in fall. Showy crocus, *Crocus speciosum*, a fall-flowering crocus, is easy to grow and hardy statewide. It flowers in fall before the leaves are fully developed. Golden crocus, *Crocus chrysanthus*, flowers earlier than the Dutch crocus, helping to extend the flowering season. And for the cooks in the group, note that *Crocus sativus* is the source of saffron. It takes 7,000 flowers to make 3 ounces—no wonder it is so expensive!

Crown Imperial

Fritillaria imperialis

Botanical Pronunciation
frit-i-LAIR-ree-a im-per-e-AL-is

Other Name Fritillaria

Bloom Period and Seasonal Color
Mid-spring with orange or yellow flowers

Mature Height × Spread
3 to 4 feet × 1 feet

The name suggests royalty, but some gardeners see a bit of Dr. Seuss in the flower. The tall plants are crowned with downward facing, bell-shaped flowers. The tuft of short grass-like leaves that top the flowers remind some of a Dr. Seuss character. Whatever you see, you will enjoy their stately appearance in the mid-spring garden. The lily-like plant fits both formal and informal garden styles. The light musky (skunky) smell won't bother you in the garden but is probably why animals leave this bulb alone. Once I made the mistake of leaving a box of these bulbs in my kitchen waiting for planting. A search of the kitchen revealed that the unidentifiable smell was coming from the bulbs, not something that rotted in my pantry.

When, Where, and How to Plant
Plant this scaly bulb in fall after the temperatures are consistently cool and before the ground freezes. Moist, well-drained soil is a must for winter survival. Add organic matter to the top 12 inches of soil to ensure good drainage in heavy soils and to increase water-holding capacity in sandy soils. Many gardeners plant the bulbs on their sides to avoid water collecting in the center leading to bulb rot. Plant the bulbs 6 inches deep and 8 to 12 inches apart. Fritillarias are said to prefer shade, but I find they grow just fine in full sun in our northern climate.

Growing Tips
Supplement rainfall in dry springs. Water thoroughly whenever the top few inches of soil begin to dry. Allow the soil to stay drier in summer. Incorporate a bulb fertilizer at the time of planting if supplemental nutrients are needed.

Regional Advice and Care
Winter survival is the biggest challenge. Cover plantings with a layer of weed-free straw, marsh hay, or evergreen boughs after the soil surface freezes. Avoid bulb rot with proper soil preparation and by planting the bulb on its side. Leaf spot and rust are occasional problems in wet springs.

Companion Planting and Design
Crown imperial's shade tolerance makes it a good addition to the shade garden. Mix it with hosta and other shade lovers that will cover the fading foliage in late spring. This tall plant makes a nice vertical accent in larger bulb plantings. I have seen wonderful plantings in the Netherlands where they had *Fritillaria* surrounded by a mix of hyacinths and daffodils that were skirted with lower growing daffodils and grape hyacinths. Or tuck a few in with shrubs or as part of the perennial border.

Try These
For those farther north or anyone looking for the more unusual, try checkered lily, *Fritillaria meleagris*. This close relative of crown imperial is hardy to Zone 3, grows 9 to 15 inches tall, and has mottled flowers that look checked. Grow it in moist soils with full sun to light shade.

Daffodil

Narcissus species and hybrids

Botanical Pronunciation
nar-SIS-us

Other Name Narcissus

Bloom Period and Seasonal Color
Early to mid-spring blooms in yellow, white, orange, pink, and green

Mature Height × Spread
6 to 24 inches × 6 to 12 inches

Daffodils are guaranteed to brighten up any spring landscape. They are one of the easiest bulbs to grow. Select several different cultivars for variety and extended bloom. The daffodil's distinctive flowers stand out from their strap-like leaves. So is it a daffodil, jonquil, or narcissus? Narcissus is the scientific name that is often used as its common name. Daffodil is a common name introduced and spread by English-speaking people. Jonquil is actually a species of this plant, *Narcissus jonquilla*. Whatever you call it, consider forcing it for your indoor enjoyment. And plant plenty of daffodils so you have extra to use as cut flowers indoors. Keep daffodils separate from other cut flowers. Sap leaking from daffodils' cut stems will plug the cut ends of other flowers.

When, Where, and How to Plant
Plant daffodil bulbs in the fall. They tolerate clay soil but perform best in areas with well-drained soil. Plant the bulbs 5 to 6 inches deep and 6 to 12 inches apart. In areas with sandy soil, you can plant daffodils up to 8 inches deep. Use closer spacing for smaller cultivars and quicker display. The wider spacing works for larger cultivars and naturalizing. The greater the spacing, the longer you have before the bulbs become overcrowded.

Growing Tips
Daffodils prefer moist soils in spring but drier soils during their dormant period in summer. Add organic matter to improve drainage. Excess nitrogen can result in lots of leaves and no flowers.

Regional Advice and Care
Animals leave this poisonous bulb alone. Remove faded flowers for a tidier look and leave the foliage on the plant until it yellows or at least six weeks after flowering. Bulb rot can be a problem in poorly drained soil. Poor flowering can be caused by excess shade, overcrowding, overfertilizing, and cold-temperatures injury to the buds. Move the daffodils, divide them, and avoid high-nitrogen fertilizers to fix the first three problems. Winter-mulch the plants that are prone to early sprouting or move them away from the house and other artificial heat sources. A hot spell at the time of flowering can prevent flower buds from opening or shorten the floral display.

Companion Planting and Design
Daffodils can be planted in perennial gardens, around trees and shrubs, or naturalized in woodland landscapes. Use smaller species in rock gardens. Mix daffodils with daylilies or hosta to mask the long lasting daffodil leaves during summer. I also like to mix daffodils with Virginia bluebells.

Try These
There are more daffodils than you can imagine, and many of them don't even look like a typical daffodil. Some have very short or double trumpets. Daffodil flowers may be all one color or a combination. Some daffodils are better for naturalizing, others are more fragrant, and still others may be better for forcing. Pick the one that fits your taste and design as I have too many favorites to list.

Dahlia

Dahlia hybrids

Botanical Pronunciation
DAH-lee-ah

Bloom Period and Seasonal Color
Midsummer to frost blooms in white, pink, red, orange, and yellow

Mature Height × Spread
1 to 5 feet × 12 to 24 inches

I am always amazed at the wide range of dahlia flower sizes, types, and colors available. With proper planting and routine maintenance, you can enjoy show-worthy dahlias right in the garden. Plus, you can reduce a bit of the work by using dahlias, like mums, for fall floral displays. Forget the hassle of starting them indoors—rather plant the tuberous roots directly in the garden each spring. The later bloom is a nice way to end the garden season. No matter when they bloom, dahlias will bring added value to your garden. They are a good nectar source for hummingbirds and butterflies, which add motion and color to the landscape. And the beautiful flowers look good on the plant or in a vase indoors.

When, Where, and How to Plant
Plant its tuberous roots indoors in mid-March for early bloom outdoors. Each section must have at least one "eye" (bud), the point of new growth. Or plant tuberous roots directly in the garden after the last spring frost. Prepare the top 12 inches of the soil and plant the roots 4 inches deep. Lay the root on its side with the eye pointing up. Stake tall cultivars at planting to avoid injuring the roots. Cover the tuberous root with soil. Dahlia plants are available in 4- to 6-inch pots from garden centers. Place the plants several inches deeper in the ground than the dahlias were growing in the container. Grow dahlias in a location with full sun to light shade in moist, well-drained soil.

Growing Tips
Mulch dahlias to keep the soil cool and moist. Make sure the plants receive adequate moisture and nutrients throughout the growing season. Move dahlias into storage after the first light frost. Pack the roots in sand and store in a cool (35 to 40 degrees Fahrenheit) dry place for winter. I prefer to divide in spring prior to planting.

Regional Advice and Care
Pinch out the growing tips and deadhead for shorter, bushier plants. To get larger blooms, train the plants to one major stem, removing side shoots as they develop. Next, remove all the flower buds that develop along the stem. Leave one bud on the end of each stem. You'll have fewer but much larger blooms. Insects such as aphids, leafhoppers, thrips, and mites can cause damage. Insecticidal soap will usually control these pests.

Companion Planting and Design
Tall dahlias make excellent background plants. Plant medium and short dahlias in small groupings throughout annual and perennial gardens. I like to use these with ornamental grasses or other fine-textured plants.

Try These
Flower types vary from the single, daisy-like flowers to the double-flowering, decorative types. The cacti flowers have twisted petals, the ball dahlias look like pom-poms, and the water lily dahlias resemble water lily flowers. Annual or bedding dahlias are smaller, less expensive, and flower from seed in the first year.

Elephant Ears

Colocasia species

Botanical Pronunciation
kol-oh-KAY-shah

Other Name Alocasia

Bloom Period and Seasonal Color
Foliage effective all season

Mature Height × Spread
Up to 5 feet tall and up to 3 feet wide

Add drama or a focal point to containers, flowerbeds, and water gardens with elephant ears. Their large foliage, sometimes variegated or heavily veined, provides a tropical feel to our northern landscapes all season long. Grown for their foliage, most types can be grown in full sun to shade as long as the soil is kept moist. The bold colorful leaves can brighten the shade and your indoor gardens. But you'll usually get the best color with more light. Cultivars of this plant can be as small as 8 inches and more than 4 feet tall. And individual leaves on larger cultivars can be several feet long and over a foot wide *Alocasia*, *Colocasia*, and *Xanthosoma* species look similar and share the common name, elephant ears.

When, Where, and How to Plant
Elephant ears can be purchased as large corms or plants. Start corms indoors in mid-March for an earlier display in the garden. Plant the corm pointed side up in a well-drained potting mix. Keep the potting mix moist and grow in a warm location. Hardened-off transplants can be moved outdoors once the soil has warmed and all danger of frost has passed.

Growing Tips
Don't be alarmed as the old leaves fade. This happens as new leaves emerge. Remove faded leaves for a tidier look. Plants may suffer scorch, or leaf browning, if grown in full sun or if the soil is allowed to dry out in hot weather. Mulch the soil with shredded leaves or evergreen needles to reduce this problem. Check the soil moisture in container grown plants at least once a day; twice a day during hot weather. Water containers thoroughly and fertilize regularly. The more water and fertilizer the plants receive the bigger they get.

Regional Care and Advice
Elephant ears are basically pest free but won't survive our winters. Those that form large corms can be grown as a houseplant or overwintered like cannas and other non-hardy bulbs. Dig them up after the first light frost. Allow the corms to dry and remove the dead foliage. Pack in peat moss and store in a cool frost-free location. Most dwarf varieties and others that are slow to develop corms do not store well dried and should be grown as houseplants in the winter.

Companion Planting and Design
Elephant ears make excellent bedding and container plants. Use them *en masse*, mixed with other shade-tolerant plants, or as a focal point. Try combining elephant ears with fine textured papyrus and shade-loving annuals and perennials. Some varieties thrive in water or bog gardens.

Try These
The arrowhead shaped burgundy-black leaves with silvery white veins make the 24-inch-tall 'African Mask' a standout in the garden. 'Mojito' has large chartreuse leaves with purple-black blotches that adds a bit of sizzle to the garden. 'Lime Zinger' has large bright yellow leaves to brighten your garden and indoor décor.

Grape Hyacinth

Muscari botryoides

Botanical Pronunciation
mus-KAR-ee bot-tree-OY-deez

Bloom Period and Seasonal Color
Early to mid-spring blooms in blue and white

Mature Height × Spread
6 to 9 inches × 4 to 6 inches

Though small in size, grape hyacinths can create great interest in the landscape. This easy-to-grow bulb is resistant to animals and multiplies quickly. I once sent my parents a bag of bulbs. Three years later my dad gave me back *three* bags of bulbs and a request not to return the favor! The name *Muscari* is derived from the Turkish name for this plant. *Botryoides* means like a bunch of grapes, which certainly describes the flowers. The flowers are nice additions to forced bulb containers and miniature cutflower arrangements. I let the seed pods develop on my grape hyacinths. I think the translucent pods add interest to the garden and to dried flower arrangements. Just be aware, you will have even more plants as they reseed.

When, Where, and How to Plant

Plant grape hyacinth bulbs in the fall. They are flexible but prefer full sun to partial shade and cool, moist, well-drained soil. Plant the bulbs 3 inches deep and 4 inches apart. Plant them in groups of at least 15 to 20 for good impact. Several hundred will really grab your attention.

Growing Tips

Make sure new plantings are well watered before the ground freezes. Supplemental watering may be needed during dry springs. Water thoroughly when the top few inches of soil are crumbly and moist. Allow the soil to go drier when the bulbs are dormant in summer.

Regional Advice and Care

Grape hyacinths are low-maintenance plants. The leaves will persist and continue to grow most of the season. They usually die back in late summer and reappear in fall, making some gardener's nervous. That's not a problem; you just need to plan for it. Grape hyacinths multiply quickly. They benefit from dividing every four or five years in the late summer or fall.

Companion Planting and Design

Plant in large masses for an impressive spring display. Mix with other, taller bulbs such as daffodils and tulips that bloom at the same time to double the blooming impact, or plant cultivars that bloom later to extend bloom time in the garden. Plant them under trees and shrubs or let them naturalize in wooded landscapes or grassy areas. Use small cultivars in the rock garden. Or create a seasonal water feature using grape hyacinths in flowing patterns like a river in the landscape.

Try These

The Armenian grape hyacinth, *Muscari armeniacum*, is a larger and more vigorous plant than the common grape hyacinth. It is often sold as grape hyacinth in some catalogues and garden centers. It is only hardy to Zone 4. Plant *Muscari botryoides album* for a white-flowering grape hyacinth. *Muscari aucheri* 'Blue Magic' flowers are true blue and hardy in Zones 4 and 5. The plumed grape hyacinth, *Muscari comosum* 'Plumosum', also hardy in Zones 4 and 5, has shredded flowers that look like plumes or tassels.

Hyacinth

Hyacinthus orientalis

Botanical Pronunciation
hy-ah-SIN-thus or-ee-en-TAL-iss

Other Name Dutch hyacinth

Bloom Period and Seasonal Color
Early to mid-spring blooms in blue, violet, white, rose, pink, yellow, salmon, and apricot

Mature Height × Spread
6 to 10 inches × 6 inches

Hyacinths are sure to brighten up a landscape or room with their large flowers and sweet fragrance. Use this plant outdoors in the garden or force it indoors. Either way, it will make a colorful addition to your spring bulb display. Just be careful when using them indoors. Their fragrance can be overpowering. One semester I transported my pot of hyacinths from campus to campus for demonstration. Despite the cold weather I drove with my windows down due to the overwhelming fragrance. Purchase pre-cooled bulbs or force your own by giving them twelve to fifteen weeks of cool (35 to 45 degrees Fahrenheit) temperatures to initiate flowering. Many gardeners and landscapers are using these animal resistant bulbs in place of tulips and other deer and rabbit favorites.

When, Where, and How to Plant
Plant hyacinth bulbs in the fall. Grow them in areas with full sun and moist, well-drained soil. Add organic matter to improve the drainage of clay soil and increase the water-holding capacity of sandy soil. Purchase medium-sized bulbs, which will produce nice-sized flowers that are less likely to flop and require staking. Keep the bulbs in a cool, dark place until you are ready to plant. Plant the bulbs 6 inches deep and 6 to 9 inches apart. Even a small grouping of 6 or 9 bulbs can put on a good show.

Growing Tips
Mulch the soil to keep the bulbs cool and moist spring through fall. Water thoroughly whenever the top few inches of soil start to dry. Fertilize according to soil test results or use a low-nitrogen slow-release fertilizer at planting or when needed in spring as leaves emerge.

Regional Advice and Care
Hyacinths are basically pest free but generally short lived in our area. They need cool summers and moist, well-drained soil to flourish and multiply. Remove faded flowers to allow all the energy to go into the bulb instead of into seed formation. Flowers will tend to get smaller each year, though; replace hyacinths every 3 or 4 years for the best flowering display. Hyacinths are subject to bulb rot. Plant them in well-drained locations and add organic matter to heavy clay soil to avoid this problem.

Companion Planting and Design
The stiff habit and large flowers give the hyacinth a formal look. Use mass plantings for an impressive spring display. I use small groupings of hyacinths scattered throughout my perennial gardens to maintain my informal design. Consider mixing hyacinths with daffodils, tulips, or winter-hardy pansies.

Try These
'Gipsy Queen' has a nice coral-colored flower that combines well with 'Pink Charm' daffodil. The flower spike covered with double raspberry red florets of 'Hollyhock' inspired its name. A close relative, *Hyacinthoides hispanica*, known as Spanish bluebells, Spanish squills, or wood hyacinth, has a more open spike of blue, bell-shaped flowers. This is a good addition to the shade garden.

Iris

Iris hybrids

Botanical Pronunciation
EYE-riss

Other Name Bearded iris

Bloom Period and Seasonal Color
Late spring to early summer blooms in wide range of colors

Mature Height × Spread
4 to 48 inches × 6 to 12 inches

The stately beauty of the iris can fill the blooming void between spring-flowering bulbs and early summer perennials. Its wide range of heights and colors makes this versatile plant work in any garden. The miniature dwarf bearded iris is the first to bloom. It is 4 to 10 inches tall, which makes it a good choice for the rock garden. The standard dwarf bearded iris blooms about seven to ten days later. It is 10 to 15 inches tall. The intermediate iris is the next to bloom and grows to 15 to 28 inches tall. The tall bearded iris is over 28 inches tall and the last to bloom. Include a variety of bearded iris to extend the flowering period in your perennial gardens.

When, Where, and How to Plant
Plant iris rhizomes late summer through early fall, preferably by September 1 so the plants can develop roots before winter. Mulch late plantings after the ground lightly freezes. Plant rhizomes in full sun and well-drained soil, just below the soil surface with the leaf fan facing outward. Each rhizome should contain at least one leaf fan. Plant iris singly or in groupings of three. In groupings, set the rhizomes next to one another, and space groupings at least 24 inches apart. Smaller cultivars can be spaced closer.

Growing Tips
Water thoroughly whenever the top few inches of soil are crumbly and moist. Avoid high-nitrogen fertilizers that promote leaf growth and discourage flowering.

Regional Advice and Care
Stake taller cultivars. Poor flowering can result from excess fertilizer, low light, overcrowding, late spring frost, and recent transplanting. Remove spent flowers. Divide overcrowded iris at least 8 weeks after flowering, preferably in late summer. Dig rhizomes and cut them into smaller pieces containing at least 1 set of leaves and several large roots. Cut the leaves back to 6 inches. Discard any damaged or insect-infested rhizomes. Iris borer is the biggest problem; remove any borers found during summer transplanting. Removing old foliage in the fall eliminates the egg-laying site of the adult moth and is often enough to control this pest. Remove leaf spot-infested leaves when found.

Companion Planting and Design
Mix iris with perennials for late spring and early summer interest. Healthy, sword-shaped leaves can provide a vertical accent in the summer garden. Iris combine nicely with most perennials especially fine textured plants.

Try These
The Siberian iris, *Iris sibirica*, tolerates moist soil, partial shade, and is less susceptible to iris borer. It grows 2 to 4 feet tall with long, grass-like leaves, which look good all summer. The fall color and persistent seed pods make this a four season plant. The crested iris, *Iris cristata*, is an early bloomer that also tolerates moist soil and shade. The short foliage persists all season, creating a nice groundcover. Reblooming (remontant) iris such as 'Immortality' may provide spring and fall blooms.

Lily

Lilium species

Botanical Pronunciation
LIL-ee-um

Other Name Hardy lily

Bloom Period and Seasonal Color
Early to midsummer blooms in white, yellow, orange, red, and pink

Mature Height × Spread
2 to 6 feet × 8 to 12 inches

The classic lily is as at home in the informal garden as it is in a more formal setting. Lilies are a little more challenging than daffodils and crocuses, but the flowers will convince you they are worth the effort. Be sure to include enough plants for cutting. The beautiful, fragrant flowers are a great addition to any arrangement. The Asiatic and Oriental hybrids are the most readily available. The Asiatic cultivars tend to be hardier than the oriental types. Their flowers are usually unscented and may face up, out, or down. The Oriental hybrids usually produce lots of showy fragrant flowers that can be trumpet-shaped, bowl-shaped, flat-faced, or with recurved petals. Many florists are forcing the Asiatic and Oriental hybrids into bloom for Easter.

When, Where, and How to Plant
Plant lily bulbs in the fall. Purchase and plant pre-cooled lily bulbs in the spring outdoors as soon as the soil is workable. Lilies are also sold as plants during the growing season. Plant whenever they are available. Grow lilies in full sun and moist, well-drained soil. Add organic matter to heavy clay soil to improve drainage. Plant lily bulbs at a depth two to three times their height. Use the minimum planting depth for lilies growing in clay soil. The deeper the bulb is planted, the greater the risk of bulb rot. Plant lilies at least three times their width apart.

Growing Tips
Mulch the soil to keep lily roots cool and moist. Avoid overwatering, especially in clay soil, since that can lead to root rot.

Regional Advice and Care
Lilies are subject to bulb rot. Proper soil preparation and watering will help prevent this problem. Deer, rabbits, and groundhogs will eat the plants down to ground level. Repellents and scare tactics may help keep these pests at bay. Apply a winter mulch after the ground freezes for added insulation and for help in getting the bulbs through our challenging winters.

Companion Planting and Design
Use lilies in large masses, small groupings, or as individual plants scattered throughout the garden. Tall lilies make excellent background or specimen plants. Mix any lilies with ornamental grasses, Russian sage, and other perennials. They are quite attractive growing up through or behind shorter plants.

Try These
'Star Gazer' is a popular Oriental lily suitable for in-ground and container gardens. The red, star-shaped flowers have recurved tips and are marked with darker spots. I like the Turk's cap lily, *Lilium martagon*. Hardy to Zone 3 and more shade tolerant, this is an excellent choice for northern gardeners. Tiger lily, *Lilium lancifolium* (formerly *Lilium tigrinum*), is a long-time favorite. Tiger lily produces lots of orange-red flowers with spotted recurved petals. It also tolerates some shade and moist soils. It and some of the other hardy lilies propagate readily from offsets (bulblets) and bulbils (black bead-like growths) that develop on the stems.

Squill

Scilla siberica

Botanical Pronunciation
SIL-a sih-BEER-ih-kah

Other Name Siberian squill

Bloom Period and Seasonal Color
Early spring blooms in blue and white

Mature Height × Spread
6 inches × 4 to 6 inches

Picture a sea of true blue flowers in the midst of the bluegrass in your front lawn. This is just one of the many uses of the Siberian squill. Its true blue color is hard to beat in the early spring garden. These early-blooming bulbs are easy to grow and hardy throughout our area. They are prolific, so give them lots of room or plan on digging and sharing them with friends and family. A few or a mass of these plants are pretty to look at and safe to touch, but do not eat them. **Note:** All parts of the squill contain digitalis-like substances that are toxic if eaten. The animals seem to know—they leave these bulbs alone.

When, Where, and How to Plant
Plant bulbs in the fall. They prefer well-drained soil but seem to tolerate less than ideal conditions. Plant the bulbs 3 inches deep and 4 to 6 inches apart. Plant them in groups of at least fifteen to twenty for good impact.

Growing Tips
Squills tolerate most soils and our climate well. Like other bulbs, they prefer moist soils when growing and a bit drier in the summer. They typically receive enough nutrients when you fertilize the lawn or garden they are growing in.

Regional Advice and Care
Properly placed squills are low-maintenance and basically pest-free plants. Crown rot can cause plants to wilt, yellow, and die. Improve soil drainage prior to planting to avoid this problem. Most gardeners have too much success—complaining that their squills have taken over the garden and moved into the lawn. I think the lawn may be a better place for this plant. Squills brighten up the spring lawn without damaging the grass. Unlike most bulbs, squills tolerate mowing once the flowers have faded. But once they are in the lawn they are difficult to remove. Broadleaf weedkillers won't work on these plants. So you must dig up the bulbs or kill them, grass and all, to remove them from the lawn. Overcrowded poor flowering bulbs can be lifted and divided every four to five years.

Companion Planting and Design
Naturalize squills in lawns and wooded landscapes, include them in rock gardens, or plant large drifts around trees and shrubs. Mix with groundcovers to add a boost of color before the groundcovers get growing. Plant them in areas where they have room to grow. Squills multiply quickly and can take over the spring garden. I like to mix them with daffodils, tulips, or hyacinths to double my bloom appeal.

Try These
Scilla siberica 'Alba' is a white-flowering Siberian squill. 'Spring Beauty' has large, blue flowers held above the leaves on taller spikes than the straight species. Two-leaved squill, *Scilla bifolia*, is another true blue flowering squill. It grows 3 to 6 inches tall and naturalizes well in sun or partial shade.

Tulip

Tulipa species and hybrids

Botanical Pronunciation
TEW-lih-pah

Bloom Period and Seasonal Color
Early through late spring blooms in all colors

Mature Height × Spread
4 to 36 inches × 6 to 8 inches

Tulips and the Tulip Time Festival in Holland, Michigan are a sure sign of spring. Whether forced in a pot or grown in the garden, tulips provide color and interest throughout the season. Select early-, mid-, and late-spring blooming tulips for a continuous display and choose the sizes, bloom types, and colors that best fit your design. Early tulips tend to be shorter, while late spring tulips are taller, reaching heights of 36 inches. Tulips come in single and double flowers. During "tulipmania" in the early 1600s, the Dutch became obsessed with tulips. They were seen as a status symbol, and people started trading money, possessions, and even family businesses for bulbs. A virus caused a streak in the flower color, which increased the excitement over and value of the tulip.

When, Where, and How to Plant
Plant tulip bulbs in the fall. Plant tulips as late as possible to avoid fall sprouting. Grow tulips in full sun and well-drained soil. Plant bulbs 5 to 6 inches deep and 6 to 9 inches apart. Those with sandy or well-drained soils can plant tulips 8 inches deep.

Growing Tips
Water tulips thoroughly whenever the top few inches of soil are crumbly and moist. This will ensure an attractive floral display during dry springs. Mulch the soil to keep bulbs cool in the summer. Excessive heat can result in poor flowering the following spring. If needed, fertilize with a low-nitrogen slow-release fertilizer at planting or in spring as leaves emerge.

Regional Advice and Care
Leave foliage in place for at least six to eight weeks after the tulips bloom. Tulips are subject to several rot diseases. Add organic matter to poorly drained soils prior to planting to reduce the risk of rot. Deer and rabbits are major pests of this plant. They will eat the flowers and trample the plants. Squirrels, mice, and chipmunks will dig, move, and eat tulip bulbs. Repellents, scare tactics, and barriers may help. Tulip hybrids tend to be short-lived. Include some of the longer-lived species tulips or plan on replacing the short-lived hybrids every few years.

Companion Planting and Design
Tulips can be planted *en masse* or scattered throughout the perennial garden in small groupings. Include small species and cultivars in rock gardens. Don't forget to plant extra tulips for cutting. I have several interplanted with perennials. I like to see my tulips popping out of *Brunnera* or *Lamium*. Mix them with pansies or smaller bulbs for a double layer of spring flowers. Include a few pesticide-free flowers in your spring salads.

Try These
It's hard to pick a favorite. Here are just a few I like. The mid-spring bloomer 'New Design' has variegated foliage and soft pink blossoms. The late spring 'Angelique' has fragrant double flowers in shades of pink. *Tulipa tarda* is a small, early blooming species tulip that has attractive seed pods for extended appeal.

GROUNDCOVERS
FOR MICHIGAN

Use groundcovers to replace struggling lawns, fill shady areas, brighten hot dry spots, and improve the growing conditions around trees and shrubs. These plants are less competitive than grass with the trees and shrubs for water and nutrients. Plus, they keep tree roots cool and moist and weed-whips and mowers away from tree trunks.

Installation and Maintenance

Many established groundcovers are relatively low maintenance, but remember that no plant is maintenance free. As much as I prefer groundcovers to grass, you can mow down or spray weeds in a lawn. Though there are a few weedkillers that work in some groundcovers, for the most part you have to pull any weeds that invade these plantings.

Increase your success and decrease maintenance by investing time and effort during planting and establishment of groundcovers. First, eliminate the existing grass and weeds. Cut an edge around the area to be planted in groundcover. Use a sod cutter to remove the grass and weeds or treat the area with a total vegetation killer. Remember, these products kill anything green that they touch. *Read* and *follow* label directions.

Fertilize and amend new groundcover beds that are not under existing trees and shrubs.

Apply the type and amount of fertilizer recommended by your soil test. Or apply 15 pounds per 1,000 square feet of a low-nitrogen (about 5%) slow-release fertilizer. Work the recommended fertilizer and 2 to 4 inches of organic matter, such as compost, aged manure, or peat moss, into the top 6 to 12 inches of the

Pachysandra is a great groundcover option to grass in difficult-to-mow areas.

soil. This will improve drainage in heavy clay soil and increase the water-holding capacity in sandy soil.

Patient gardeners who prefer a non-chemical approach can try this method. It's also great for creating groundcover beds under trees and around shrubs. Edge the bed and cut the existing grass short. Cover with several layers of newspaper or a layer of cardboard and top with woodchip mulch. The covered grass will eventually die, and the newspapers or cardboard will decompose over the following few months, improving the soil.

Dead nettle (*Lamium*) 'Beacon Silver'.

Planting Under Trees

Many groundcovers are planted under trees and shrubs. Do not add soil on top of tree roots or deeply till the soil surrounding established trees and shrubs. That can injure or kill the trees and shrubs.

Start by killing or removing the grass around established plantings. Dig a hole larger than the groundcover's rootball and plant it in the existing soil. Broadcast the recommended fertilizer over the soil surface and water in. Next, mulch with an organic material such as shredded leaves, twice-shredded bark, or pine needles. As the mulch breaks down, it will improve the soil below. Be patient; it takes plants longer to fill under established trees.

Proper soil preparation will reduce the need to fertilize. If plants need a nutrient boost, apply 15 pounds of a low-nitrogen (around 5%) slow-release fertilizer per 1,000 square feet in spring. This provides season-long results and won't damage plants even during drought.

Water new plantings thoroughly and often enough to keep the soil slightly moist. Check new plantings under trees more often. Once established, many groundcovers can survive on natural rainfall. You may need to lend a hand during drought or with plants growing under the dense canopy of oaks, maples, and evergreens. For best results, water established plants thoroughly but only when the top 4 to 6 inches start to dry.

Weeds are the biggest problem these plants face. Mulch plantings to reduce weed infestations, or plant the groundcovers a little closer so they will fill in quickly to crowd out the weeds. Planting closer means more plants and more money, and the groundcovers may need dividing sooner. Remove weeds as soon as they appear, especially when the groundcovers are getting established. Once the groundcover fills in, there will be fewer weeds. Invest some time and hard work now for years of beauty.

Barrenwort

Epimedium × rubrum

Botanical Pronunciation
ep-ih-MEE-dee-um ex ROO-brum

Other Name Bishop's Hat

Bloom Period and Seasonal Color
May blooms in red

Mature Height × Spread
8 to 12 inches × 8 to 12 inches

Hardiness Zones Hardy to Zones 4 and 5

Barrenwort's changing character can provide year-round interest in your landscape. The new growth emerges green with a touch of red. Its heart-shaped leaves are held on wiry stems, giving them a delicate, airy appearance. The red flowers emerge in May or June as the new leaves develop. In the fall, the leaves will turn reddish bronze. Old leaves persist through the winter, adding interest to the winter perennial garden. Add to your enjoyment by using them as cut flowers. Use them in small containers alone or as a filler with other flowers. Pick partially opened flowers in the morning or evening for best results. You will be pleasantly surprised by their vase life. Barrenwort is a long-lived plant that can remain in the same location for many years.

When, Where, and How to Plant

Plant barrenwort in the spring for best results. Winter mulch late plantings after the ground freezes. Divide plants in spring or early summer after the new leaves reach full size. Plants tolerate full sun as long as the soil is kept moist. Barrenwort prefers moist, well-drained soil, but established plants will tolerate dry shade. Purchase barrenwort plants from garden centers and nurseries. Prepare the site prior to planting. Space plants 9 to 12 inches apart and plant at the same depth they were growing in their container. Division is needed only if you want to start new plants for other areas. Dig, divide, and replant in spring or early summer after the new leaves are full sized.

Growing Tips

Water the plants during dry periods. Mulching will help conserve moisture and lengthen the time between waterings. Give these slow growers, and those competing with tree roots, a boost of fertilizer as needed. Use a low-nitrogen fertilizer in the spring.

Regional Advice and Care

Barrenworts are slow growers, which gives fast-growing weeds an opportunity. Pull weeds as they appear. Avoid cultivating near the plants, which could damage the barrenwort's shallow roots. Once the barrenworts fill in, they will crowd out the weeds and reduce the time you spend on this task. Cut back old foliage in late winter or early spring before new growth begins. This will make the flowers more visible. Daring Zone 3 gardeners may want to try a plant or two. I have had reports of success from a few of your fellow gardeners.

Companion Planting and Design

Use barrenwort in small groupings, mixed with other shade lovers, and in rock gardens. Or grow these dry shade tolerant groundcovers under trees where grass won't grow. Sedges, hostas, and ferns make a nice backdrop for the delicate heart-shaped leaves.

Try These

Yellow barrenwort, *Epimedium × versicolor* 'Sulphureum', (shown) grows 10 to 12 inches tall and has yellow flowers and is more tolerant of dry, shady sites than the other barrenworts. A new introduction, *E. grandiflorum* 'Rose Queen', has pink flowers and is hardy in Zones 4 and 5.

Bearberry

Arctostaphylos uva-ursi

Botanical Pronunciation
ark-toe-STAF-il-lohs oo-vah-ER-see

Other Name Kinnikinick

Bloom Period and Seasonal Color
May blooms of white tinged pink

Mature Height × Spread
6 to 12 inches tall × 2 to 4 feet wide

Include this beautiful native groundcover for multiple seasons of color in your landscape. The glossy dark green leaves form a dense mat providing a nice backdrop for the small urn-shaped white to pink spring flowers. Small red berries appear in late summer and persist into winter. The growing season ends with a colorful display of bronze to red fall leaves that persist through winter. All this subtle beauty on one small plant and it's durable too. Use this adaptable plant in difficult locations. It thrives in poor soils and dry locations and those subject to deicing salts. Watch for bees and other beneficial insects that visit the flowers and birds that will feast on the berries, adding color and motion to your garden.

When, Where, and How to Plant

Invest some time in soil preparation to ensure long-term success. Bearberry is quite an adaptable plant but must have good drainage to thrive. And even though it prefers acid soil it seems to adapt to alkaline soils. Plant bearberry in a location sheltered from winter wind and sun to avoid winter burn on the evergreen foliage. Start with transplants for best results. You will have less success with bare-root cuttings. Plant 12 to 24 inches apart and be patient; these are slow to get growing, but once established in well-drained soil, it can grow well beyond its average 2- to 4-foot spread.

Growing Tips

Avoid overfertilization that not only stimulates growth of the bearberry, but also the weeds that can quickly take over the planting. Instead, use a low-nitrogen slow-release fertilizer when a nutrient boost is needed. Pull weeds as they appear to avoid competition for water and nutrients with the slow growing bearberry. Weed control is important to maintain a healthy and vigorous planting.

Regional Advice and Care

Basically pest-free though mildew, rust, and galls can be a problem. This slow grower seldom needs pruning. Remove damaged, rubbing, and stray branches as needed. And since transplanting can be difficult, be patient; it may take a couple years for the plants to get growing. Your patience will be rewarded.

Companion Planting and Design

Use bearberries in natural plantings and wildlife gardens. Look to nature for ideas. The bearberry can be found growing on sandy dunes and banks or in partially shaded woodland areas. Or include them as groundcover in informal and even formal settings. You can also use them as an edging plant in mixed borders or shrub beds. Or plant on hillsides and banks or allow the plant to cascade over the edge of a raised bed, terrace, or curb. They make a great substitute for creeping juniper once it is established.

Try These

'Massachusetts' is probably the most commonly grown and readily available cultivar. It has small, dark green leaves and produces an abundance of flowers and fruit. It also shows good disease resistance.

Bugleweed

Ajuga reptans

Botanical Pronunciation
ah-JEW-gah REP-tanz

Other Name Ajuga

Bloom Period and Seasonal Color
May through June blooms in violet
and blue-purple

Mature Height × Spread
6 to 9 inches × 24 to 36 inches

Bugleweed is a beautiful evergreen ground-cover. The strap-like leaves create a thick mat of green, bronze, or variegated foliage. New and interesting cultivars are continually appearing in garden centers. These come in a variety of leaf and flower colors. Select a cultivar that is hardy to your location and complements your landscape design. The foliage creates a nice backdrop to the spikes of purple-blue flowers that appear in May. This member of the mint family spreads in all directions by stolons. These horizontal stems lie on the soil surface, producing new plants along the way. One healthy plant can fill a 3-square-foot area in a season. You'll need to regularly edge the planting beds to slow the spreading bugleweed.

When, Where, and How to Plant
Plant container-grown bugleweed in the spring or early summer to allow the plants to become established before our tough winters. Bugleweed can be grown in sun or shade but flowers best in full sun with moist, well-drained soil. Avoid open or exposed areas where this plant may suffer winter kill. Bugleweed plants are available from garden centers and perennial nurseries in flats and containers. Space plants 12 inches apart. Divisions can be made anytime, but you will get the best results if plants are divided in spring or early summer.

Growing Tips
Mulch new plantings to conserve moisture and reduce weeds. Water established plants during drought. Minimal fertilization is needed to keep

these plants healthy. Broadleaf weedkillers applied to the lawn will help control stray bugleweed.

Regional Advice and Care
Bugleweed is a quick-growing plant that will eventually crowd out the weeds. Remove weeds as they appear. Cut off or mow faded flowers to prevent reseeding and to keep the plants looking good. Lift and divide crowded plants. These fast growers may need to be divided as often as every two to three years to avoid overcrowding and reduce the risk of crown rot. Overgrown plants often have dead centers or fail to bloom. Use a shovel or garden fork to dig out the plants. Cut the clump into several sections. Replant the divisions at 12-inch intervals in a prepared site. Bugleweed is susceptible to crown rot. Avoid this disease by growing plants in well-drained soil.

Companion Planting and Design
Bugleweed is a quick, mat-forming plant that works well under trees, in rock gardens, or as a ground-cover in large beds. Avoid growing it next to lawn areas where its aggressive nature can be a problem. Interplant with hostas. The bugleweeds help keep down the weeds until the hostas fill in.

Try These
Ajuga reptans 'Catlin's Giant' is one of the largest bugleweed cultivars. It has 8-inch bronze leaves and blue flowers. 'Chocolate Chip' has narrow burgundy-bronze foliage, and 'Burgundy Glow' provides added color with its green, white, and dark pink leaves.

Deadnettle

Lamium maculatum

Botanical Pronunciation
LAY-mee-um mak-yew-LAY-tum

Other Name Lamium

Bloom Period and Seasonal Color
May through midsummer blooms in rose-purple

Mature Height × Spread
8 to 12 inches × 3 feet

Deadnettle is such an ugly name for such a pretty plant! The green and white foliage brightens shady locations all season. Delicate rose-purple flowers rise above the leaves for added beauty in May and June. Deadnettle works equally well in large or small plantings. Once established, it will grow well in dry shade found under dense shade trees. Many gardeners in our region lost a few deadnettle in the winter of 2002–2003. I found that most gardeners looked at it as nature helping to thin the planting. My lamium quickly filled in by the end of the following summer. Deadnettle is similar to variegated yellow archangel. Both plants have similar growing requirements and uses. Deadnettle tends to grow in a clump form, while variegated yellow archangel is more spreading and harder to contain.

When, Where, and How to Plant

Plant container-grown deadnettle plants anytime throughout the growing season. Divide plants in early spring for best results. The leaves may scorch or brown if grown in full sun. It prefers moist, well-drained soil and will become open and a bit leggy in dry conditions. Prepare the soil prior to planting as described in the chapter introduction. Dig a hole larger than the rootball and plant deadnettle in the existing soil. Mulch the soil with organic matter. Deadnettle plants are available from garden centers and perennial nurseries in flats and containers. Plant them at the same level they were growing in the pot. Space these plants 12 to 18 inches apart.

Growing Tips

Mulch new plantings to conserve moisture and reduce weeds. Water new plantings during dry periods. Check established plants during drought periods. Water thoroughly whenever the top few inches dry.

Regional Advice and Care

Spotted deadnettle is basically pest free. Weed control is critical in the first year, so remove weeds as they appear. Once established, deadnettle will quickly fill in, keeping weed growth to a minimum. Prune plants growing in dry shade to encourage fuller, more compact growth. Lift and divide overgrown plants, which often have dead centers or fail to bloom. Use a shovel or garden fork to dig out plants. Cut the clump into several sections. Replant divisions at 12-inch intervals in a prepared site.

Companion Planting and Design

Deadnettle makes an excellent groundcover for shaded areas. Use it under trees where grass won't grow. I also like to use it as an edging plant or in rock gardens. It can be a little aggressive for some garden settings, so pick its neighbors carefully. The attractive foliage of deadnettle has made it a popular addition to hanging baskets and containers.

Try These

'Beacon Silver' and 'White Nancy' are popular deadnettle cultivars with their silver leaves edges in green. 'Beacon Silver' has pink flowers and 'White Nancy' has white blooms. 'Pink Chablis' sports long-lasting pink flowers while 'Purple Dragon' has purple flowers that stand out above the heavily variegated leaves.

Foamflower

Tiarella species

Botanical Pronunciation
tee-ar-EL-lah

Other Name False mitrewort

Bloom Period and Seasonal Color
May into June blooms white, pale pink, or rose flowers

Mature Height × Spread
6 to 12 inches × 12 to 24 inches

Foamflower was one of the first perennials I grew in my small city lot twenty some years ago. A friend gave me a plant that I tucked it into a shady side yard. I didn't think much about it until the second season when it was covered with a foamy cloud of blooms for *months*. Since then I have added more cultivars to the shady bed under my street tree. The shape and texture of this native's foliage and the variety of colorful leaves found in the many cultivars makes this a good choice for groundcover and perennial beds. The spikes of white star-shaped flowers are sure to impress. That's what my neighbors must think as some of them are harvesting the flowers as they walk by!

When, Where, and How to Plant

Grow this woodland native in partial to full shade and cool moist soil. You'll get the best results with the least effort if you grow these plants in partial shade. I have seen and even grown a few plants that survived in full sun as long as the soil is cool and moist. Add organic matter to the soil as they grow best in organic soils. Plants are available in 4-inch and 6-inch containers as well as one-gallon pots. Plant 12 to 18 inches apart.

Growing Tips

Mulch with shredded leaves or evergreen needles to keep the soil cool and moist and weeds under control. Water thoroughly and as needed to keep the soil moist but not wet. Drought stress can cause brown leaf edges (scorch) and overall decline of the plants.

Regional Advice and Care

Monitor plantings for frost heaving in spring. These shallow rooted plants can be pushed out of the soil when winter temperatures fluctuate and snow cover is lacking. As the soil freezes and thaws pushes plants out of the ground. Consistently cold temperatures and snow cover are the best solutions. Just reset plants at the proper depth and water as needed in spring. Cover plantings with a few evergreen boughs after the ground freezes if this is a common problem in your garden.

Companion Planting and Design

This woodland native is at home in shaded natural plantings. They combine nicely with hosta, coralbells, astilbe, and ferns. The foliage makes a nice backdrop for spring flowering bulbs. Combine these with coralbells to create a tapestry of color and texture under a shade tree.

Try These

I like to try any of the new cultivars I find in the garden center. Their small size allows even small space gardeners to become collectors. 'Elizabeth Oliver' has been around for a while but still deserves a spot in the garden. The leaves have purple markings in the center and are topped by large pinkish fragrant flowers. 'Pink Skyrocket' has the largest pink flowers that are held above shiny green foliage with a black blotch in the center.

Ginger

Asarum species

Botanical Pronunciation
ah-SAR-um

Other Name
Wild and European ginger

Bloom Period and Seasonal Color
Early May blooms in greenish purple or brown

Mature Height × Spread
6 to 12 inches × 12 inches

Can't grow anything under that spruce tree? Try wild ginger. Both European and wild ginger can take heavy shade and moist conditions that most plants won't tolerate. The ginger flower often goes unnoticed. It is a greenish purple or brown, bell-shaped flower. The large leaves mask the flowers lying on the soil surface. Wild ginger, *Asarum canadense*, is native, hardy throughout the region, and tolerant of the rigors of northern gardens. European ginger, *Asarum europaeum*, is an evergreen. The spicy fragrance released by ginger's cut leaves, flowers, and rhizomes gave these plants their common name. Though not related to the culinary ginger, *Zingiber officinale*, European settlers candied or dried the roots of wild ginger to use in cooking.

When, Where, and How to Plant
Plant container-grown ginger in early spring. Space plants 8 to 12 inches apart. Divisions can be made and planted in early spring before growth. Both European and wild ginger prefer full to dense shade but will tolerate partial shade. Plant them in moist soil with lots of organic matter. They prefer an acid soil, but I have had luck growing them in the high-pH soil. Grow the European ginger in a protected location for best results.

Growing Tips
Mulch new plantings with shredded leaves, twice-shredded bark, pine needles, or another organic matter. The mulching will help conserve moisture, reduce weeds, and add organic matter to the soil as it breaks down. Water established plants thoroughly, wetting the top 6 inches of the soil, during dry period. Water again when the top few inches of soil starts to dry.

Regional Advice and Care
These are low maintenance, pest-free plants. I find European ginger a bit more challenging. It is more particular about the growing conditions, often struggles through the winter, and is slow to establish. Grow in a location free of winter wind and winter sun to avoid winter damage. Canadian ginger will tolerate the rigors of northern gardens and once established spreads quickly. You'll eventually have plenty of plants to move into other gardens or share with friends. Remove weeds as they appear.

Companion Planting and Design
Use them as groundcovers under trees and shrubs. The glossy green leaves of European ginger reflect the light and help brighten shady locations. Wild ginger is hardier and is a good choice for native woodland gardens. Both European ginger and wild ginger combine well with ferns, hostas, astilbe, and other shade-tolerant plants. The native wild ginger, *Asarum canadense* (shown), has large, deeply veined, kidney-shaped leaves.

Try These
Zone 5 and 6 gardeners may want to try *Asarum splendens*. This ginger has narrow, heart-shaped leaves with silver variegation. The unique shape and color are a welcome addition to the shade garden. My plants are a couple years old, slowly taking root but a beautiful addition to my shade garden.

Mother of Thyme

Thymus serpyllum

Botanical Pronunciation
TY-mus sir-FYE-lum

Other Name Creeping thyme

Bloom Period and Seasonal Color
Summer blooms in purple

Mature Height × Spread
3 to 6 inches × 18 inches

Thyme has long been used for its fragrance and flavor. History is full of examples of how Roman soldiers, European royalty, and common folks used this fragrant herb in cooking and as a deodorant. In the garden, women's long skirts would brush over the thyme groundcover releasing its fragrance and masking less desirable odors. Mother of thyme is a close relative of the thyme most used for cooking. Its creeping growth habit makes it a good groundcover for sunny, dry locations. Add attractive leaves and a summer-long bloom, and you have a groundcover fit for most landscapes. This plant is listed under several different botanical names. That may be why there is some variability in the plants sold as creeping thyme or mother-of-thyme.

When, Where, and How to Plant
Start seeds of thyme indoors in early spring. Germination requires light and 55- to 60-degree Fahrenheit temperatures to germinate. Lift and divide established plants in the spring. Plant container-grown thyme throughout the growing season. I like to get it in the ground early so it has time to get established before winter. You can also take cuttings of new growth to root and plant later in the summer. Grow thyme in full sun and well-drained soil. Add 2 to 4 inches of organic matter to heavy clay soils to improve drainage. It will tolerate light shade but does best in full sun and poor, dry soil. Space plants 6 to 18 inches apart.

Growing Tips
Only fertilize if your plants show signs of nutrient deficiencies. Excess fertilizer results in tall, weak, and unattractive growth. Avoid overwatering. Wet soil will lead to root rot and winter dieback.

Regional Advice and Care
Winter dieback can be a problem in extremely cold winters or poorly drained locations. Fortunately, stems will often root and survive even when the parent plant dies. Prune back plants in the spring after leaves begin to sprout but before flowering begins. Don't disturb the rooted stems you want to keep. Spring pruning will remove winter damage and give the plants a neat appearance. Root rot can be a problem when thyme is overwatered or grown in poorly drained soils. Lift and divide overgrown plants in spring or early summer using a shovel or garden fork to dig out plants.

Companion Planting and Design
Use thyme as a groundcover on slopes, in rock gardens, near walkways, and between steppers where it can be seen. The lovely fragrance and attractive flowers add to its landscape value. Thyme will tolerate light traffic, which will release its fragrance. Use thyme in hot dry locations surrounding stone walkways in place of the traditional bluegrass lawn.

Try These
For a change of color try 'Albus' with white flowers, 'Coccinea' with red flowers, or 'Pink Chintz' with pink flowers. 'Elfin', as its name implies, is small, 2 by 5 inches, and slow growing.

Pachysandra

Pachysandra terminalis

Botanical Pronunciation
pak-ih-SAN-drah ter-min-AL-iss

Other Name Japanese spurge

Bloom Period and Seasonal Color
April to May blooms in white

Mature Height × Spread
6 to 8 inches × spreading

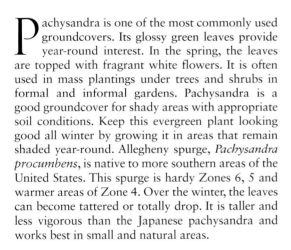

Pachysandra is one of the most commonly used groundcovers. Its glossy green leaves provide year-round interest. In the spring, the leaves are topped with fragrant white flowers. It is often used in mass plantings under trees and shrubs in formal and informal gardens. Pachysandra is a good groundcover for shady areas with appropriate soil conditions. Keep this evergreen plant looking good all winter by growing it in areas that remain shaded year-round. Allegheny spurge, *Pachysandra procumbens*, is native to more southern areas of the United States. This spurge is hardy Zones 6, 5 and warmer areas of Zone 4. Over the winter, the leaves can become tattered or totally drop. It is taller and less vigorous than the Japanese pachysandra and works best in small and natural areas.

When, Where, and How to Plant
Plant divisions and rooted cuttings of pachysandra in spring or early summer. Plant container-grown plants anytime during the growing season. Earlier plantings allow transplants to establish before winter. Plants will yellow when grown in full sun. Winter wind can also cause yellowing. Avoid winter damage by planting this evergreen groundcover in a protected location or winter-mulch plantings in exposed sites. Pachysandra needs moist, well-drained soil to thrive. Plant container plants at the same level they were growing in the pot, 12 inches apart.

Growing Tips
Mulch new plantings to conserve moisture and reduce weeds. Water thoroughly when the top few inches are moist and crumbly. Fertilize plants in the spring with a low-nitrogen fertilizer if needed in spring.

Regional Advice and Care
Remove weeds as they appear. Mulching helps reduce weeds and improve the soil. Leaf blight, root rot, and euonymus scale can be devastating problems. Proper soil preparation, placement, and care will help prevent these problems. Remove blight-infected leaves as soon as they appear. Water in the morning, if needed, to avoid wet leaves at night. Treat euonymus scale when the young shell-less scales are active. This coincides with the beginning of Japanese tree lilac and catalpa bloom. Use insecticidal soap at that time and then twice more at ten- to twelve-day intervals. Soil-applied systemic insecticides labeled for this pest can be applied according to label directions.

Companion Planting and Design
Grow this groundcover under trees and shrubs. It can be used in small or large groundcover beds on flat or sloped surfaces.

Try These
The 'Green Carpet' cultivar of Japanese pachysandra is a low-growing plant. The compact growth and deep green leaves make this the preferred choice for many landscapers. The less vigorous 'Variegata' has mottled white foliage. Use this choice for small locations or to create contrast in shade gardens. *Pachysandra procumbens* 'Pixie' is a miniature cultivar of the Allegheny spurge. It's slow growing to 4 inches.

Potentilla

Potentilla species

Botanical Pronunciation
poe-ten-TIL-lah

Other Name Cinquefoil

Bloom Period and Seasonal Color
May to June blooms in white or bright yellow

Mature Height × Spread
3 to 10 inches × 12 to 24 inches

Potentilla is a good groundcover for those gardening in rocky and sandy soils. The growth habit and dissected foliage is similar to barren strawberry. Select a species best suited for your growing conditions and your landscape design. Some cinquefoils lose most or all of their leaves for the winter, while others are evergreen. Flowers are typically yellow or white, although there are some newer red-flowering cultivars. These plants are related to the popular summer-blooming shrubs used in many landscapes. A close look at the flowers will help you see the family connection. The genus name *Potentilla* comes from the Latin word *potens*, meaning "powerful." The word refers to the medicinal properties this group of plants is supposed to have.

When, Where, and How to Plant
Plant container-grown potentillas throughout the summer. Dig and divide overgrown plantings in the spring. Grow potentillas in full sun or partially shaded locations. They need good drainage and tolerate infertile soils. Proper soil preparation is critical when planting potentilla in clay. Work at least 2 inches of organic matter into the top 6 to 12 inches of soil. Space plants or divisions 6 to 12 inches apart, depending on the species.

Growing Tips
Water new plantings as needed until they are established. Most species are drought tolerant once established. All benefit from supplemental watering during extended dry periods. Mulch new plantings to conserve moisture and reduce weeds. Avoid excess fertilizer than can lead to poor growth and reduced flowering

Regional Advice and Care
Remove weeds as they appear. Some species benefit from pruning whenever the plants appear unkempt. With a shovel or garden fork, lift and divide overgrown plants. These often have dead centers or fail to bloom. Cut the clump into several sections and replant the divisions at 12-inch intervals in a prepared site. Root rot and winter dieback is common in heavy and poorly drained soils. Improve drainage or use a more suitable groundcover in these areas.

Companion Planting and Design
Use potentilla for rock gardens, on dry slopes, or as a groundcover in open, rocky areas. I saw a wonderful combination of blue fescue and potentilla. The potentilla covered the ground beneath the grass. The yellow potentilla flowers peeked through the blue leaves of the fescue. It was a nice texture and color combination—good for full sun and dry locations.

Try These
'Fire Flames' is an evergreen potentilla with bright red flowers. It grows 15 to 24 inches tall and is hardy throughout the region. Spring cinquefoil, *Potentilla verna*, is deciduous, grows 2 to 3 inches tall, and has yellow flowers in late spring. Use wineleaf cinquefoil, *Potentilla tridentata*, as a groundcover in rock gardens and on dry slopes. This hardy evergreen spreader is 2 to 6 inches tall with white flowers.

Sweet Woodruff

Galium odoratum

Botanical Pronunciation
GAL-ee-um oh-dor-AY-tum

Other Name Woodruff

Bloom Period and Seasonal Color
May and June blooms in white

Mature Height × Spread
6 to 8 inches × spreading

Don't let the delicate appearance of sweet woodruff fool you. Its bright green, fragrant leaves will cover the ground from early spring through late fall. The white flowers cover the plant for several weeks. Consider adding a little patch to your garden or put a large planting under some trees and shrubs. Try adding a planting near the patio or deck or garden bench where you can enjoy the fragrance. I have mine under a serviceberry tree near my front door. The fragrance greets me on warm summer evenings. It's a little landscape aromatherapy to end my work day. Extend its fragrant impact by adding dried leaves to potpourris and sachets. The fresh leaves and flowers have long been used to flavor May wine and other spring drinks.

When, Where, and How to Plant
Plant container-grown sweet woodruff throughout the season. Dig, divide, and plant divisions from established plantings in early spring for best results. Woodruff prefers shade and moist, well-drained soil but tolerates a wide range of conditions. It tends to burn out in full sun and dry locations. Reduce maintenance and improve the plant's appearance by growing it in full to part shade with moist soils. Space plants 12 inches apart.

Growing Tips
Keep the soil near new plantings moist but not wet. Water established plants thoroughly and only when the top few inches of soil feel crumbly and moist. Mulch new plantings with shredded leaves or other organic matter to conserve moisture and reduce weeds. Apply a low-nitrogen fertilizer in the spring if needed to improve flowering.

Regional Advice and Care
Woodruff will quickly cover an area; just remove weeds as they appear. Woodruff maintains an even and attractive growth habit throughout the summer. You can clip it back several times during the summer to create a more formal appearance. Poor flowering and a fungal leaf spot may be a problem on rare occasions. Remove disease-infected leaves. In severe cases, you will need to remove infected plants, amend the soil with organic matter, and wait for the surrounding plants to fill in the bare spots. Lift and divide overgrown plants. Cut the clump into several sections and replant the divisions at 12-inch intervals in a prepared site.

Companion Planting and Design
In shady spots, it makes a nice edging or rock garden plant. Try using it under crabapples for double blooming pleasure. Or mix it with hostas as a spring-flowering backdrop. Allow the sweet woodruff to wander through perennial gardens and mixed borders. It is a greater weaver plant providing fine texture unity in planting beds.

Try These
Galium odorata is the best choice for use as a groundcover. *Galium triflorum* is native to moist forests. It has a taller, looser habit but has the same nice fragrance. The dried vanilla scented leaves were often used to stuff mattresses, thus the common name bedstraw.

LAWNS
FOR MICHIGAN

Grass is a unifying element and a functional part of any landscape design. Grassy areas provide walkways, play areas, and something to keep your feet from getting muddy when it rains. No matter how much effort and money you invest in grass seed or sod, your lawn will be only as good as the soil it is grown in. Taking the time to plan carefully before the first seed is sown or the sod is laid will help ensure a healthy, attractive lawn you can be proud of. After the soil is properly prepared, selecting the right grass for growing conditions in your area will also improve chances for a lush, green, outdoor carpet. Once the grass is established, mowing, watering, and fertilizing properly are the three keys to maintaining a healthy and attractive lawn.

The Grasses
Kentucky Bluegrass

Kentucky bluegrass *(Poa pratensis)* is a traditional favorite for northern lawns. This cool-weather grass is well suited to our northern climate. It is green most of the year when the ground isn't frozen or covered with snow. Bluegrass may go dormant during hot, dry periods in July and August, but as soon as the weather cools and rains return, the grass turns green and begins to grow. Bluegrass lawns can be started from seed or sod. Grow it in full sun with moist, well-drained soil. It does not perform well in extremely wet or dry locations. Bluegrass lawns will thin and eventually fail in heavily shaded areas. Use a blend of three to five cultivars to provide greater resistance to disease.

Fescue

Fine fescues' (*Festuca* species) low-maintenance requirements and their shade and drought tolerance make it one of the top three grasses in our region. It is much more tolerant of shade, drought, and acidic and infertile soils than bluegrass. You will find a large percentage of fine fescue in shade-tolerant lawn seed mixes. Although fescue will tolerate full sun, especially in northern parts of the state, it needs cool soil temperatures for best results. Overfertilization can lead to leaf spot and other fungal diseases. Fertilize pure stands of fescue growing in the shade only when the leaves are pale or the plants stop growing. One-half pound of actual nitrogen per thousand square feet applied in the fall is often enough for 100 percent fine fescue lawns growing in the shade.

The creeping red, *Festuca rubra,* is the most commonly used fine fescue. It blends well with Kentucky bluegrass. Creeping red spreads slowly by rhizomes, so it is sluggish when recovering from injury. This fescue will tolerate drought and shade but not

Kentucky bluegrass (*Poa pratensis*) is a great lawngrass choice for our area.

heat. Once established, it can be left unmowed for a meadow-like effect. Chewings fescue, *Festuca rubra commutata,* is a bunch-type fescue that has the same growth requirements as creeping red. Its bunching habit makes it more difficult to create an even stand. Hard fescue, *Festuca longifolia,* is often combined with sheep fescue, *Festuca ovina,* for low-maintenance lawns. Both are bunch-type grasses, and the lower-growing varieties require less frequent mowing.

Rhizomatous tall fescue is a turf-type tall fescue. It grows well in sun or shade, has good color, pest resistance, quickly fills in damaged areas, and tolerates high traffic. Once established, this deeply rooted grass is drought tolerant.

Perennial Ryegrass

Turf-type perennial ryegrass, *Lolium perenne,* is an important part of lawn seed mixes. It germinates quickly and aids in the establishment of seeded lawns. The versatility

The fine blades of Kentucky bluegrass shown in close-up.

of perennial rye, its improved quality, and the availability of hardier cultivars have made this a major component in most grass seed mixes. Straight ryegrass is often used to overseed high traffic or other thin areas of the lawn. Many new turf-type perennial ryegrasses are being introduced. Select the hardiest and most disease-resistant cultivars available. Annual ryegrass, *Lolium multiflorum,* is the quick-start grass of old mixtures. It is an annual that dies within the first year. Its coarse texture blends poorly with other grasses. Quick-fix miracle grasses contain a large percentage of this grass. They provide a quick-growing, short-lived lawn and should be avoided.

Choices for Lawn Establishment

New lawns can be started from seed or sod. Seed mixes provide a wider variety of grasses and cultivars to choose from, allowing you to best match the grass with the growing conditions. Seed is cheaper than sod, but be patient—it takes about two months to establish a lawn from seed. Sod gives you an instant lawn at an additional cost. Most sod is best suited for sunny areas, though some growers are providing some that are more shade tolerant. Many gardeners sod the front yard and seed the back yard for fairly fast results at a lower overall cost.

Soil Preparation

Whether you seed or sod, start by taking a close look at the earth beneath your feet. Start with a soil test to determine how much and what type of fertilizer your lawn needs. Spread no more than the recommended lime, phosphorus, and potassium combination over the soil surface and till it into the top 6 inches of the soil. Phosphorous containing fertilizers can only be used when establishing new lawns or if a soil test shows it is needed on established lawns. If soil test recommendations are not available, spread four to eight pounds of a low-nitrogen slow-release fertilizer (no lime) over the soil surface. Lightly rake the fertilizer into the soil prior to seeding.

If your yard does not have at least 4 to 6 inches of good topsoil, you will also need to add blended topsoil or amend the existing soil by adding organic matter. Add 2 to 3 inches, equal to two to three cubic yards per thousand square feet, of peat moss, compost, aged manure, or another organic material to the top 4 to 6 inches of the existing soil. This can be incorporated at the same time as the fertilizer, lime, or sulfur recommended by the soil test. Do not add sand. Mixing sand into clay soil can result in poor growing conditions. Allow the soil to settle, and rake it smooth, leveling high areas and filling in low areas. With healthy soil in place, the next step is choosing the right grass for your yard.

Seeding the Lawn

Use one or a mixture of the cool-weather grasses previously described. Bluegrass works best in full sun while fescues really prefer the shade. Sun mixes contain mostly bluegrass and ryegrass with a smaller percent of fescue for shady areas. Shade mixes are the opposite, mostly fescues and ryegrass with a small percent of bluegrass to take over in sunny locations. Select a mix containing a variety of disease-resistant cultivars. Don't use zoysia, a warm-weather grass; it is better for southern states where the summers are long and hot. The best time to seed is August 15 through September 20 when temperatures cool. May is the second best time to seed. Apply half the recommend rate of seed over the entire lawn moving in a north-south direction. The remaining seed should be applied in an east-west direction to ensure good coverage.

Rake the seed into the soil surface and then roll the yard with an empty lawn roller, which will help guarantee good contact with the soil. Mulch the newly seeded lawn with weed-free straw, marsh hay, one of the season-extending fabrics, or other suitable mulch. Keep the surface of the soil moist until the grass seeds germinate, then water thoroughly but less frequently.

Sodding

Soil preparation is just as important for sodded lawns. Sod can be laid anytime it is available and the ground is not frozen. Sod is purchased in rolls 1½ by 6 feet (traditional size), though some garden centers now carry rolls 2 by 4 feet. Start by laying the first roll of sod next to a walk or driveway. Butt the ends of the sod pieces together, overlapping them slightly to compensate for shrinkage. Stagger the joints, just like you were laying bricks, for a nice finished look. Water frequently enough to keep the soil beneath the sod moist. Start watering thoroughly but less frequently once the sod roots into the soil and resists a light tug.

Caring for Your Lawn

Mowing

A healthy lawn is the best defense against weeds and disease. Proper mowing, watering, and fertilization will keep your grass green and healthy. Keep bluegrass lawns cut to a height of 2½, preferably 3½, inches. The taller grass will be more drought tolerant and better able to compete with weeds. No more than one-third of the total height should be cut at each mowing. Leave clippings on the lawn to decompose, adding moisture and nutrients to the soil. Be sure your mower blade is sharp. This will make your job easier, and the newly cut lawn will look better.

Watering

Ideally, lawns should receive 1 inch of water per week. Use a sprinkler, if needed, to supplement rainfall. Water thoroughly but only when the top 4 to 6 inches of soil are crumbly and moist or when your footprints are left in the grass. That's usually once a week in clay soil and twice a week in sandy, fast-draining soil. Avoid using quick-release, high-nitrogen fertilizers (especially in summer) on non-irrigated lawns. This can damage the grass plants during the hot dry months of summer. Conserve water and allow your lawn to go dormant during hot dry weather. Once dormant, keep it dormant until the rains return. Do provide ¼ inch of water every three to four weeks during extended drought to keep the crown of the grass alive yet keeping the lawn dormant.

Fertilizing

Fertilizer is the third component of a healthy yard. Our lawns generally need three to four pounds of actual nitrogen per thousand square feet a year. Use the annual holiday fertilization schedule: Memorial Day, Labor Day, and the final application of fertilizer between Halloween and Thanksgiving but before the ground freezes. Consider using a low-nitrogen slow-release fertilizer that encourages slow steady growth that needs less mowing. And it won't burn if an unexpected drought follows your application. Low maintenance lawns are fertilized only once in late fall.

Weed Control

When weeds appear, it's a sure sign that the grass isn't vigorous or healthy enough to keep them at bay. Do some detective work to determine why weeds have invaded your lawn. Is the area too shady? Is the soil compact, or is the grass not receiving needed water and nutrients? Correct the conditions for long-term weed control. You may decide instead to live with a few weeds rather than using chemicals or adjusting your yard-maintenance efforts in some other way. It's up to you to determine the quality desired and the time and effort you are willing to invest. If you do decide to use an herbicide, be sure to read and follow all label directions carefully. These really are plant killers. They can't tell the difference between a dandelion and a geranium, so use them carefully to minimize the risk to you, the landscape, and the environment. Timing is critical for successful treatment. Fall applications are most effective against perennial weeds like plantain and dandelions. Treat that bothersome creeping Charlie in spring when it is in full bloom or in fall, around late October, after a hard frost. All those chemicals you previously used unsuccessfully will work if applied at the right time. Crabgrass killers are applied in early spring before the seeds of this annual grass sprout. When the soil temperatures reach 50 degrees (soon after the forsythia bloom), it is time to apply the crabgrass pre-emergent. Perennial grass weeds like quack and bent are more difficult. Anything that kills them will kill your good grass. Spot treat large infestations with a total vegetation killer such as Roundup® or Finale®. Then reseed to get new grass growing before the weeds take over.

Reduce your exposure by spot treating problem areas with broadleaf weedkillers. You do not need to treat the entire lawn and should not need to be treating it every year. Yearly applications indicate poor grass-growing conditions that need to be fixed. Gardeners looking for a safer option may want to try a new weed killer made of corn gluten meal. It prevents many seeds, including weeds, from germinating. It won't kill existing weeds, but it reduces the weed population by as much as 85 percent after three years of spring and fall applications. A new broadleaf weedkiller containing HEDTA (FeHEDTA) is now available and research continues on other organic products. These are appealing alternatives for many lawn owners whose children and pets play on the grass.

Thatch Control

Thatch is a problem on highly managed lawns. Lots of fertilizer and water encourage thick, dense growth. As the old grass plants die, they have no way to reach the soil surface to decompose. The old grass stems, leaf coverings, and roots—not grass clipping—form the thatch layer. Control thatch when it becomes ½ inch or thicker. You can topdress the lawn with ¼ inch of soil to help compost the thatch in place. This is good for the lawn, but hard on your back. Core aeration is another method to control thatch. The core-aerating machine removes plugs from the soil. It opens the lawn, allowing the thatch to decompose. Dethatching machines and verti-cut mowers physically remove the thatch. Be prepared: the lawn will look awful when you finish. Overseed thin lawns after dethatching or aeration to thicken up the lawn. You will have better seed germination once the thatch is removed. Core aeration and dethatching should be done in the spring or fall when the lawn is actively growing.

Pest Control

A healthy lawn is relatively free of insects and disease. Even with proper care, your lawn may be attacked by disease or insects. Proper diagnosis is the first step in managing the problem. Check with your local University Extension service, reliable Internet sites, or *Minnesota Lawn Guide* or *Wisconsin Lawn Guide* (both from Cool Springs Press) for more details on possible problems and control.

A lush green lawn highlights a beautiful flower bed.

ORNAMENTAL GRASSES
FOR MICHIGAN

Ornamental grasses have become an important part of the American gardening scene. With their long, narrow leaves, these distinctive plants provide motion and sound in a landscape. A gentle breeze makes the tall moor grass flowers dance and the switch grass rustle.

Most ornamental grasses bloom at some point during the growing season. The flowers on some, such as blue fescue, are secondary to the foliage, while those of others, such as the miscanthus, steal the show from the greenery. The seedheads also add winter color to an otherwise barren garden since the dried leaves and flowers often remain intact on the plant. They also can be enjoyed in a vase indoors.

Porcupine grass, *Miscanthus sinensis* 'Strictus'

Selecting Ornamental Grasses

It is important to select ornamental grasses that are best suited to the growing conditions in your area. Most grasses prefer full sun and well-drained soil. A few, like hakonechloa, will tolerate shade and moist soils. New grasses are continually being introduced. If you get the opportunity, check out the ornamental grass collection at the University of Minnesota Landscape Arboretum located just west of the Twin Cities. Dr. Mary Meyer has been evaluating hardiness of grasses since 1987 and published her results in *Ornamental Grasses for Cold Climates*, which is available from the University of Minnesota Extension Service. Those trying to push plant hardiness can do a bit of their own research. Try a few test plants in protected sites in your landscape. Remember cold temperatures, snow cover, and soil drainage all influence the ornamental grasses' ability to survive our harsh winters. You may have better or worse results in the microclimates of your own garden.

Avoid aggressive grasses that can take over your garden and invasive grasses that can escape the garden and invade and disrupt our natural spaces. If in doubt check with your local Extension service, nearby botanic garden or nature center, or one of the invasive plant lists online.

Many of the ornamental grasses are substantial plants, so it's important to allow sufficient space for them to grow and bloom. I have quite a few grasses in my small city lot, but I use single specimens of various species and varieties to add interest, texture, and sound. In larger settings, ornamental grasses make great screens, as well as background or hillside plantings. However, remember your screen will be missing from the late winter, when you trim back the plants, through early summer, when they again reach full size.

Consider light when placing grasses in the garden. Not just for growth, but also beauty. Sunlight glistening through fluffy or icy seedheads can provide added beauty. Combine ornamental grasses with trees, shrubs, and other perennials that provide winter interest. This will give you a nice garden rather than a lone plant to view in winter.

Planting Basics

Many ornamental grasses come in containers that are one gallon or larger. That means you will need a shovel, not a trowel, for planting. Dig the planting hole the same depth and two to three times wider than the rootball. Plant the grass at the same level it was growing in the container. Gently loosen potbound and girdling roots before filling the hole with soil. Established grasses rarely need watering or fertilizing except in extreme droughts or where the soil is sandy. Follow soil test recommendations when fertilizing ornamental grasses. If these aren't available, err on the side of moderation. Most grasses need little to no fertilizer when grown in well-prepared soil that is top-dressed every other year with compost.

Ornamental grasses provide a great tall backdrop for perennials in the border. In this shot are *Sedum* 'Autumn Joy', *Rudbeckia* 'Goldsturm', *Betula* 'Whitespire', and *Miscanthus sinensis*.

Cut back ornamental grasses in late winter before growth begins. I use hand pruners for my small plantings. A weed whip or electric hedge trimmer will make larger jobs go much faster. Compost the debris. Spring is a good time to dig, divide, and transplant ornamental grasses that are overgrown, dead in the center, or performing poorly.

Ornamental grasses can make a big impact in the home landscape. With proper selection, you can use ornamental grasses to add low-maintenance, year-round interest to your landscape.

Blue Fescue

Festuca glauca

Botanical Pronunciation
fess-TOO-ka GLOK-ah

Other Name Gray fescue

Bloom Period and Seasonal Color
Midsummer blooms in blue-green followed by beige seedheads

Mature Height × Spread
6 to 10 inches × 10 inches

Blue fescue has long been used in our perennial gardens and landscapes. This small grass is a good fit in large and even small city lots. Blue fescue forms a tuft of narrow, blue-green leaves that contrast nicely with bold textured perennials and shrubs. Its colorful, fine texture blends well in rock and perennial gardens. Or try using it *en masse* as a groundcover. This salt-tolerant plant is a good solution for garden areas subjected to winter deicing salts. I have seen it growing successfully in boulevard plantings, parking lot islands, and groundcover beds next to salted sidewalks. Use it in areas where its evergreen foliage can be enjoyed throughout the winter—when it's not buried under a blanket of snow.

When, Where, and How to Plant

Plant container-grown blue fescue during the growing season. I prefer spring and early summer. That allows the grass time to become established before our harsh winter. Divide and transplant blue fescue in the spring. Plant blue fescue in well-drained soil. Add organic matter to soil with a heavy clay content to improve drainage. Blue fescue is available in pots from perennial nurseries, garden centers, and catalogues. Space the plants 1 foot apart or a bit closer together for a denser, groundcover effect.

Growing Tips

Blue fescue is a relatively low-maintenance plant. Avoid overwatering and overfertilizing, which can lead to poor growth, root rot, and dead plants.

Regional Advice and Care

Blue fescue can be short-lived, especially in poorly drained soils. Try dividing these plants every three or four years to increase vigor. Or replace them with new plants as needed. Although blue fescue is an evergreen, parts of the plant turn brown during the winter. You can trim back the older leaves in late winter before growth begins, or just let the new growth mask the old leaves as they fade away. A light combing with your fingers through the foliage will help dislodge the brown leaves. I have done both, and my plants looked fine and remained healthy either way.

Companion Planting and Design

This small grass makes a good edging plant, groundcover, or addition to the rock garden. The fine texture creates a nice contrast to bolder, coarser-textured plants. The blue-green foliage makes blue fescue a nice addition to any garden. Try combining this plant with one of the purple-leaved coralbells or hardy geraniums. Blue fescue also works well in rock gardens. For a similar but bigger (2 feet × 2 feet) and slightly coarser look try blue oat grass (*Helictotrichon sempervirens*). This combines nicely with bronzed leafed penstemons and many other perennials.

Try These

'Elijah Blue' is an excellent cultivar that grows 8 inches tall and has powdery blue foliage. *Festuca amethystina* is slightly bigger and more tolerant of clay soils.

Bluestem

Schizachyrium scoparium

Botanical Pronunciation
skiz-ah-KEER-ee-um skoe-PAR-ee-um

Other Name Little bluestem

Bloom Period and Seasonal Color
Fall blooms in pinkish white

Mature Height × Spread
1½ to 3 feet × 2 feet

Bluestem, also known as little bluestem and sometimes sold as *Andropogon scoparius*, was a major element in our native prairie landscape. Its beauty and year-round interest have helped this native grass find its way into the home landscape. The fine-textured green to blue-green foliage fits well in naturalized or perennial gardens. The late-summer flowers quickly give way to showy silvery white seedheads and striking orange-red fall color. This short grass forms loose, upright clumps. Its compact size makes it a practical choice for even the smallest city lot. If you like natives but don't have room for a prairie, try incorporating this and other natives into your perennial gardens. This creates a less abrupt transition from formal to naturalized, readily blends with surrounding yards, and is easier to manage on a smaller plots.

When, Where, and How to Plant

Plant container-grown bluestem during the growing season. I prefer spring and early summer, which gives the grass time to become established before our harsh winter. Divide and transplant little bluestem in the spring. Seed large plantings of little bluestem in the spring or fall. The seed must be stratified (cold treated) to germinate. Little bluestem and short prairie seed mixes are available from several local quality prairie seed companies. Purchase clean seed that is free of stems, fluff, bracts, and leaves. Although clean seed costs more, you get more seed and less debris for your money. Quality companies will provide soil preparation and planting guidelines. Plant little bluestem in areas with well-drained soil, adding organic matter to heavy soils to improve drainage. Space plants at least 2 feet apart.

Growing Tips

When placed in an appropriate spot, bluestem requires very little maintenance. Avoid overfertilizing. Plants tend to flop over when they receive excessive nitrogen or are grown in nutrient-rich soils.

Regional Advice and Care

Cut down old stems in the late winter before growth begins. Poor growth will occur in wet, poorly drained soils. Dig up struggling plants in the early spring and move them to a location with better drainage, or add organic matter to the soil to improve drainage before replanting.

Companion Planting and Design

Little bluestem can add year-round interest to the garden with its beauty and bird appeal. The fine-textured green to blue-green foliage fits well in naturalized or perennial gardens. Combine them with asters, coneflowers, and other natives. A mass planting of little bluestem can be quite impressive in a large landscape.

Try These

Look for local strains of bluestem for seeding and natural plantings. An introduction by Dr. Meyer is 'Blue Heaven'™, taller and more upright with dark blue foliage turning burgundy in fall. 'The Blues' is another upright cultivar with blue-green foliage turning red-orange in fall. Big bluestem, *Andropogon gerardi*, is a much larger (4 to 7 feet or taller) cousin to little bluestem. Its suited to large landscapes and salt-tolerant.

Feather Reed Grass

Calamagrostis × acutiflora 'Stricta'

Botanical Pronunciation
Kal-ah-mah-GROSS-tiss ex
ah-kew-tih-FLOOR-ah strict ah

Other Name Reed grass

Bloom Period and Seasonal Color
July blooms in pink

Mature Height × Spread
4 to 5 feet × 2 feet

Feather reed grass has demonstrated its hardiness, durability, and beauty for many years in our landscapes. The wheat-like seedheads and stiff, upright leaves provide year-round interest. Feather reed grass is tall enough to demand attention in a large yard yet small enough to fit into more limited spaces. This tough plant tolerates a wider range of growing conditions than most grasses. I have observed it growing and thriving in difficult sites subject to stressful winters, droughty summers, deicing salt, clay soil, and reflected heat. An ice cream shop in a busy part of town uses feather reed grass in a narrow planting bed between a wall and the parking lot, and it always looks good, especially while you're checking out the flavor of the day.

When, Where, and How to Plant

Plant container-grown feather reed grass during the growing season. I prefer to plant in the spring and early summer, which gives the grass time to get established before our harsh winter. Divide and transplant feather reed grass in the spring. It prefers moist, well-drained soil but will tolerate clay and wet soil with good drainage. Plant at the same level it was growing in the pot. Gently loosen potbound and girdling roots (ones that encircle the grass) before planting. Space plants at least 2 feet apart.

Growing Tips

Feather reed grass is a low-maintenance plant. It is one of the tougher, more reliably hardy ornamental grasses, and it attracts birds to the garden. Water established plants only during extended droughts.

Water thoroughly, moistening the top 6 inches of soil. Wait until the top 4 inches of soil are crumbly and slightly moist before watering again.

Regional Advice and Care

Feather reed grass has no serious insect or disease problems. Cut it back to just above ground level in late winter before growth begins. Divide plants as they outgrow their location or when divisions are needed for other garden areas.

Companion Planting and Design

Feather reed grows stiffly upright. This makes it a good choice for a background plant or as a vertical accent in the landscape. Use it as a low screen to block the view of a compost pile, neighbor's doghouse, or storage area. Its moisture tolerance makes it suitable for placement alongside a pool or pond. Feather reed grass is also salt tolerant. Mix feather reed grass with other perennials and shrubs to expand your landscape's seasonal interest.

Try These

'Karl Foerster' is a popular cultivar due to its slightly smaller size and earlier bloom. Overdam feather reed grass, *Calamagrostis acutiflora* 'Overdam' ('Oredam'), is also stiffly upright, a bit shorter (24 to 30 inches), and has variegated leaves. Korean feather reed grass, *Calamagrostis arundinacea brachytricha*, has the same growth habit but tends to be a little shorter and flowers later in the summer. It combines nicely with purple coneflower.

Fountain Grass

Pennisetum setaceum

Botanical Pronunciation
pen-nih-SEE-tum sah-TAY-see-um

Other Name Annual fountain grass

Bloom Period and Seasonal Color
Midsummer through fall blooms in pink
to purplish pink

Mature Height × Spread
3 feet × 18 to 24 inches

Fountain grass is an annual that is bound to brighten flowerbeds and container gardens. This traditional favorite has been used in boulevard and park plantings for years and still generates attention from everyone. It forms an upright clump up to 3 feet tall, but in container gardens, its limited root area keeps plants a bit shorter. Its light airy texture makes it a perfect filler in annual, perennial, and container gardens. Try it in place of spike plant for a vertical accent in planters. Fountain grass has feathery foxtail flowers that extend beyond the leaves and attract birds to the garden. In late fall, the seedheads will shatter and the leaves will brown, but the plant form will remain intact and provide winter interest.

When, Where, and How to Plant
Fortunately fountain grass is now more readily available. It is sold in 4- and 6-inch pots as well as gallon containers. Plant in properly prepared soil at the same depth it was growing in the pot. You can also start plants from seeds. Sow seeds in late winter according to seed packet directions. Be patient as it takes seeds three to four weeks to sprout. Plant hardened-off transplants outdoors in the spring after all danger of frost is past, spacing plants 1 or 2 feet apart. Excessive shade can result in poor flowering and floppy plants. Fountain grass prefers moist, well-drained soil but will tolerate a wide range of conditions including clay soil.

Growing Tips
Fountain grass is a low-maintenance garden plant, but specimens grown in containers need extra attention. Check the soil moisture in container gardens at least once a day and water thoroughly as needed. Use a slow-release low-nitrogen fertilizer at the start of the season. You can add a midseason nutrient boost if needed. In the garden, water thoroughly whenever the top 4 inches of soil feel crumbly but slightly moist.

Regional Advice and Care
Fountain grass is relatively pest free. No deadheading is needed to keep this plant covered with flowers throughout the growing season.

Companion Planting and Design
Include fountain grass in containers for a vertical accent. I often grow a single fountain grass plant in a funky container like an old metal bucket, child's sand bucket, basket, or even a purse. Use fountain grass *en masse* or mixed with annuals and perennials. I combined the red leafed variety with 'Gartenmeister' fuchsia and wire vine for a nice partial-shade combination.

Try These
The traditional red leafed cultivars will always be in my gardens. But newer cultivars have moved into my containers. 'Fireworks' lives up to its name with its burgundy, pink, and white leaves. *Pennisetum glaucum* 'Jade Princess' grows 3 to 4 feet tall and has wide chartreuse leaves topped with dark maroon seedheads. Perennial fountain grass, *Pennisetum alopecuroides*, is marginally hardy in Zone 4a. Try dwarf 'Hameln' that some claim is a bit hardier.

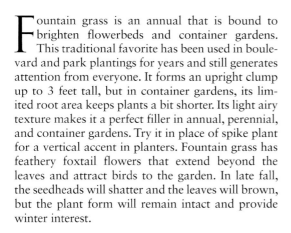

Hakonechloa

Hakonechloa macra 'Aureola'

Botanical Pronunciation
hak-on-eh-KLO-ah MAK-rah ah-ree-OH-la

Other Name Japanese forest grass

Bloom Period and Seasonal Color
Late summer blooms tinged with pink

Mature Height × Spread
20 to 24 inches × 20 to 24 inches

Hardiness Zones Hardy to Zone 4

Very few grasses tolerate moist shady conditions, but this one does. Its variegated foliage forms attractive mounds in the flower garden. It may remind you of the spider plants many of us have grown indoors. Its bamboo-like foliage also makes this grass suitable for Japanese gardens. Pink flowers appear in late summer. Though it's not very showy, I find the light, airy flowers a nice addition to the overall appearance. The flower display is followed by a pink tinge of fall color. Consider this award winning plant if you're looking for something different for your shade or container garden. Its unique features along with its shade and moisture tolerance won it the title of 2009 Perennial Plant of the Year.

When, Where, and How to Plant
Plant container-grown hakonechloa during the growing season. Divide and transplant hakonechloa in the spring. This is one of the few ornamental grasses that will tolerate shade and moist soil. Add organic matter to heavy clay soil to improve drainage and to sandy soil to increase its capacity to hold water. Plant hakonechloa early in the season and in a protected location to increase its chances of winter survival. Space plants 18 to 24 inches apart.

Growing Tips
Keep the soil moist, but not wet, throughout the season. Mulching will help conserve water and minimize weeds. Water thoroughly whenever the top few inches of soil are crumbly and slightly moist. This is key to establishing these plants. Hakanochloa can

also be used in container plantings. Check the soil moisture in container gardens at least once a day. Fertilize planters with a low-nitrogen slow-release fertilizer at the start of the season.

Regional Advice and Care
Hakonechloa is a low-maintenance plant. It is slow to get established, so be patient. Leaf scorch or brown leaf edges can occur on plants grown in full sun or in dry soil. Loss of variegation is common in heavily shaded areas. Extremely cold and fluctuating winter temperatures as well as poor drainage can kill this plant; use a winter mulch to help it survive the cold. Cover the plants with evergreen boughs or weed-free straw after the ground freezes. Remove the mulch in the spring. Sink potted hakonechloa into the soil for the winter or move into an unheated garage. Water whenever the soil is thawed and dry.

Companion Planting and Design
Use it as a specimen plant near the front of a shady border. The variegated leaves brighten up the shade and the colorful narrow foliage contrast nicely with the bold leaves of hosta. Hakonechloa also combines well with other shade plants like ferns and astilbe.

Try These
'Albo Striata' tends to be more sun tolerant and some of the new introductions like 'Naomi' have more purplish fall color. Those in cold regions may want to start with the hardier more vigorous Hakone grass, *Hakonechloa macra*.

Miscanthus

Miscanthus sinensis

Botanical Pronunciation
mis-KAN-thus sih-NEN-sis

Other Name Silver grass

Bloom Period and Seasonal Color
Fall blooms in pale pink to red

Mature Height × Spread
3 to 7 feet × 4 feet

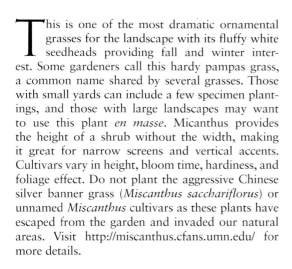

This is one of the most dramatic ornamental grasses for the landscape with its fluffy white seedheads providing fall and winter interest. Some gardeners call this hardy pampas grass, a common name shared by several grasses. Those with small yards can include a few specimen plantings, and those with large landscapes may want to use this plant *en masse*. Micanthus provides the height of a shrub without the width, making it great for narrow screens and vertical accents. Cultivars vary in height, bloom time, hardiness, and foliage effect. Do not plant the aggressive Chinese silver banner grass (*Miscanthus sacchariflorus*) or unnamed *Miscanthus* cultivars as these plants have escaped from the garden and invaded our natural areas. Visit http://miscanthus.cfans.umn.edu/ for more details.

When, Where, and How to Plant
Plant container-grown miscanthus during the growing season, preferably in spring and early summer so the grass has time to become established before winter. Space plants at least 3 feet apart. Divide and transplant miscanthus in the spring. Miscanthus prefers moist, well-drained soil. It will tolerate clay soil, although I prefer to add organic matter to the soil prior to planting. In shady areas, it tends to flop over and flower poorly.

Growing Tips
Plants are slow to emerge in spring, so be patient. Root prune to invigorate sparsely leaved miscanthus plants struggling after a hard winter. Take a sharp spade and cut through the crown and roots in two directions. The plant will fill in by the following season. Use these in large containers for a dramatic display. Move containers into an unheated garage, surround with woodchips or sink the pot in the ground to insulate the roots. Water anytime the soil is thawed and dry.

Regional Advice and Care
Miscanthus is a low-maintenance plant. Lift and divide every four or five years when the center of the plant dies out or becomes floppy. Rust, a fungal disease, can occasionally be a problem during wet, humid weather. Adjust watering if necessary and remove infected leaves as soon as they appear. Cut the plants back in late winter before new growth begins.

Companion Planting and Design
Use these large grasses as screens, hedges, background plants, and to attract birds. Individual plants make good specimens in the landscape, in a flower garden, or near water. One of my favorite combinations includes tamarisk, *Hydrangea paniculata* 'Tardiva', boltonia, and silver feather miscanthus. You can't go wrong with this grass among most perennials, shrub roses, and flowering shrubs.

Try These
Maiden grass, *Miscanthus sinensis* 'Gracillimus', grows 5 to 6 feet tall and is grown for its fine foliage. The cold weather often arrives before its late season blooms. Variegated miscanthus, *Miscanthus sinensis* 'Variegatus', is somewhat shade tolerant, grows 5 to 6 feet tall, and is hardy throughout our region.

Moor Grass

Molinia caerulea

Botanical Pronunciation
Mo-LEEN-ee-uh sir-oo-LEE-ah

Other Name Purple moor grass

Bloom Period and Seasonal Color
Midsummer blooms in purple

Mature Height × Spread
1 to 2 feet × 1 to 2 feet

U se moor grass to add motion and color to your perennial garden. Native to the wet moorlands of Eurasia, it is more tolerant of wet soils than most grasses. Moor grass forms a tuft of green leaves that easily blends with other plants. The real surprise comes in midsummer when the flowers shoot several feet above the foliage. The purple flowers are open, airy, and blend well with the background. This, along with the shorter foliage, makes it easy to use throughout the flower garden and landscape. Or use it like sheer curtains in your home to create a bit of see-through privacy. In the fall, the leaves and flowers turn yellow, creating a colorful display, especially when grown in front of evergreens.

When, Where, and How to Plant

Plant container-grown moor grass during the growing season. I prefer spring and early summer so the grass has time to get established before our harsh winter. Divide and transplant moor grass in the spring. It prefers moist, well-drained soil. Moor grass is available in pots from perennial nurseries, garden centers, and catalogs. Plant container-grown moor grass at the same level it was growing in the pot. Gently loosen potbound and girdling roots before planting. Space plants 18 to 24 inches apart.

Growing Tips

Native to the wet lowlands of Eurasia, this grass prefers moist soil. Mulch the soil surrounding the grass to help keep roots moist. Water thoroughly as needed during dry spells.

Regional Advice and Care

Moor grass is a low-maintenance plant. It is slow to get established. Use larger plants and divisions to get flowers in the first or second year. Some gardeners have reported problems with voles feeding on the roots and crowns of this grass. Watch for damage and dig, divide, and replant healthy sections in the spring. Moor grass is self-cleaning. The leaves and flower stems drop from the plants in the winter. A little spring cleanup may be all that is needed.

Companion Planting and Design

Moor grass forms dramatic tufts of foliage 1 to 2 feet tall and wide. The flowers shoot several feet above the plant. The fine, airy blooms allow you to see through to the rest of the garden. That feature makes moor grass a good choice as a specimen plant or in a small grouping in the perennial garden. Use moor grass as a sheer divider between various sections of your landscape.

Try These

Variegated purple moor grass, *Molinia caerulea* 'Variegata', is 18 to 24 inches tall. The flowers rise 6 to 12 inches above the white-striped foliage. This shorter plant makes a nice edging, groundcover, or rock garden plant. Tall moor grass, *Molinia caerulea* subspecies *arundinaceae*, foliage grows 2 to 3 feet tall. The cultivars 'Skyracer' reaches 7 to 8 feet in bloom while 'Transparent' is shorter, 5 to 6 feet in bloom, with seemingly transparent flower stems.

Prairie Dropseed

Sporobolus heterolepis

Botanical Pronunciation
spor-OB-oh-lus het-er-oh-LEP-sis

Bloom Period and Seasonal Color
Summer pale pink blooms

Mature Height × Spread
3 to 3½ feet × 24 inches

This beautiful native grass is suited to any landscape. Its smaller size fits into any size landscape while providing year-round beauty. In late summer, the grassy leaves are topped with fragrant delicate flowers. The seedheads persist through winter, capturing dew and ice crystals to add a little sheen to the garden. This is what sold me on the plant. The leaves turn a yellow-orange in fall and eventually fade to beige; they provide motion, sound, and beauty in the winter landscape. This grass is equally at home in a perennial, rock, or naturalized garden. I like to tuck a couple of these in amongst my perennials and watch the birds come to visit. Or consider adding several to create an impressive winter display.

When, Where and How to Plant

Grow prairie dropseed in full sun and well-drained soils. Plants can be started from seeds in spring or fall. Select quality seed free from debris. Though it costs more, you are paying for seed, not the debris you don't need. Purchase seed from a quality source that provides detailed information on soil preparation and planting rates. Plants are also available from some garden centers and catalogues. Plant dormant bare-root plants as soon as they arrive and container plants throughout the season. Dig a hole two to three times wider than the rootball. Plant prairie dropseed at the same depth it was growing in the nursery. Loosen any tangled roots and girdled roots before planting. Backfill with existing soil, gently tamp, and water in well.

Growing Tips

This native takes several years to dig its roots in and start blooming—so be patient. Water recent transplants often enough to keep soil slightly moist. Once established, these plants are fairly drought tolerant and only need occasional watering during drought.

Regional Advice and Care

This native grass is low maintenance and basically pest free. Allow the plants to stand for winter interest. Cut them back in late winter and compost the leaf debris.

Companion Planting and Design

Use as a specimen or plant *en masse*. The airy foliage looks great with ornamental shrubs and dwarf conifers. Or add prairie dropseed to your perennial garden. It looks good with airy perennials such as coreopsis and boltonia as well as the bolder plants of heliopssis and sedum. And don't forget to look to nature for some ideas. Try combining it with its native companions such as aster, coneflowers, and rudbeckia. A hillside covered with prairie dropseed is a site and fragrance to behold. Or line a walkway or flank an entrance where visitors will delight in the beautiful texture and late summer unique fragrance of this grass. In downtown Chicago, near Navy Pier, you can find this native combined with sun-loving coleus and threadleaf coreopsis for a more formal design.

Try These

'Tara' is a dwarf cultivar with stiff, more upright habit.

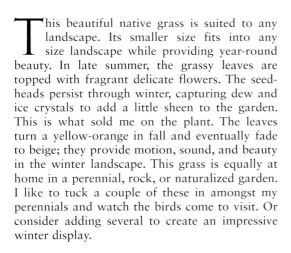

Sedge

Carex species

Botanical Pronunciation
KARE-ex

Other Name Ornamental sedge

Bloom Period and Seasonal Color
Late spring or early summer, green
turning brown

Mature Height × Spread
6 to 24 inches × 6 to 24 inches

You may have heard the old saying "sedges have edges." Their triangular stem gives their identity away. Though not a true grass, many of these grass lookalikes tolerate the moist shade that most grasses detest. These clump-growing plants with long narrow leaves make nice fillers, groundcovers, and specimen plantings. Their fine texture creates a welcome contrast to the bold textures of hosta, ginger, and ligularia often found in shade gardens. Consider replacing sparse lawns and bare spots in wet shaded parts of the landscape with sedges. Use *Carex pennsylvanica* or other native sedges to create a no mow grass-like look for these challenging areas. Plus, many provide food for the birds. Hardiness and shade and moisture tolerance varies with species.

When, Where, and How to Plant
Plant bare-root sedges as soon as they arrive. Container-grown sedges can be planted throughout the season. I prefer spring or early summer so they establish before summer heat or winter cold. Most sedges prefer full to part shade and moist to wet soils. Hardiness has been a concern with many ornamental types. Look for hardier introductions and try planting just one or two before investing in large numbers. It may take you several tries to find the best location.

Growing Tips
Check soil moisture throughout the season. Most sedges prefer moist soils and may need supplemental watering. Hardiness can be a bigger problem in clay soils that stay excessively wet in winter. Add

organic matter to clay soils to improve drainage while maintaining moisture.

Regional Advice and Care
Native sedges are low maintenance if planted in the proper environment. Ornamental sedges can be a bit more difficult to grow successfully in our climate. Place these in microclimates that have the right soil, moisture, and shelter in the winter. Let plants stand for winter. They provide interest and overwintering increases winter hardiness. Cut back dead foliage in spring or allow new leaves to grow through the old.

Companion Planting and Design
Sedges are good alternatives for grass in moist shady areas. Use it as a groundcover under shade tolerant viburnums and dogwoods, or mix in a few spring wildflowers. Don't forget to add a few sedges to the shade or hosta garden. The fine-texture leaves provide a colorful contrast to the bold leaves of hostas.

Try These
Carex morrowii 'Bowles Golden' has been the standard ornamental sedge for northern gardens. The chartreuse foliage brightens the shade and looks great against the large blue-green leaves of hosta. My new favorite is variegated cultivar of our native palm sedge, *Carex muskingumensis* 'Oehme'. The leaves emerge green then develop yellow edges on the leaves. The foliage glistens in the sun and the plants are suited to rain gardens. *Carex morrowii* 'Ice Dance' is a vigorous plant whose wider leaves with white variegation add color and interest to gardens.

Switchgrass

Panicum virgatum

Botanical Pronunciation
PAN-ih-kum ver-GAY-tum

Other Name Panicum

Bloom Period and Seasonal Color
Midsummer to late summer blooms in pink to red to silver

Mature Height × Spread
3 to 8 feet × 3 feet

Bring a little of our native prairie into your backyard. Plant some switchgrass as a backdrop for a flower garden, as a screen, *en masse*, on a hillside, or as part of a native garden. The straight species will spread by underground rhizomes and seed, so give it plenty of room to grow. Use some of the cultivated varieties in your perennial gardens. Switchgrass grows in tall, upright clumps. The colorful flowers look like fireworks exploding 1 to 2 feet above the leaves. This "flowerworks" display is complemented by the beautiful golden yellow fall color. And watch for the wildlife that enjoys this plant. Finches feed on the seeds, and the larvae of Leonard's skipper (*Heperia leonardus*) and tawny edge skipper (*Polites themistochies*) feed on the leaves.

When, Where, and How to Plant
Plant container-grown switchgrass during the growing season. I prefer spring and early summer, which gives the grass time to become established before winter. Divide and transplant switchgrass in spring. Space plants 30 to 36 inches apart. Seed large areas of switchgrass in the spring or fall. Switchgrass and prairie seed mixes are available from several quality prairie seed companies in our area. Purchase clean seed that is free of stems, fluff, bracts, and leaves and is from a local source. Seeds collected outside our region can be overly aggressive. The quality companies will provide soil preparation and planting guidelines.

Growing Tips
Shade-grown plants tend to be more open and fall over. Move them to a sunnier location. Switchgrass prefers moist soil but will tolerate wet to dry soil and exposure to deicing salt.

Regional Advice and Care
Switchgrass is a low-maintenance plant. The biggest problem is keeping plantings of the straight species under control. Plants spread by seeds and rhizomes. Weed out strays and dig and divide sprawling clumps to keep them under control. Consider cultivated varieties that are much less aggressive, for home gardens and landscapes. Rust and fungal leaf spot may occasionally occur. Adjust watering if necessary and remove infected leaves as soon as they appear.

Companion Planting and Design
Use it near roadsides, paved areas, and walkways that are salted in winter. Switchgrass also works well as a specimen plant, background plant, or as a mass planting. Try combining switchgrass with plants you would see it with in nature. The bold textures of coneflowers, black-eyed Susans, sunflowers, and goldenrods contrast nicely with the light, airy appearance of switchgrass.

Try These
Heavy metal switchgrass, *Panicum virgatum* 'Heavy Metal', is a narrow, upright plant that grows 3 to 5 feet tall. It has metallic blue leaves that turn bright yellow in the fall. 'Northwind' is stiffly upright with blue foliage and reaches heights of 6 feet. 'Shenandoah' is 36 inches tall with bright red foliage that appears in June, followed by red flowers later in summer. 'Strictum' is 5 feet tall and narrowly upright with green foliage.

PERENNIALS

FOR MICHIGAN

Whether you are adding a few or a few hundred perennials to your landscape, proper selection, planting, and care are essential to perennial gardening success.

Shade garden favorites include hostas, Solomon's seal (*Polygonatum biflorum*), and maidenhair fern (*Adiantum pedatum*).

Start with the Soil

Evaluate and prepare the soil as described in the general introduction. Perennials growing in a properly prepared soil only need an inch of compost spread over the soil surface every other year. And if fertilizer is needed, use a low-nitrogen slow-release fertilizer if soil test results are not available.

Most perennials are sold bare root or grown in containers. Store bare-root plants in a cool, but not freezing, location until you are ready to plant. Keep the roots moist and packed in peat moss, sawdust, or another similar material. Move dormant bare-root plants into the garden as soon as the soil is workable and ready for planting. Pot up bare-root plants that begin to grow in transport or storage. Grow in a sunny window indoors or outdoors in the protection of a coldframe. Move these plants into the garden after hardening off and the danger of severe weather has passed.

Preparation Pays Off

Container-grown plants are grown and sold in pots. Some are grown outdoors and can be planted as soon as they are purchased. Others are grown in greenhouses and need to be hardened off before planting. Here's how: store potted perennials in a shaded location and water daily until they can be planted in the garden. Water and allow the potted plants to drain prior to planting. Remove container-grown plants from the pot. Loosen potbound roots to encourage root development into the surrounding soil. Plant these at the same level they were growing in the container in a hole two to three times wider than the rootball.

Water established plants thoroughly, at least 6 inches deep, whenever the top 3 inches of soil are crumbly and slightly moist. Mulch perennials with a 1- to 2-inch layer of organic material such as twice-shredded bark, shredded leaves, or evergreen needles. Organic mulches conserve moisture, moderate soil temperature, suppress weeds, and improve the soil as it decomposes.

Banish Weeds

Weeds compete with perennials for water and nutrients and often harbor insect and diseases. Pull these invaders as soon as they appear and mulch to help prevent weed seeds from sprouting. You may choose to enlist help controlling quackgrass, bindweed, and other hard-to-control perennial weeds. Spot treat with a total vegetation killer containing glyphosate. These materials are absorbed by the leaves and move through the plant, killing the roots and all. Protect nearby plants that can also be killed by these herbicides. Once the chemical enters the soil, it won't harm the plants.

Remove all disease- and insect-infested plant debris in the fall to reduce the source of infection for next year. Leave the seedheads and healthy foliage for winter interest, to attract birds, and to increase hardiness. Cut back and compost this winter interest in late winter or early spring before growth begins.

Perennials Care

Perennials can be divided to improve their health and appearance or to start new plants. Divide perennials that are too big for the location, flower poorly, flop over, or open in the center. In general, lift and divide spring-flowering plants in late summer and fall-flowering plants in the spring. Summer bloomers can be divided in spring or late summer.

Winter-mulch late plantings, tender perennials, and those subject to frost heaving. Cover the plants with evergreen branches, weed-free straw, or marsh hay after the ground freezes. Remove the mulch in the spring as new growth begins. Winter mulching keeps the soil temperature consistently cold. That eliminates frost heaving caused by the freezing and thawing of soil throughout the winter. Frost heaving damages plant roots and can even push perennials right out of the soil.

Despite the long list of chores, perennial gardening can be relatively low maintenance and definitely worth the effort. The best part, I think, is the seasonal change.

Peonies have many species and forms, including this one, *Paeonia lactiflora* 'Bowl of Beauty'.

Amsonia

Amsonia hubrichtii

Botanical Pronunciation
am-SO-nee-ah hew-BRIK-tee-eye

Other Name Blue star

Bloom Period and Seasonal Color
Steel blue flowers in May and June

Mature Height × Spread
2 to 3 feet × 2 to 3 feet

Multiple seasons of interest was just one of many attributes that made the Perennial Plant Association membership pick amsonia as a Perennial Plant of the Year. Its airy fine foliage is a nice backdrop for the icy blue spring flowers. Their star-shaped flowers gave rise to the common name blue star. And watch for butterflies that come to sip on their nectar! The airy foliage helps soften the bold texture of sedums, coneflowers, and rudbeckia. It also makes a nice plant to weave throughout large perennial beds. The narrow leaves turn a clear yellow in fall and just glow in the garden. Leave these plants to stand for winter to provide texture among the bolder textures in the winter garden.

When, Where, and How to Plant
Start plants from seeds in spring. Plant dormant container and bare-root plants in spring when severe weather has passed and soil is workable. Plant hardened-off, potted, and container-grown amsonia in the garden after the danger of frost has passed. Grow these plants in full sun and moist well-drained soils for best results. Plants will flop when grown in too much shade. Water new plantings thoroughly and often enough to keep the soil slightly moist. They will tolerate drier soils once established. Space plants 3 feet apart.

Growing Tips
Avoid high-nitrogen fertilizers and excess fertilization, which can cause plants to flop open. Instead, topdress the soil with an inch of compost every other year. Water established plants thoroughly whenever the top few inches of soil are crumbly and slightly moist. These plants seldom need dividing. Dig and divide in spring or fall to propagate more plants.

Regional Advice and Care
After flowering, cut the plants back to 6 to 8 inches above the ground for denser growth. Or take the low-maintenance approach and mix it with neighboring plants that benefit from the more open airy growth. And more good news—this plant has no serious pests.

Companion Planting and Design
Use the fine texture to soften structures and bold textured plants. The icy blue flowers help tone down hot colors like orange and yellow in the garden. One of my favorite combinations included tiger eye sumac, globemaster allium, and willow amsonia in front of a dark green arborvitae hedge. The color and texture of this combination was everchanging and looked good year-round. Use these moisture and somewhat drought tolerant plants in rain gardens. Mass plantings have a shrub-like appearance. Partner them with purple-foliaged plants. The summer and fall color combinations are outstanding.

Try These
Amsonia × 'Blue Ice' is 15 inches tall, has deep lavender-blue flowers atop wider leaves. *Amsonia montana* 'Short Stack' grows 10 inches tall, has wider green leaves, and sky blue flowers.

Aster

Symphytrichum species

Botanical Pronunciation
sim-fee-oh-TRIK-um

Bloom Period and Seasonal Color
Late summer through fall blooms in purple, white, and pink

Mature Height × Spread
2 to 5 feet × 1 to 3 feet

Asters can add a last flash of color to the landscape before the snow falls. They are equally at home in formal and naturalized gardens. Include asters in your garden design to help attract butterflies, for use as cut flowers, and for a little winter interest. A little early season care or garden design can keep these stately beauties upright and attractive. Select the color and size that best fits your landscape design and is hardy in your area. The New England aster, *Symphytrichum novae-angliae*, is among the most well-known asters. It is native and grows 4 to 6 feet tall. The New York aster, *Aster novi-belgii*, grows 3 to 5 feet tall. Asters were once used to dye wool a greenish gold color.

When, Where, and How to Plant
Plant dormant container and bare-root asters in spring after the danger of severe weather has passed. Plant hardened-off potted and container-grown perennials anytime during the growing season. Plant less hardy species and cultivars early in the season to give them time to establish before winter. Grow asters in well-drained soil. Prepare the soil before planting, and space asters at least 2 feet apart with the crown even with the soil surface.

Growing Tips
Water new plantings thoroughly whenever the top 4 inches are crumbly and moist. Mulch asters to conserve moisture and reduce weed problems. Avoid excess fertilization that can reduce flowering and increase floppy growth.

Regional Advice and Care
Pinch back tall asters to 6 inches throughout June. Cut the stems above a set of leaves to reduce toppling and encourage full, compact growth with lots of flowers. Taller species may still need staking. Or use grow-through stakes or sturdy neighboring plants for added support. Divide asters every three years to control the growth of taller plants and increase the vigor of less hardy species. Let the plants stand for winter to increase hardiness and add a little winter interest. Cover the base of less hardy asters with evergreen branches, weed-free straw, or marsh hay after the ground freezes. Asters are susceptible to wilt and powdery mildew. Remove wilt-infested plants. Proper spacing and placement will minimize problems with powdery mildew, which won't kill the plant but just looks bad.

Companion Planting and Design
Asters make great additions to perennial and cut-flower gardens. Use them with ornamental grasses and goldenrod for a dramatic fall display.

Try These
S. dumosus 'Wood's Light Blue' is a compact New York aster with light blue flowers; it has shown mildew and rust resistance. 'Purple Dome' is a compact cultivar of New England aster that grows 18 inches tall and requires no pinching. 'Alma Potschke' is another New England aster guaranteed to grab your attention. Its bright pink flowers seem to leap out of the garden. It grows 3 to 4 feet tall and usually needs staking.

Astilbe

Astilbe species

Botanical Pronunciation
ah-STILL-bee

Other Name False spirea

Bloom Period and Seasonal Color
Summer blooms in white, pink, red, salmon, and lavender

Mature Height × Spread
1 to 4 feet × 2 to 3 feet

Astilbes can add color, attractive foliage, and texture to the shadier side of your landscape. Select a variety of astilbes with different bloom times to provide summer-long color. Leave seedheads of late bloomers intact. They will persist over winter adding additional texture and interest. Astilbes make great cut flowers and are even grown as flowering potted plants in some areas. Cut astilbe when the flowers are halfway open for the maximum vase life. The light feathery flowers and fern like foliage make this a great filler plant in the vase or shade garden. Select an area with moist soil and partial shade for the best looking plants with minimal care. Or use the more drought-tolerant dwarf Chinese astilbe for late summer bloom.

When, Where, and How to Plant

Plant dormant container and bare-root astilbe in spring after the danger of severe weather has passed. Plant hardened-off potted and container-grown perennials anytime during the growing season. Plant them early in the season, before September 1, to give them time to establish before winter. Grow astilbe in moist, well-drained soil. No matter where it is planted, astilbe needs moist, not wet, soil for best results. Prepare the soil prior to planting; add several inches of organic matter to improve both drainage and the water-holding capacity of the soil. Plant small cultivars 12 to 15 inches apart and larger cultivars at least 24 inches apart.

Growing Tips

Moisture and fertilization are the keys to growing healthy astilbes. Water thoroughly and often enough to keep the soil moist. Mulch the soil surface with a 1- or 2-inch layer of organic material to keep the roots cool and moist and to suppress weeds. Fertilize astilbe in the spring before growth begins or in the fall as plants are going dormant. Astilbe can take a year or two to get growing. Use a low-nitrogen, slow-release fertilizer to help get them growing.

Regional Advice and Care

Deadheading will not encourage reblooming but tidies up the summer garden. Seedheads add a bit of winter interest. Let healthy foliage stand for the winter. This helps increase hardiness, and the stems catch the snow for added insulation. Regular dividing every three years seems to help revitalize astilbe.

Companion Planting and Design

Use astilbe for its foliage and flower effect in shade gardens. Shorter cultivars work well in shady rock gardens with moist soil. Try using astilbes with ferns and hosta. The combination of foliage shape, texture, and color make for an attractive display.

Try These

Color Flash® has pink flowers held above burgundy, purple, and green foliage that matures to gold tones in fall. Flamingo astilbe, *Astilbe × arendsii* 'Flamingo', has full, fragrant pink flowers June through July. The drought-tolerant dwarf Chinese astilbe, 12 to 15 inches tall, has a rosy-lavender flower in mid- to late summer.

Baptisia

Baptisia australis

Botanical Pronunciation
bap-TIZ-ee-ah oss-TRAL-iss

Other Name Blue false indigo

Bloom Period and Seasonal Color
Blue flowers in May and June

Mature Height × Spread
3 to 4 feet × 3 to 4 feet

This North American native can be found growing in woods, thickets, and along stream banks in the eastern United States. In the garden you can find it in formal, informal, and naturalized settings. Selected as a Perennial Plant of the Year, this beauty has blue flowers that look much like those of lupines but is much easier to grow. The blue-green foliage covers this large upright perennial and looks good all season. Showy black seedpods appear in late summer and fall and last into winter. These are great in dried flower arrangements and were once popular rattles for kids. Early settlers used this plant as a substitute, albeit inferior, for *Indigofera*, the West Indies indigo plant used for dyeing.

When, Where, and How to Plant
Start plants from seeds. Their hard seed coat requires scarification, etching through the seedcoat, to enhance germination. Some gardeners find a cold treatment also helps. Purchase small plants as they recover more quickly from transplanting. Plant dormant container and bare-root plants after severe weather has passed and the soil is workable. Plant hardened-off transplants in the garden after the danger of frost has passed. Grow these perennials in full sun and well-drained soils. Avoid shade where the plants tend to flop. They do tolerate a wide range of soils from rocky sand to clay and poor soils with low fertility. Water new plantings thoroughly and often enough to keep the roots moist. Space at least three 3 apart.

Growing Tips
This is a low-maintenance plant when properly sited. Water established plants thoroughly during extended dry periods. Avoid high-nitrogen fertilizers and excess fertilization that can lead to floppy open growth. Be patient as these plants get established. They look pretty sparse when young but quickly fill in and flourish by the third season. You can pinch off faded flowers to encourage more blooms or go even more low maintenance and skip the extra bloom and enjoy the seedpods earlier.

Regional Advice and Care
Baptisia have no serious pests. These large plants grow into large, shrub-sized clumps with deep extensive roots. They really are best left undisturbed. Plants have been growing and flourishing for several decades and never been divided.

Companion Planting and Design
Use these large plants and their attractive blue-green foliage as a backdrop for other perennials. It combines nicely with other perennials and ornamental and native grasses in perennial and meadow gardens as well as mixed borders. Combine with bulbs for added spring appeal.

Try These
Prairieblues™ has an upright growth habit and long, deep blue-violet flowers that last for a month. 'Purple Smoke' has smoky violet-blue and purple flowers on black stems. Our native white wild baptisia (*Baptisia alba*, formerly *B. leucantha*) is found in our prairies, savannahs, and open woods.

Beebalm

Monarda didyma

Botanical Pronunciation
mo-NAR-dah DID-ih-mah

Other Name Monarda

Bloom Period and Seasonal Color
Summer blooms in red or violet

Mature Height × Spread
Up to 4 feet × 3 feet

This lovely flower fits in formal, informal, or naturalized settings. The unique, almost Dr. Seuss–like, flowers sit atop fragrant foliage. The tubular flowers attract hummingbirds, butterflies, and, as the common name suggests, bees! Cut a few flowers to enjoy in a vase indoors. Allow seedheads to develop later in the season. They add texture and interest to the winter garden. The fragrant foliage adds a little aromatherapy as you thin and weed your way around the plant. This species is native to the eastern United States. Our native wild bergamot, *Monarda fistulosa*, has lilac-purple to pale pink flowers and is hardy to Zone 3. Beebalm leaves have long been steeped to make tea.

When, Where, and How to Plant
Plant dormant container and bare-root plants as soon as the soil is workable. Plant hardened-off transplants throughout the season. Place in an area with moist soils and full sun for healthy and attractive plants. Those grown in shade are more susceptible to powdery mildew and tend to spread faster. Add organic matter to the soil to improve drainage in clay soils and water holding ability in sandy soils. Space at least 2 feet apart.

Growing Tips
Drought-stressed plants are less attractive and more susceptible to powdery mildew. Water thoroughly whenever the top 3 to 4 inches of soil are moist and crumbly. Mulch with shredded leaves, evergreen needles, or other organic matter to conserve moisture and reduce weeds. Avoid high-nitrogen and excess fertilization that can increase disease, reduce

flowering, and promote faster growth on this naturally assertive plant.

Regional Advice and Care
Remove one-fourth of the plant stems in early spring to increase light penetration and air circulation through the plant. This reduces problems with powdery mildew and encourages stiffer stems. Deadhead for added bloom and to limit unwanted seedlings. Allow a few late blooms to go to seed for winter interest. Remove unwanted seedlings in early spring to keep plantings contained. The young leaves are easily identified by their citrus-mint fragrance. Divide plants every three years or as needed to control its spread.

Companion Planting and Design
The bold red flowers stand out nicely against an evergreen background. Mix with swamp sunflower, coreopsis, or other yellow flowers to create a bold focal point. Use an evergreen, tall ornamental grass, or deciduous plant behind beebalm to create a nice combination for year-round interest.

Try These
These have good mildew resistance. *M. bradburiana*, eastern beebalm, which is 1 to 2 feet tall and wide, has pinkish lavender flowers in May, is mildew resistant and drought tolerant. 'Fire Marshall' is a 2- to 3-foot-tall red-pink introduction from the Chicagoland Grows® Plant Introduction Program. The hybrid 'Raspberry Wine' has rich raspberry color. 'Cambridge Scarlet' has bright scarlet flowers. 'Marshall's Delight' has a long bloom period and rosy-pink flowers.

Bellflower

Campanula species

Botanical Pronunciation
kam-PAN-yew-lah

Other Name Harebells

Bloom Period and Seasonal Color
Late spring to summer blooms in blue, white, and purple

Mature Height × Spread
6 to 36 inches × 6 to 36 inches

Bellflower's beautiful, blue-and-white, bell-shaped flowers are unmistakable. The commonly grown bellflowers are native to Europe and Asia. There are several bellflowers native to our region. The tall bellflower, *Campanula americana*, is native to moist, shady locations. The same goes for Marsh bellflower, *Campanula aparinoides*, which can be found in swamps and grassy swales throughout the eastern United States. You may find the common harebell, *Campanula rotundifolia*, in cedar glades. The European or creeping bellflower, *Campanula rapunculoides*, should be avoided. It has long spikes of blue bell-shaped flowers and has widely naturalized in our region. This tall garden plant spreads by rhizomes and seeds, quickly engulfing a perennial garden and escaping into nearby natural areas. It takes several years to get this plant out of the garden.

When, Where, and How to Plant
Plant dormant bellflowers in spring after the danger of severe weather has passed. Plant hardened-off transplants anytime during the growing season. Grow them in full sun to partial shade in moist soil with good drainage. Bellflowers have a difficult time surviving our winter in poorly drained soils. Add several inches of organic matter to the top 12 inches of soil prior to planting. Space them 12 to 24 inches apart.

Growing Tips
Healthy bellflowers require minimal care. Water thoroughly whenever the top 3 to 4 inches of soil are moist and crumbly. Mulch the soil to keep the roots

cool and moist and to help reduce weed problems. Avoid excess nitrogen fertilizer that leads to floppy growth and poor flowering. Instead, spread a 1-inch layer of compost over the soil every other year.

Regional Advice and Care
Some species, like the clustered bellflower, may need to be staked even when properly fed. Cut back floppy plants after blooming to encourage fresh compact growth. Remove faded flowers to encourage repeat blooming and reduce problems with reseeding. Be careful not to remove the developing buds. Divide overgrown and poorly flowering bellflowers in early spring for best results.

Companion Planting and Design
Use campanulas in formal or more naturalized settings. The stately spikes of flowers on upright forms create a vertical accent or serve as background plants in the landscape. The mounded types of bellflowers easily blend with other flowers, and they work well in rock gardens or as edging.

Try These
'Pink Octopus' has narrow, weeping pink petals and blooms all summer long. Some gardeners have complained about excessive reseeding but I have not found this a problem. Serbian bellflower, *Campanula poscharskyana*, forms a 12-inch mound, covered with pale blue flowers in late spring and early summer. It often continues throughout the summer. The Clips series of Carpathian bellflower, *Campanula carpatica*, 6- to 12-inch plants, have white, blue, or dark blue flowers throughout the summer.

Bergenia

Bergenia species

Botanical Pronunciation
ber-GEN-ee-ah

Other Name Pigsqueak

Bloom Period and Seasonal Color
Pink, salmon, red, white, violet flowers in early to late spring

Mature Height × Spread
12 to 18 inches × 12 inches

You'll love 'em or hate 'em. That's what I find when I talk to gardeners and horticulture professionals about this plant. The large, cabbage-like leaves are green through the growing season, then turning a purplish red in fall. The colorful leaves are evergreen adding a nice touch of color when not blanketed with snow. In spring white or pink flowers emerge and peek out above the new foliage. Use the bold leaves of bergenia as a foil for or contrast with nearby bulbs, annuals, and finer textured perennials. Include the long-lasting flowers in spring bouquets and the bold leaves in flower arrangements. Rub the leaves between your finger and thumb and hear it squeak like a pig! Thus the source of its common name, pigsqueak.

When, Where, and How to Plant

Sow seeds in spring. Start seeds indoors or directly in the garden. Follow directions on the seed packet. Plant dormant container and bare-root plants in spring as soon as the soil is workable and severe weather has passed. Plant hardened-off potted and container-grown bergenia throughout the growing season. Grow these adaptable plants in full sun or part shade. They tolerate a wide range of soil conditions, including dry shade, but perform best in moist well-drained organic soil. Water new plantings thoroughly and often enough to keep the roots slightly moist. Space plants 12 inches apart.

Growing Tips

Bergenia are low maintenance plants. Minimal fertilizer is needed when grown in properly prepared soil. Topdress the soil with 1 to 2 inches of compost every other year. This continues to improve the soil and provide plants with needed nutrients. Follow soil test recommendations or use a low-nitrogen slow-release fertilizer if the plants need a nutrient boost. Water thoroughly whenever the top few inches of soil are crumbly and slightly moist. Mulch to conserve moisture and suppress weeds. Remove flower stems for neater appearance. Divide bergenia growing in moist soils and ideal growing conditions every four years. Those on drier sites will seldom need dividing.

Regional Advice and Care

Leaves may be tattered and brown after one of our harsh or open winters. Remove damaged leaves in spring before or as new growth emerges. And don't be discouraged when flower buds are damaged in cold winters; the foliage is still an asset. There are no serious pests.

Companion Planting and Design

Use in dry shade under the dense canopied tree, or en masse as a groundcover. I prefer it in smaller groupings in containers, rock gardeners, or as a filler in perennial gardens and mixed borders.

Try These

'Winterglut' has outstanding red fall and winter color; purplish pink flowers rise 16 inches above the foliage. 'Pink Dragonfly' forms a low clump with long narrow leaves that turn plum in the fall and tall coral flowers.

Black Cohosh

Actaea racemosa

Botanical Pronunciation
ak-TAY-ah rass-ih-MOE-sah

Other Name Cimicifuga

Bloom Period and Seasonal Color
White flowers in late June to July

Mature Height × Spread
4 to 6 feet in bloom × 2 to 4 feet

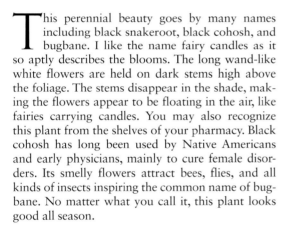

This perennial beauty goes by many names including black snakeroot, black cohosh, and bugbane. I like the name fairy candles as it so aptly describes the blooms. The long wand-like white flowers are held on dark stems high above the foliage. The stems disappear in the shade, making the flowers appear to be floating in the air, like fairies carrying candles. You may also recognize this plant from the shelves of your pharmacy. Black cohosh has long been used by Native Americans and early physicians, mainly to cure female disorders. Its smelly flowers attract bees, flies, and all kinds of insects inspiring the common name of bugbane. No matter what you call it, this plant looks good all season.

When, Where, and How to Plant
Plant dormant container and bare-root plants in spring as soon as severe weather has passed and the soil is workable. Plant actively growing potted or container-grown plants, properly hardened-off, in spring after the danger of frost has passed. Grow black cohosh in cooler areas of the garden in moist organic soils for best results. They prefer part to full shade but will tolerate more sunlight if the roots are kept cool and moist. Water new plantings often enough to keep the roots moist.

Growing Tips
Topdress the soil with compost every other year. Little additional fertilizer is needed. Mulch and water established plants when the top few inches of soil are crumbly and slightly moist. These plants rarely need dividing. If more plants are desired, divide the summer blooming black cohosh in spring or fall and the fall bloomers in spring for best results.

Regional Advice and Care
Leaves will scorch in hot dry conditions. Leave the seedpods on the plants to feed the birds and add winter interest to the landscape.

Companion Planting and Design
Use both the midsummer (*Actaea racemosa*) and late summer-fall blooming (*Actaea ramosa* and *A. simplex*) black cohosh in the same planting to extend your bloom time. These also look great with another moist shade tolerant plant, *Ligularia* 'The Rocket'. Their summer blooms are held high over the foliage mingling to brighten the shade. Include the fragrant fall blooming *A. ramosa* in outdoor living spaces or other areas where their fragrance can be enjoyed. Prevent purple-leaved cultivars from disappearing in the shade by combining them with complementary-colored plants like golden variegated hakone grass. Use black cohosh in naturalized areas or as vertical accents in shade gardens. Leave the seedpods stand for winter interest and food for the birds.

Try These
These late bloomers all have fragrant flowers. 'Hillside Black Beauty' has dark purple foliage topped with white flowers. 'James Compton' has purple-bronze foliage and creamy white flowers. 'Chocoholic' has broader bronze-purple leaves and mauve-pink maturing to white flowers.

Black-eyed Susan

Rudbeckia species

Botanical Pronunciation
rud-BEK-ee-ah

Other Name Gloriosa daisy

Bloom Period and Seasonal Color
Summer and fall blooms in yellow with
black centers

Mature Height × Spread
24 to 36 inches × 18 to 48 inches

Black-eyed Susans are sure to attract the attention of your neighbors as well as passing butterflies and birds. Their dramatic yellow flowers brighten formal, informal, and naturalized plantings. These plants will bloom continuously throughout summer and fall without deadheading. As the flowers fade, the attractive seedheads form. Harvest a few flowers and seedheads to enjoy indoors. Leave the rest intact for winter interest. You and the finches will enjoy them all winter long. The common black-eyed Susan, *Rudbeckia hirta*, is susceptible to powdery mildew and tends to be a short-lived perennial. It easily reseeds, so its presence will be long-lived in the garden. Many of the new introductions like 'Prairie Sun', 'Becky Mix', and 'Goldilocks' are being sold and used as annuals.

When, Where, and How to Plant
In early spring or fall, sprinkle seeds on prepared soil, lightly rake, tamp, and water to ensure good seed-soil contact. See the chapter introduction for guidelines for planting bare-root and potted plants. Rudbeckias tolerate a wide range of soils but prefer moist, well-drained soil and full sun. Space plants at least 2 to 3 feet apart.

Growing Tips
Water new plantings thoroughly whenever the top few inches of soil are moist and crumbly. Once established, these plants can tolerate dry periods. Mulch the soil to conserve moisture and reduce weed problems. Proper soil preparation and top-dressing with an inch or two of compost every other year provides all the nutrients this plant needs.

Regional Advice and Care
Black-eyed Susans are low-maintenance plants. They will quickly grow and crowd out weeds. Rudbeckias will bloom continuously summer through fall without deadheading. As the flowers fade, the attractive seedheads provide fall and winter interest. Powdery mildew can be a cosmetic problem on some species. Select mildew-resistant plants and grow them in areas with full sun and good air circulation. Several fungal and a bacterial leaf spot diseases have recently attacked rudbeckias. Remove infested leaves and do a thorough fall cleanup. If the problem continues, treat plants as they emerge in spring with a copper-containing fungicide. Follow label directions. Some gardeners and growers report fewer problems on *R. fulgida* and *R. fulgida* 'Viette's Little Suzy'.

Companion Planting and Design
Combine with other native plants and grasses for a naturalized or meadow effect. Combine with tall red angelica or porcupine grass (*Miscanthus sinensis* 'Strictus') for a bit of color echoing in the garden.

Try These
R. subtomentosa 'Henry Eilers' grows 3 to 5 feet tall with good branching and rolled yellow rays ("petals") surrounding a bright brown center. The great coneflower, *R. maxima*, has large bluish green leaves and is 5 to 6 feet when in bloom. *R. nitida* 'Herbstonne' has large yellow flowers on 7-foot-tall plants. The native three-lobed coneflower (*R. triloba*) blooms longer than 'Goldsturm' and grows 2 to 3 feet tall.

Bleeding Heart

Dicentra spectabilis

Botanical Pronunciation
dy-SEN-trah spek-TAB-ill-iss

Other Name Japanese bleeding heart

Bloom Period and Seasonal Color
Spring to early summer blooms in rose-red and white

Mature Height × Spread
2 to 3 feet × 3 feet

Bleeding heart is an old-fashioned favorite among gardeners. Many of us include this plant more for sentimental than ornamental reasons. Perhaps your grandmother grew bleeding hearts when you were a child. In any case, the beautiful, heart-shaped flowers add interest and color to shade gardens. Use the flowers for cutting or check with your florist who may sell them as potted blooming plants. Bleeding heart is a fun plant for kids. Pull a flower apart to reveal a dancing lady, slippers, bathtub, sword, and other items that combine to make great stories. Check children's gardening books for the many stories. Check out the flowers on its cousin, our native Dutchman's breeches (*Dicentra cucullaria*), to see where this spring bloomer gets its name.

When, Where, and How to Plant

Plant dormant container and bare-root bleeding hearts in the spring after the danger of severe weather has passed. Plant hardened-off potted and container-grown perennials whenever plants are available. Grow bleeding hearts in partial to full shade with moist soil. The plants will turn yellow and go dormant earlier when they are grown in full sun and dry soils. Space plants 24 to 30 inches apart.

Growing Tips

Bleeding hearts are relatively low-maintenance plants. Water plants thoroughly whenever the top few inches of soil are crumbly and moist. Mulch the soil with a 1- to 2-inch layer of organic material. This helps conserve moisture and reduce weed problems.

Regional Advice and Care

Remove faded flowers to encourage a longer bloom period and discourage reseeding. Young seedlings can be moved in early spring to a desired location, or share them with your perennial gardening friends. The leaves normally yellow and brown and the plants go dormant in July. Prune bleeding heart plants back halfway after flowering to avoid the summer dormancy. The pruned plants send up new foliage that stays green throughout the season. Plants can stay in the same location for many years. Divide plants in early spring to start new plants or to reduce the size of those that have outgrown their location.

Companion Planting and Design

These large plants need lots of room. Make plans to cover the bare spot left when these plants die out in midsummer. Or keep them towards the back of the garden, making their midsummer departure less noticeable. Combine them with hosta, ferns, and other shade tolerant perennials.

Try These

Valentine® has deep red flowers and bronzy gray-green leaves. Fringed bleeding heart, *Dicentra eximia* (shown), grows 12 to 18 inches tall and wide. Its lacy foliage stays green all summer. These plants are covered with flowers in early summer but continue producing blooms all season. 'King of Hearts' has blue-green foliage and rosy pink flowers throughout the summer. 'Burning Hearts' has fringed leaves with fragrant summer-long deep red flowers on compact 10- to 12-inch-tall plants.

Butterfly Weed

Asclepias tuberosa

Botanical Pronunciation
ah-SKLEE-pee-us too-ber-OH-sah

Other Name Milkweed

Bloom Period and Seasonal Color
Summer into fall blooms in orange, red, and yellow

Mature Height × Spread
18 to 30 inches × 12 inches

This is no "weed" that needs to be removed from the garden. It's a beautiful plant that deserves a home in most landscapes. The deep orange flowers and the monarch butterflies they attract brighten the landscape from midsummer into fall. Watch for the black-green-and-yellow-striped caterpillars. They feed on the leaves, form cocoons, and soon turn into beautiful butterflies that nectar on the flowers. Kids and adults love to watch this amazing process. A side benefit for the butterfly is that the toxins in the plant make the butterfly distasteful to their predators. Don't use insecticides on this plant if you want to enjoy the monarch butterflies. Butterfly weed is native and is now available as plants and seeds from garden centers, perennial nurseries, and catalogs.

When, Where, and How to Plant

Sow purchased seeds in early spring on prepared soil and lightly rake. Tamp and water to ensure good seed-soil contact. Butterfly weed is difficult to transplant, so plant seeds in their permanent location. Plant container-grown plants anytime during the growing season. See the chapter introduction for planting directions. Grow this plant in full sun and well-drained soil. Established plants tolerate drought and perform well in poor soil. Space plants 12 inches apart.

Growing Tips

Water new plantings thoroughly whenever the top few inches of soil are crumbly and moist. Mulch the soil to conserve moisture and reduce weed problems. Established plants are drought tolerant. This native plant needs little fertilizer.

Regional Advice and Care

Butterfly weed is slow to establish. The seedlings that plant themselves often do the best. They seem to find the perfect spot and thrive. Move, propagate, transplant, and divide butterfly weed in early spring. Dig deep to avoid damaging the taproot. Butterfly weeds are late to emerge in the spring. Mark their location by leaving last year's stems stand or with plant labels or spring-flowering bulbs. Remove the first set of flowers as they fade to encourage a second flush of blooms. Allow the second flush of flowers to set seed for added interest and additional plants. Aphids are a problem, but many of the insecticides that kill these will harm visiting butterflies. Let the ladybugs take care of the aphids. If that doesn't work, spot-spray the aphids with insecticidal soap, but don't spray caterpillars.

Companion Planting and Design

Use in perennial gardens or naturalized areas. Butterfly weed competes with grass, making it a good addition to meadow and prairie plantings. The orange flowers combine nicely with blue-flowered plants such as the wild petunia (*Ruellia*).

Try These

Most plants have orange flowers, but there are some available with red or yellow blooms. The cultivar 'Gay Butterflies' has all 3 flower colors. 'Hello Yellow' grows 2 to 3 feet tall and produces flat topped clusters of bright yellow flowers. Swamp milkweed, *Asclepias incarnata*, is native and tolerates moist soils.

Catmint

Nepeta × faassenii

Botanical Pronunciation
NEP-eh-tah ex fah-SEEN-ee-eye

Other Name Nepeta

Bloom Period and Seasonal Color
Late spring through fall in lavender-blue

Mature Height × Spread
18 to 30 inches × 10 to 30 inches

Catmint is out of the doghouse and into the garden thanks to the non-aggressive cultivars now available. Catmint's fragrant gray-green foliage is covered with lavender to blue flowers from June through August. Use this plant as a substitute for lavender. Its hardy nature makes it much easier to grow in our area. I have heard mixed reports on how attractive this plant is to cats. One gardener told me she found her cat rolling in this plant every morning. She was so frustrated she placed thorny rose prunings in the middle of the plant. The next morning the stems were removed and the cat was contentedly lying in the catmint. I have had no problems but I do have many stray cats visiting my landscape.

When, Where, and How to Plant
Plant dormant container and bare-root plants as soon as the soil is workable. Hardened-off transplants can be planted anytime throughout the growing season. Grow catmint in full sun with well-drained soils. Add several inches of organic matter to heavy soils to improve drainage. Plant catmint at the same depth it was growing in the nursery. Water for soil settling, and cover exposed roots as needed. Space plants 18 to 24 inches apart.

Growing Tips
Water new plantings thoroughly whenever the top 3 to 4 inches of soil are moist and crumbly. Mulch the soil to conserve moisture and suppress weeds. Established plants are drought tolerant. Overwatering and rainy seasons can lead to yellow foliage and floppy growth. Proper soil preparation and topdressing with compost every other year usually provide sufficient nutrients for these perennials. Avoid high-nitrogen fertilizers that can lead to floppy growth.

Regional Advice and Care
Select sterile and less aggressive cultivars. They offer all the beauty without fighting to keep the plant inbounds. Deadheading is not needed for repeat bloom. Remove spent flowers for a tidier appearance or to prevent reseeding. Cut back floppy plants by two-thirds after the first flush of blooms. This encourages more compact growth and prevents open centers.

Companion Planting and Design
Use catmint as a groundcover or edging plant with roses. Sedums and yellow daylilies also make good planting partners. The light airy foliage and flowers are easy to blend and make catmint a great filler in full-sun perennials gardens.

Try These
'Walker's Low' is a 24- to 36-inch mounding plant that does little if any reseeding (I've heard a few complaints, but I've seen none in my garden). Junior Walker™ is a compact 18-inch non-reseeding catmint. 'Six Hills Giant' grows into clumps up to 30 inches and has sterile seeds. Or try its close non-aggressive relative *Calamintha nepeta nepeta*. It's heat and drought tolerant with the fine texture of baby's breath. 'Blue Cloud' and 'White Cloud' grow 15 inches and are covered all summer with blue or white flowers as their names imply.

Columbine

Aquilegia hybrids

Botanical Pronunciation
ak-will-EE-jah

Bloom Period and Seasonal Color
Late spring to early summer blooms in yellow, red, pink, blue, purple, and white

Mature Height × Spread
1 to 3 feet × 1 to 2 feet

This delicate beauty has blue-green leaves that make a nice base for the long, flowering stems. The flowers can be single or bicolored with long or short spurs. You, the hummingbirds, and butterflies will enjoy the flowers from late spring through early, even mid-, summer. Be sure to include them in the garden where you can sit and watch the hummingbirds feed. Plant extras so you can pick a few to enjoy indoors as well. The native columbine, *Aquilegia canadensis*, has red and yellow nodding flowers. It is easy to grow, self-seeds, and will quickly fill in shady areas. Columbine's jester's cap-like flowers fit as it's the symbol for folly. Or perhaps you see an eagle's claw, as the botanical name *Aquilegia* means eagle.

When, Where, and How to Plant

Plant dormant container and bare-root perennials in spring as soon as the soil is workable. Plant hardened-off transplants anytime during the growing season. Grow columbine in full to part sun with moist soil. Plants will deteriorate in dry soil and rot in overly wet conditions. Space plants 12 inches apart.

Growing Tips

Columbines are fairly low-maintenance plants. Water thoroughly whenever the top few inches of soil are moist and crumbly. Mulch the soil to help conserve moisture and reduce weed problems. Proper soil preparation and topdressing with compost every other year usually provide adequate nutrients.

Regional Advice and Care

Remove faded flowers to encourage rebloom and prevent reseeding of hybrids whose unpredictable offspring can overrun the garden. Deadheading also channels energy back into the roots instead of seed, increasing the longevity of short-lived cultivars. Leave a few seedheads on the plants for winter interest. Columbine seldom needs dividing. You can divide plants in late summer and preferably by September 1 to become re-established by winter. Leafminers are the biggest pest. These insects feed between the upper and lower leaf surfaces leaving a white, snake-like pattern in the leaves. It doesn't hurt the plant; it just looks bad. Cut severely damaged plants back to ground level after flowering to encourage fresh new foliage. Columbine sawfly is a more recent pest problem. It eats the leaves causing the gardeners, not the plants, great stress. Remove and destroy the problem insects by hand to avoid injuring visiting hummingbirds and butterflies.

Combination Planting and Design

Combine with ferns, hosta, and other shade-loving plants. Mix them with these and other perennials to mask the foliage that tends to deteriorate over the summer.

Try These

So many new varieties with single, double, and frilly flowers! 'Nora Barlow' has pink and white double flowers on 20- to 24-inch-tall plants. 'McKana Hybrids' grow 30 inches tall and come in a variety of colors. 'Song Bird' cultivars are 24 to 30 inches tall with vibrant flowers.

Coralbells

Heuchera sanguinea

Botanical Pronunciation
HEW-ker-ah san-GWIN-ee-ah

Other Name Alum root

Bloom Period and Seasonal Color
Late spring to early summer blooms in red, pink, and white

Mature Height × Spread
12 to 20 inches × 12 to 20 inches

Use coralbells as groundcovers, edging plants, or specimens in sun or shade locations. The foliage looks good throughout the growing season and in mild winters. The small bell-shaped flowers are held high above the leaves. These light, airy blooms allow you to see through to the back of the border. And bring a few of the flowers indoors to enjoy in floral arrangements. Most gardeners select hybrids and cultivars with attractive foliage and flowers. Cultivars are available with white, red, and pink flowers. They may have green, amber, purple, plain, or variegated foliage in a wide range of shapes. There are over fifty species of coralbells native to North America. Our native alum root, *Heuchera richardsonii*, has green flowers and coarse textured leaves.

When, Where, and How to Plant

See chapter introduction for planting directions. Plant in spring and early summer to allow the plants to get established and reduce the risk of frost heaving. Coralbells perform best in partial shade with moist, well-drained soil. They will tolerate dry shade. Heavy shade allows nice foliage but fewer flowers. Some cultivars will scorch in the hot afternoon sun. Space plants 12 inches apart.

Growing Tips

Water thoroughly whenever the top 3 to 4 inches of soil are moist and crumbly. Mulch them with a 1- to 2-inch layer of organic material to conserve moisture and reduce weeds. Proper soil preparation and topdressing with compost every other year usually provide sufficient nutrients.

Regional Advice and Care

Shallow-rooted coralbells are subject to frost heaving. Plants are pushed out of soil as the ground freezes and thaws over the winter. To prevent this, mulch the plants in early winter after the ground freezes. Check coralbells in the spring and replant frost-heaved plants so the crown is just below the soil surface. Coralbells need dividing about every three years to prevent woody stems or when they outgrow their location. Divide in spring to allow plants time to reestablish before winter. Remove browned leaves in the spring before new growth begins. The green ones can be left in place. Deadhead coralbells to encourage season-long bloom.

Companion Planting and Design

Use them as groundcovers, edging plants, or rock garden plants in sun and shade locations. The purple-leafed forms look nice with blue oat and fountain grasses. Mix coralbells with ferns, salvias or veronicas, and threadleaf coreopsis.

Try These

Heuchera villosa types are reportedly more heat tolerant. 'Big Top', a *villosa* type, looked good growing in full sun throughout the extreme heat and drought of 2012. *Heuchera* × 'Raspberry Ice' has pewter gray-green leaves with raspberry veining and two-toned pink flowers. 'Plum Pudding' has silvery marked, plum-colored leaves with pink, bell-shaped flowers that appear in June. *Heucherella* is a cross between *Heuchera* and foamflower (*Tiarella*).

Coreopsis

Coreopsis species

Botanical Pronunciation kor-ee-OP-sis

Other Name Tickseed

Bloom Period and Seasonal Color
Late spring to late summer blooms in yellow

Mature Height × Spread
18 to 36 inches × 18 to 36 inches

Coreopsis is a good choice for sunny, dry gardens. The small daisy-like flowers are great for cutting and for attracting butterflies. Use them in formal and informal perennial gardens or in wildflower and naturalized plantings. Threadleaf coreopsis is a good choice for beginning and low maintenance gardeners. Its fine-textured foliage is covered most of the season with small, yellow flowers. And—the best part—it requires no deadheading for season-long bloom. The name "coreopsis" comes from the Greek words *koris*, meaning a bug, and *opsis*, meaning resemblance. The seeds are thought to look like ticks. Thus the common name, tickseed. *Coreopsis tripteris* and *C. palmata* are two of more than 100 native coreopsis that can be found in our dry prairies.

When, Where, and How to Plant
Plant dormant container and bare-root coreopsis in the spring after the danger of severe weather has passed. Plant hardened-off, container-grown, and field-potted perennials any time during the growing season. Grow coreopsis in moist, well-drained soil. Established plants of most species will tolerate dry conditions. Space plants 12 to 24 inches apart.

Growing Tips
Proper soil preparation, plant selection, and planting will help reduce future maintenance. Keep the soil around new plantings moist but not wet. Water thoroughly whenever the top 3 to 4 inches begin to dry. Some species prefer dry soil and will topple over in moist soil. Check the plant tag for watering recommendations for the plants you buy. Established

plants of many species can tolerate drought. Mulch to conserve moisture and reduce weeds. Avoid high-nitrogen fertilizer and excess fertilization that can decrease flowering and increase floppiness.

Regional Advice and Care
Some of the coreopsis species need deadheading. This encourages a second flush of flowers and reduces problems with self-seeding. One plant of mouse ear coreopsis has turned into many plants scattered throughout one of my perennial gardens. A little spring weeding and deadheading will keep this plant in check. Divide overgrown and floppy plants in the spring. The threadleaf coreopsis is not as aggressive as others and seldom needs deadheading. Dig and divide threadleaf coreopsis (*Coreopsis verticillata*), about every four years to increase vigor and eliminate the need for deadheading.

Companion Planting and Design
Use coreopsis in the perennial, wildflower, or naturalized garden. They look nice when grown with salvias, ornamental grasses, and sedums.

Try These
Threadleaf coreopsis is my first choice. This attractive plant tolerates drought and needs no staking or deadheading. 'Zagreb' is 12 to 18 inches tall with clear yellow flowers. The taller cultivar 'Moonbeam' is less hardy in heavy soils. *C. grandiflora* 'Sunfire' has yellow petals with maroon centers. Another *grandiflora*, 'Early Sunrise', is a Fleuroselect gold medal and All American Selections winner. It has bright yellow semi-double flowers.

Cranesbill Geranium

Geranium sanguineum

Botanical Pronunciation
jer-AY-nee-um san-GWIN-ee-um

Bloom Period and Seasonal Color
Late spring through summer blooms in pink, lavender, and white

Mature Height × Spread
8 to 15 inches × 24 inches

Use this long-blooming plant, also called perennial geranium, to provide several seasons of interest in your landscape. The fragrant, lobed leaves form an attractive mound. The white, pink, or lavender blooms appear in late spring through early summer. Sporadic flowers follow throughout the summer. Watch for hummingbirds and butterflies looking for a meal from this garden beauty. A close look at the seedheads will reveal the source of this plant's common name. They resemble a crane's bill. In the fall, the leaves turn red and will often persist through a mild winter. Try the cultivar 'Max Frei' for a longer season of bloom on a smaller, 8-inch plant. *Geranium* × 'Rozanne' has larger, cup-shaped, deep blue flowers that tolerate the heat and brighten the garden all summer.

When, Where, and How to Plant
Plant dormant container and bare-root geraniums in early spring as soon as the ground is workable. Plant hardened-off transplants anytime during the growing season. Grow perennial geraniums in full sun or partial shade locations with moist well-drained soils. Established plants will tolerate drought. Amend the soil prior to planting. Space plants 18 to 24 inches apart.

Growing Tips
Water the soil thoroughly whenever the top 3 to 4 inches are crumbly and moist. Mulch the soil with 1 to 2 inches of an organic material to conserve moisture and suppress weeds. Minimal fertilization is needed when the soil is properly prepared and top-dressed with compost every other year.

Regional Advice and Care
Deadheading will not increase the sporadic bloom. Trim plants back after the main flower display when the leaves are spotted, discolored, or unkempt. Use a hedge clipper to prune plants back to about 4 inches, exposing the new growth near soil surface. These new leaves will grow quickly, giving the plant a fresh new look for the remainder of the season and throughout the winter. Geraniums occasionally suffer from leaf spot and rust. As a control, clip back the plants and perform a good fall cleanup. Dig and divide geraniums when they outgrow their location. Or use a sharp spade and just remove a portion of the outside edge of the plant.

Companion Planting and Design
Geraniums make nice groundcovers, edging plants, and additions to the rock garden. Mix them with dwarf conifers or use them to hide the ugly ankles of small deciduous shrubs. Plant them with bearded iris, ornamental grasses, and other perennials.

Try These
G. pratense 'Dark Reiter' has dark purple dissected foliage and lavender flowers. Bigroot geranium (*G. macrorrhizum*) produces pink or white flowers from May through June and sporadically the rest of season atop fragrant foliage looks good all season, turning red in fall. It is more heat and drought tolerant than the cranesbill geranium. 'Variegatum' has magenta pink flowers and creamy variegated leaves. *Geranium* × *cantabrigiense* 'Biokovo' is also good for dry shade.

Daylily

Hemerocallis species and hybrids

Botanical Pronunciation
ham-er-oh-KAL-iss

Bloom Period and Seasonal Color
Summer through fall blooms in most colors

Mature Height × Spread
1 to 4 feet × 2 to 3 feet

Daylilies are versatile plants that can fit in any garden. The long, grass-like leaves are effective all season. The individual flowers last a day, but the flower display can last up to one month on an individual plant. The repeat-blooming hybrids provide a summer-long floral display. Enjoy them indoors as cut flowers. Some daylily flowers are fragrant, and they all are edible. Use them fresh, in salads, stuffed and cooked, or in soups. The orange daylily (*Hemerocallis fulva*), often called ditch lily, is seen growing wild in our drainage ditches and is considered in invasive in much of the United States. Remove these aggressive daylilies and replace them with one of the many finer cultivars that are not invading our native habitats.

When, Where, and How to Plant

Grow in full sun to partial shade. Pastel-colored daylilies tend to fade in full sun, and poor flowering and floppy growth may occur in heavy shade. Daylilies prefer moist, well-drained soil but will tolerate a wide range of conditions including heavy clay. See planting instructions in the chapter introduction. Space plants 1½ to 3 feet apart.

Growing Tips

Water thoroughly whenever the top 3 to 4 inches of soil are moist and crumbly. Mulch the soil to conserve moisture and suppress weeds. Established plants are fairly drought tolerant. Most daylily cultivars grow fast and need minimal fertilization. Excess nitrogen can cause unattractive growth and poor flowering. Repeat bloomers benefit from regular division and light fertilization in spring.

Regional Advice and Care

Gardeners who like things neat and tidy may find these a bit high maintenance. Each daylily flower lasts one day, fades, and then hangs on the stem. Daily deadheading is needed for meticulous gardeners. Once all flowers have bloomed, remove the flower stem back to the leaves. Animals also love the blossoms. Scare tactics and repellents can be used to discourage these pests. Use a repellent labeled for food crops if you plan to eat the blossoms. Pull out or clip back discolored foliage in mid- to late summer. Established daylilies form a tangle of thick fleshy roots that make digging and dividing difficult for the gardener. Divide plants every three years to make this job easier.

Companion Planting and Design

Use daylilies as groundcovers, cut flowers, edibles, or in the perennial border. They combine nicely with Russian sage, ornamental grasses, and sedum. For cutflowers, select stems with tight buds for a longer flower display or remove fresh blossoms and place them on tables around the house for an evening of enjoyment.

Try These

Earlybird Cardinal™ grows 21 inches tall and produces abundant watermelon red flowers with a chartreuse throat in mid-June. Golden Zebra® bears golden yellow flowers that sit atop unique green-and-white striped foliage 'Strawberry Candy' is a repeat bloomer with coral-pink flowers and a strawberry-red eye.

Delphinium

Delphinium elatum

Botanical Pronunciation
del-FIN-ee-um

Other Name Larkspur

Bloom Period and Seasonal Color
Early to midsummer blooms in blue, purple, white, red, pink, and yellow

Mature Height × Spread
4 to 6 feet × 2 feet

Stately spikes of blue-and-white delphinium flowers stir up visions of an English cottage garden. These visions may have enticed you, like many gardeners, to add these high-maintenance plants to your garden. Every time you see a beautiful flowering plant or a bouquet of blossoms, you are ready to try again. Join the club. Some gardeners buy flowering plants and treat them like annuals. If they return, they consider it a bonus. I know gardeners who have no problem growing these plants. One gardener even asked me for advice—her delphiniums were only 8 feet instead of their normal 12-foot height. Wear gloves when working with these plants as the leaves may irritate sensitive skin. And, don't eat; the seeds and young plants are poisonous.

When, Where, and How to Plant
Plant hardened-off perennials in spring and early summer so the delphiniums have time to establish before winter. Grow delphiniums in cool sunny location or an area with light afternoon shade in hot locations. Plant in moist, well-drained soil. Place the plants in a protected site with good air circulation. Space 24 inches apart.

Growing Tips
Summer heat and poor drainage are the stressors that weaken delphiniums, shortening their lives and making them more susceptible to their many pest problems. Start with proper soil preparation, placement in the garden, and continue toward success with watering. Water thoroughly whenever the top few inches of soil are moist and crumbly. Mulch plants with a 1- to 2-inch layer of organic material to conserve moisture, keep roots cool, and reduce weed problems. Fertilize delphiniums lightly in the spring as growth begins and again in the summer, after you clip back the faded foliage. Follow soil test recommendations or use a low-nitrogen slow-release fertilizer.

Regional Advice and Care
Deadhead flowers to encourage a second flush of blossoms. Prune back plants once all the flowers have faded to encourage new growth and blossoms. Consider skipping the fall bloom the first year to increase the chance of winter survival. Stake tall cultivars to prevent flopping and wind damage. Regular division improves plant vigor and hardiness. Divide in early spring as growth begins. Check plants frequently for insects and disease problems. They are susceptible to powdery mildew, blight, leaf spot, crown rot, canker, aphids, mites, borers, and leafminers. Buy healthy transplants and grow them in the right conditions to minimize pest problems.

Companion Planting and Design
These plants make a great backdrop for other perennials, or as a vertical accent or specimen plant. Mix them with threadleaf coreopsis, beebalm, and most perennials.

Try These
The New Millenium hybrids are bred for strong stems and greater survival in our less-than-ideal growing conditions. Or try our native prairie and woodland one, *Delphinium carolinianum*. It may not be as showy, but it is more at home in our environment.

Ferns

Athyrium, Matteuccia, Osmunda et al

Botanical Pronunciation
ah-THEER-ee-um, mah-TOO-kee-ah,
oz-MUN-dah

Bloom Period and Seasonal Color
Season-long foliage in shades of green

Mature Height × Spread
1 to 5 feet × 1 to 3 feet

Ferns' wonderful texture, shades of green, and interesting forms can add interest to shady gardens. You may be familiar with our native ostrich fern, *Matteuccia struthiopteris*. It has been used next to homes as a foundation planting for decades. Its long lacy upright fronds reach heights of 5 feet. These fast growers quickly fill the space provided. You may also know that ostrich ferns will brown out in the heat and drought of midsummer. Minimize scorch by planting them in a north or east location, mulching, and keeping the soil moist. But this is not the only choice. Ferns come in a variety of sizes, leaf shapes, and textures. Some are even suited for the sun, making them a plant for any garden.

When, Where, and How to Plant
Plant dormant container and bare-root ferns in spring after the danger of severe weather has passed. Hardened-off, container-grown, and field potted plants can be planted anytime during the season. Plant tender ferns early in the season to give them time to get established before winter. Most ferns prefer shady locations with moist soil. Prepare the soil prior to planting. Add several inches of organic matter into the top 8 to 12 inches of soil. Spacing depends on the species grown and varies from 12 to 36 inches.

Growing Tips
Water ferns thoroughly whenever the top few inches of soil are crumbly and moist. Mulch ferns with an organic material to conserve moisture, improve the soil, and reduce weed problems. Proper soil preparation and topdressing with compost every other year are usually all you need to keep ferns healthy and attractive.

Regional Advice and Care
Fast growing ferns benefit from division while slow growing ones seldom need attention. Divide overgrown ferns in spring as growth begins. Let fronds stand for winter. This adds beauty to the winter garden and increases winter hardiness. Prune out old fronds in late winter or allow the new growth to mask the old leaves.

Companion Planting and Design
Use taller ferns as background plants in the shade garden. Lower-growing ferns can be used as groundcovers and edging plants. Ferns combine well with hosta, astilbe, ginger, daylilies, and other shade lovers.

Try These
Japanese painted fern, *Athyrium niponicum* 'Pictum', was a Perennial Plant of the Year and is hardy to Zone 4. The fronds are gray-green with a maroon stalk and a silver flush to the leaves. Autumn fern, *Dryopteris erythrosora*, has beautiful emerging copper fronds. The hayscented fern, *Dennstaedtia punctilobula*; interrupted fern, *Osmunda claytoniana*; and lady fern, *Athyrium filix-femina*, all tolerate the sun, but provide shade from afternoon sun and keep soil moist for best results. A cultivar of our native lady fern, 'Lady in Red' has red stems and lacy fronds.

Gayfeather

Liatris spicata

Botanical Pronunciation
lee-AY-tris spih-KAY-tah

Other Name Blazing star

Bloom Period and Seasonal Color
Midsummer to fall blooms in lavender, rose, and white

Mature Height × Spread
12 to 36 inches × 18 inches

The North American native gayfeather is equally at home in our perennial gardens. Whorls of dark green leaves are topped with spikes of purple, rose, or white flowers. These attract wildlife to the garden and make long-lasting cut flowers. In winter, birds will stop by to feed on the seeds hidden in the fluffy seedheads. This native has also been an important crop in the floral industry. It is grown here and around the world for use as a cut flower. Don't confuse this with the invasive loosestrife. A closer look will help you tell the two apart. Gayfeather flowers open from the top down. Purple loosestrife, with its shorter and broader leaves, has purple flowers that open from the bottom up.

When, Where, and How to Plant
Plant gayfeather rhizomes in spring or fall. Place the woody corm or rhizome 1 to 2 inches below the soil surface. Plant hardened-off, potted, and container-grown perennials anytime during the growing season. Grow gayfeather in full sun and well-drained soil. These plants will tolerate some light shade but not wet feet. Space plants 15 to 20 inches apart.

Growing Tips
Gayfeathers are low-maintenance plants. Water thoroughly whenever the top few inches of soil start to dry. Once established, these plants are very drought tolerant. Mulch new plantings to conserve moisture and reduce weed problems. Avoid high-nitrogen fertilizer and excess fertilization, which can lead to floppy growth and poor flowering.

Regional Advice and Care
Deadhead plants when most of the flower spike has bloomed. Cut the flower stem back to the first whorl of leaves; this will encourage a second flush of flowers. Let flowers dry and form their fluffy seedheads. The plants will self-seed if the seedheads are left on the plant. I have supplied gayfeathers to several friends, a park, and all my gardens from *one* plant. Gayfeather plants seldom need staking, but those grown in rich, moist soil or shade are more likely to topple. Use commercially available grow-through stakes or surrounding plants to provide support. Divide overgrown gayfeathers and give away extras in spring as growth begins.

Companion Planting and Design
Mix gayfeather with other sun-loving perennials. Its upright growth habit makes it a good vertical accent and background plant for the perennial garden. Or combine it with grasses and other native plants to create a naturalized garden.

Try These
'Alba' produces white flowers and 'Kobold' is a compact cultivar. Its smaller size, 18 to 30 inches tall, makes 'Kobold' easier to blend into most home gardens. The profusion of dark purple flowers will provide enjoyment in the garden and flower vase. Several species are native to our area, easy to grow, and commercially available. The most common include the tall blazing star, *Liatris pycnostachya*, and rough blazing star, *Liatris aspera*.

Goldenrod

Solidago species

Botanical Pronunciation
Sol-ih-DAY-go

Bloom Period and Seasonal Color
Yellow blooms midsummer to fall

Mature Height × Spread
2 to 6 feet × 1 to 3 feet

They're at it again. Those pesky taxonomists taking a closer look at our plants and changing the names. In the long run it will help us have a better understanding of the plants. But as gardeners and even horticulturists it can be frustrating keeping up with the nuances of the name changes. My apologies to taxonomists if I slip into old habits. Goldenrod not only varies in name (some now go by *Oligonevron*) but also preferred growing conditions. Most prefer full sun and well-drained soils, though others like moister soils. All make great cut flowers, and none of them are the cause of hay fever. It is the less noticeable green flowered ragweed that often grows next to this showy plant that is the real culprit.

When, Where, and How to Plant
Start seed indoors in warm, 70-degree-Fahrenheit soil. Do not cover seeds as they need light to germinate. Keep the sterile seed starting mix moist and watch for seeds to sprout in 2 to 3 weeks. Move hardened-off transplants outdoors after the danger of frost. See the chapter introduction for bare-root and container planting instructions. Grow goldenrod in full sun and well-drained soils unless otherwise directed on the tag or cultivars listed here. Space plants 1 to 2 feet apart depending on species and cultivar.

Growing Tips
Water established plants thoroughly whenever the top few inches of soil are crumbly and slightly moist. Drought tolerant goldenrods will only need supplemental watering during extended drought. Mulch the soil with shredded leaves, evergreen needles, or other organic mulch to conserve moisture, suppress weeds, and improve the soil as they decompose. Avoid excess fertilization and high-nitrogen fertilizers that can promote rampant growth. Instead, spread a 1-inch layer of compost over the soil surface (topdress) every other year. Divide overgrown plants in spring for best results and minimal impact on flowering.

Regional Advice and Care
Deadhead plants for increased bloom and to reduce reseeding. Save a few mature blooms to use in cut and dried flower arrangements. Mildew, rust, and leaf spot are usually only a problem when goldenrod is improperly sited, overplanted, or during cool wet weather. Remove diseased plants in fall. Otherwise leave the plants stand for winter.

Companion Planting and Design
A hillside filled with New England aster and goldenrod mimcs a Monet painting. Or combine baptisia, fireworks goldenrod, tiger eye sumac, and prairie dropseed for a naturalized planting. Give self-seeding varieties plenty of room to naturalize with other equally assertive plants.

Try These
Solidago rugosa 'Fireworks' grows 3 to 4 feet tall with arching flower panicles that resemble fireworks. 'Golden Baby' grows 1½ to 2 feet tall with dense horizontal blooms and tolerates poor dry soils. *Solidago cutleri* 'Gold Rush' has dense panicles of yellow flowers on 12-inch plants.

Hellebore

Helleborus orientalis

Botanical Pronunciation
hel-LEB-or-us or-ee-en-TALL-iss

Other Name Lenten rose

Bloom Period and Seasonal Color
Purple, pink, white, black, red, yellow, and green flowers in early spring

Mature Height × Spread
15 to 18 inches × 15 inches

Include a few hellebores in the shady corners of your landscape. Their evergreen foliage, long bloom, and low maintenance make this a good choice for most gardeners. And the deer usually leave it be. If you have planted hellebores in the past and failed, don't worry. It took me a couple tries to find the right spot in my garden. But once I did, the established plants provided color all season with minimal care. They've even survived severe heat and drought. The colorful parts of the flower are actually sepals, mostly downward facing. New hybrids and cultivars are being introduced with upward and outward-facing "flowers" in a variety of colors. **Note:** Look, but don't eat, these poisonous plants.

When, Where, and How to Plant
You can start plants from seed though you will have better results transplanting the seedlings your plants produce. Plant dormant container and bare-root plants after severe weather has passed and the soil is workable. Plant hardened-off transplants anytime during the growing season. Grow hellebores in full to partial shade in moist, organic soils. Water new plantings thoroughly and often enough to keep the roots moist. Space plant 12 to 15 inches apart.

Growing Tips
Plants may not bloom the first year after planting. Established plants are drought tolerant but prefer moist well-drained soils. Water these during extended dry periods or whenever the top few inches of soil are crumbly and moist. Topdress soil with an inch of compost every other year. Follow soil test recommendations or use a low-nitrogen slow-release fertilizer if a nutrient boost is needed. Divide plants as needed or to propagate new plants in spring. Make sure each division has several leaf buds and roots. Dig overcrowded seedlings and share or move to new location.

Regional Advice and Care
Hellebores' evergreen foliage may be tattered or scorched after an extremely harsh or open winter. Avoid the problem by growing plants in a protected spot or apply a winter mulch after the ground freezes. Blackspot and crown rot are usually only a problem in wet weather and poorly drained soils.

Companion Planting and Design
Use in containers or mixed with other shade tolerant perennials. Or plant en masse at the base of shade tolerant shrubs. Combine with peonies for extended bloom and year round beauty.

Try These
Christmas rose (*Helleborus niger*), white with pink tinged flowers, appears earlier than the Lenten rose. Grow in a protected spot where you can enjoy the early blooms. 'Winter Jewels'™ series are vigorous plants with various flower colors. 'Onyx Odyssey' is purple-black double flowering in this series. *Helleborus* × *ballardiae* 'Pink Frost' (Zone 5) has upward facing flowers in shades of pink, white, and rose. 'Ivory Prince' (Zone 5) is very early with blue-green foliage ivory flowers with pink-chartreuse blush.

Hosta

Hosta species and cultivars

Botanical Pronunciation
HOSS-tah

Other Name Funkia

Bloom Period and Seasonal Color
Summer and fall blooms in white and lavender, yellow fall color

Mature Height × Spread
2 to 36 inches × 36 inches

Hostas are low-maintenance, quick-growing, shade-tolerant perennials. These features have helped make hosta one of the most popular perennials in the landscape. The variety of leaf sizes, shapes, colors, and textures and yellow fall color adds to its landscape value. Plants are topped with white or lavender, sometimes fragrant, flowers. Plant hosta where you can enjoy hummingbirds nectaring on the flowers in summer, juncos feeding on the seeds in winter, or the fragrance. Gather design ideas with a visit to Hidden Lake Gardens in Tipton, Michigan. Their hosta hillside features more than 800 varieties of hosta. Hosta enthusiasts may want to join the American Hosta Society, www.americanhostasociety.org.

When, Where, and How to Plant
Plant dormant container and bare-root hostas in spring after the danger of severe weather has passed. Plant hardened-off transplants anytime during the growing season. Grow hosta in shady locations with moist, organic soil. Your plants will have the best leaf color in partial shade. Avoid afternoon sun that can cause leaf edges to brown or scorch. Hosta prefer rich organic soil. Spacing depends on size of the variety grown.

Growing Tips
Hosta are low-maintenance plants. Water established plants thoroughly whenever the top few inches of soil are crumbly and moist and mulch. Hosta will scorch in dry soil.

Regional Advice and Care
Early-sprouting hosta may suffer frost damage. New growth will help mask some of the browned leaves. Many gardeners remove the flowers as they sprout or as the flowers fade to improve their appearance. I like to leave the seedheads for winter interest and to attract birds. You can divide hostas almost anytime during the growing season. Winter-mulch fall-divided plants for added winter protection. Slugs and earwigs are the major pests. Beer-baited traps tucked under the hosta leaves will help capture the slugs. The newer iron phosphate–based baits are eco-friendly and provide good slug control. Hosta with thicker and heavier leaves, such as 'Inniswood', tend to resist slug damage. Crumpled paper or tubes can be used to trap earwigs. Deer and rabbits love hosta. Repellents, scare tactics, and fences around small perennial plantings may help, or you can replace hosta with the more deer-resistant *Pulmonaria*.

Companion Planting and Design
Use hosta alone or in groupings in shade gardens. Combine hosta with ferns and astilbes for an interesting shade garden. Or use them *en masse* as a groundcover or edging plant.

Try These
There are too many hostas for me to narrow the list. The American Hosta Growers Association Hosta of the Year selections are a good place to start. *H. clausa* has "closed" purple flowers in late summer. 'Cherry Berry' is compact with green-and-white variegated leaves with cherry red flower stems and seedpods.

Joe-Pye Weed

Eupatorium fistulosum

Botanical Pronunciation
yew-pah-TOR-ee-um fist-u-LO-sum

Bloom Period and Seasonal Color
Mid- to late summer through fall, purple flowers

Mature Height × Spread
Up to 8 feet × 3 feet

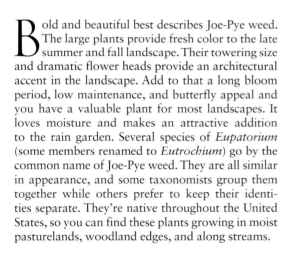

Bold and beautiful best describes Joe-Pye weed. The large plants provide fresh color to the late summer and fall landscape. Their towering size and dramatic flower heads provide an architectural accent in the landscape. Add to that a long bloom period, low maintenance, and butterfly appeal and you have a valuable plant for most landscapes. It loves moisture and makes an attractive addition to the rain garden. Several species of *Eupatorium* (some members renamed to *Eutrochium*) go by the common name of Joe-Pye weed. They are all similar in appearance, and some taxonomists group them together while others prefer to keep their identities separate. They're native throughout the United States, so you can find these plants growing in moist pasturelands, woodland edges, and along streams.

When, Where, and How to Plant
Plant dormant container and bare-root perennials in spring as soon as severe weather has passed. Container-grown plants can be added to the garden anytime during the growing season. Plants can be grown from seed. Start seeds indoors in a moist starter mix at 55 to 60 degrees Fahrenheit. Hardened-off transplants can be moved outdoors after the danger of frost. Grow Joe-Pye weed in full sun with moist soil. Plants growing in shade tend to grow tall and leggy, and those growing in droughty soils are not as robust and attractive. Space plants 3 feet apart.

Growing Tips
Keep soil moist for best results. Water thoroughly whenever the top few inches are moist and crumbly. Mulch to conserve moisture and suppress weeds. Minimal fertilizer is needed for this robust plant.

Regional Advice and Care
Cut plants back to 6 inches in early June to reduce the height by several feet. 'Gateway' is free flowering and requires little or no deadheading. Dig and divide overgrown plants in early spring. Regular division keeps plants vigorous and needing less deadheading. Leave the seedheads on and plants standing for winter interest. You may occasionally see leaf spot disease or powdery mildew. Good cleanup is usually sufficient to control these diseases.

Companion Planting and Design
This is a beautiful background plant or focal point. It is equally at home in the formal garden or the rain garden. Try growing it near a water feature and combine with heliopsis, swamp sunflower, and miscanthus grass. Or anchor it to the garden with smaller ornamental grasses and daylilies.

Try These
'Gateway' is 5 to 6 feet tall and provides a long period of bloom with no deadheading needed. The smaller scale and low maintenance make it a great landscape plant. Pinch these plants back in early June for fuller growth. *Eutrochium dubium* 'Baby Joe' grows 2 to 3 feet tall with mauve flowers atop red stems; 'Phantom' is a bit taller at 2 to 4 feet; *E. rugosum* 'Chocolate' grows 3 to 5 feet tall with white flowers and purple-chocolate leaves.

Lavender

Lavandula angustifolia

Botanical Pronunciation
lah-VAN-dew-la an-gus-tih-FOE-lee-ah

Other Name English lavender

Bloom Period and Seasonal Color
Lavender and purple blooms in summer

Mature Height × Spread
12 to 24 inches × 12 to 24 inches

The wonderful fragrance, silvery gray foliage, and beautiful purple summer blooms makes lavender worth the risk and effort of growing it in a northern garden. Grow this popular herb in full sun and well-drained soils for the best chance of success. Lavender has long been used in potpourris and sachets. You may want to do the same. Oil of lavender is used in perfumes and bath oils. The flowers are great fresh and maintain their fragrance and color when dried. Tuck a few sprigs of this calming herb under your pillow to help reduce stress so you can relax at night. And look for some tasty recipes like lavender lemonade and scones to get the full benefit from your gardening efforts.

When, Where, and How to Plant

Start seeds indoors six to eight weeks prior to last spring frost. Some gardeners have found five weeks of cold treatment (stratification) increases germination success. To stratify: place seeds in a baggie filled with moistened seed starter mix and refrigerate. Remove from storage, sprinkle seeds on soil surface and lightly tamp. Do not cover as these seeds need light to germinate. Keep the planting mix warm and moist. Seeds should sprout in two to three weeks. Harden off transplants before moving them outdoors. Or purchase transplants from garden catalogues or garden centers. They may be in the perennials or herb section. See the chapter introduction for planting instructions. Plant lavender in spring to provide plants sufficient time to establish roots before winter. Grow plants in full sun with good drainage. Water new plantings often

enough to keep the roots moist but not wet. Space plants 12 inches apart.

Growing Tips

Once established lavender is drought tolerant and should only be watered when the top few inches of soil are dry. Overwatering and poor drainage, especially in winter, can kill lavender. Skip the mulch if your soils tend to be damp or wet. Avoid high-nitrogen fertilizers and excess fertilization. Instead topdress the soil with an inch of compost every other year. Remove faded flowers to prolong bloom. Harvest mature blooms to use in crafts and bouquets.

Regional Advice and Care

Root rot and wet soils in winter are the biggest killers of lavender in our area. Grow lavender in full sun and well-drained soils for overwintering success. Wait for new growth to begin before pruning. Start by pruning out dead stems, then shape the remaining plant.

Companion Planting and Design

Grow lavender with roses, a traditional combination that still works. Or use in containers to improve drainage and longevity.

Try These

'Hidcote' and 'Munstead' grow 12 to 18 inches tall and are the hardiest cultivars. Grow French or Spanish lavender (*Lavandula stoechas*) with the unique thicker flower spike with tuft of petals on top as an annual since it is not hardy here.

Mum

Chrysanthemum × *morifolium*

Botanical Pronunciation
kris-AN-theh-mum ex mor-ih-FOE-lee-um

Bloom Period and Seasonal Color
Late summer through frost blooms in yellow, orange, rust, red, bronze, white, and lavender

Mature Height × Spread
1 to 2 feet × 1 to 2 feet

Mums are often called "the last smile of the departing year." It's a good description of their frost-tolerant fall flower display. One plant can provide over a hundred blossoms for cutting and garden use. Consider adding a few mums to your perennial gardens, annual flower display, or fall container gardens. A single fall flower show will convince you they are well worth the price. They can be single or semi-double like the daisy, anemone, brush, or spoon types. The double-flowering pompons, quill, spider, or buttons tend to be more rounded with many more petals. Many gardeners have given up growing mums as perennials but thanks to the University of Minnesota's breeding programs, there are new hardy mums being introduced into the market.

When, Where, and How to Plant
Plant dormant container and bare-root mums in spring after the danger of severe weather has passed. Plant hardened-off transplants in spring or late summer. Spring planting increases plant hardiness and overwintering success. Grow mums in full sun with moist, well-drained soil. Increase winter hardiness by growing them in protected sites with good drainage. Space plants 2 to 3 feet apart.

Growing Tips
Further increase success by selecting hardy cultivars and providing proper care. Water established plants thoroughly whenever the top few inches of soil start to dry. Fertilize mums early in the growing season according to soil test recommendations or with a low-nitrogen slow-release fertilizer.

Regional Advice and Care
Pinch back taller cultivars for compact growth and increased flower production. Start pinching mums in late May or early June. Cut plants back just above a set of leaves to a height of 6 inches. Stop pinching by late June so blooming will occur prior to snowfall. Leave the plants intact for the winter for increased hardiness. The stems help capture snow and insulate the plants. For added protection, cover plants with a few evergreen branches after the ground freezes.

Companion Planting and Design
Many botanical gardens, estates, and home gardeners treat mums as annuals. Use them alone for a splash of fall color or *en masse* for a more formal, breathtaking display. I like to use mums in containers. A few plants go a long way in brightening up the landscape.

Try These
'My Favorite Mum'™ really *is* my favorite mum. Bred at the University of Minnesota, it is now sold as Mammoth™ Mum and is hardy to Zone 3. These 3-foot-tall plants come in colors of white, bronze, coral, dark pink, red, and lavender. A garden mum relative *Chrysanthemum* × *rubellum* is hardier. 'Clara Curtis' has rosy pink flowers and grows 2 to 3 feet tall. 'Duchess of Edinburgh' has dull red flowers. 'Matchsticks' spoon-shaped petals of golden yellow and red grow 18 inches tall; it is hardy only to Zone 5.

Oriental Poppy

Papaver orientale

Botanical Pronunciation
pa-PAH-ver or-ee-en-TALL-ee

Bloom Period and Seasonal Color
Late spring to early summer blooms in orange-red, red, pink, and white

Mature Height × Spread
1 to 4 feet × 2 feet

I think I fell in love with poppies when I saw Georgia O'Keefe's painting of the red and orange flowers. The flowers are just as beautiful in the garden as they are in her art. They can be a bit difficult to get started, but your efforts will be rewarded with years of enjoyment. Poppies make great cut flowers. Cut the flowers when the bud is in an upright position. Some floral designers singe the end of the stem, while others feel it is unnecessary and possibly detrimental. See what works best for you. Don't forget to pick the dried seedpods to use in wreaths and dried arrangements. Select cultivars propagated from root cuttings, not seed, to maintain the true characteristics of the plant.

When, Where, and How to Plant
Plant hardened-off transplants in spring. Divide poppies, only if needed, in August and September. Grow in a sunny location with good drainage. Poppies do not respond well to transplanting, making them difficult to establish. However, once established, they are very long-lived. Good soil drainage is critical for growing success. Minimize transplanting stress by carefully handling the plants. Plant poppies at the same depth they were growing in the containers and 2 feet apart.

Growing Tips
Established poppies are low-maintenance plants. Winter-mulch new late-season plantings with evergreen branches after the ground freezes. This will help them through their first winter and increase establishment success. Many gardeners, including me, are not successful on their first attempt at planting poppies. It has taken me several tries to find the best spot to successfully grow poppies.

Regional Advice and Care
Deadheading is not necessary and will not encourage a second flush of flowers. You can leave the large, attractive seedheads for added interest. Remove the faded leaves in midsummer. A small rosette of leaves may develop in the fall. Leave these in place over the winter. New growth in spring will cover any of the leaves damaged during cold weather. Pull, don't dig, weeds as soon as they appear. Cultivation can damage the poppy's roots.

Companion Planting and Design
Used *en masse*, these large flowered plants will steal the show. I have seen them used effectively in naturalized settings and formal gardens. Plan for the void left by these earlier bloomers. By midsummer, the plants dry up and die back to ground level. Plant late-blooming perennials nearby to fill the void left by the poppy.

Try These
'Watermelon' has watermelon pink flowers, 'Allegro' has bold orange-red flowers and dark markings at the base, and 'Prince of Orange' has more orange than red flowers. 'Beauty of Livermore' produces 4- to 6-inch scarlet red flowers while 'Pink Ruffles' has pink fringed petals. Include 'Louvre' for its wavy white petals that are blushed pink at the base.

Peony

Paeonia hybrids

Botanical Pronunciation
pay-OH-nee-ah

Bloom Period and Seasonal Color
Late spring to early summer blooms in white, pink, red, and salmon

Mature Height × Spread
3 feet × 3 feet

Peonies provide a long season of interest in the landscape. The new growth comes up red and soon turns green as the leaves enlarge. The large flowers can be single, semi-double, or double. Many are fragrant, and all of them work well as cut flowers. Once the flowers fade, the leaves remain green and attractive throughout the season. In the fall, the leaves turn a nice purple before dying back to the ground. Select the peony cultivar with the color and flower type that is best suited to your landscape. Choose a cultivar with fragrance if this is a desired feature. Some retailers sell unnamed peonies that may not have the attributes you want. Check with quality garden centers, nurseries, and catalogs for named cultivars.

When, Where, and How to Plant

Plant rhizomes in fall before the ground freezes or in spring after the danger of severe weather has passed. Plant hardened-off transplants anytime during the growing season. They will tolerate light shade but will fail to bloom in excess shade. Peonies will survive in heavy clay soil but need good drainage. Plant the rhizomes with the buds (eyes) 2 inches below the soil surface. Space peonies 3 feet apart.

Growing Tips

Water established peonies whenever the top few inches of soil are crumbly and moist. Mulching not only helps conserve moisture and reduce weeds, it can also help reduce some soilborne diseases. Properly prepare the soil, add mulch, and topdress with compost every other year for healthy and attractive plants.

Regional Advice and Care

Once established, peonies can remain in place for many years. Removing the large terminal bud results in many smaller flowers on each stem. These are less subject to flopping. Removing the side buds and leaving just the terminal bud results in fewer, but larger, blossoms. Using a peony cage provides support to peonies in full bloom. Plants can fail to bloom the spring after transplanting and when grown in too much shade, planted too deep, or overfertilized. Peonies are subject to several fungal diseases. Remove faded flowers and infected parts as soon as they appear. This combined with fall cleanup will usually control problems.

Companion Planting and Design

Use them as specimen plants, mixed with shrubs in foundation plantings, or as a background plant for other flowers. Mix with dwarf conifers, low growing ornamental grasses, and other perennials.

Try These

There are lots of beautiful cultivars available. I like the American Peony Society's gold medal 'Sea Shell Pink'. It has fragrant single flowers and doesn't need staking. Fern leaf peony, *Paeonia tenuifolia*, has cutleaf foliage and impressive red flowers. 'Bartzella' is a cross between the tree and herbaceous peony. The large yellow flowers are incredible. 'Abalone Pearl' has slightly fragrant coral-pink flowers on sturdy stems. 'Buckeye Belle' has semi-double velvet red blooms on sturdy stems.

Phlox

Phlox species

Botanical Pronunciation
FLOX

Bloom Period and Seasonal Color
Spring or summer to fall blooms in blue, purple, pink, rose, red, and white

Mature Height × Spread
3 to 48 inches × 24 inches

Use a few creeping phlox plants to give your spring landscape a little pizzazz. But don't go overboard; it will just be green the remainder of the season. Creeping or moss phlox, *Phlox subulata*, grows 3 to 6 inches tall and creeps along the ground. One plant can quickly cover a 2-foot-square area. Its evergreen foliage and early spring bloom make it a popular perennial. Garden phlox, *Phlox paniculata*, is another popular phlox with gardeners as well as the butterflies and hummingbirds. This phlox grows 3 to 4 feet tall, making it a nice background, cut flower, or specimen plant in the perennial border. Select mildew-resistant cultivars or the similar, more mildew-resistant, wild sweet William (*Phlox maculata*) for garden phlox.

When, Where, and How to Plant
Plant potted and container-grown phlox anytime during the growing season. See chapter introductions for planting directions. Creeping phlox is often sold as half flats rooted in sand. These can be planted as is or divided into smaller sections. Grow phlox in full sun with moist, well-drained soil. Creeping phlox prefer well-drained soils and are drought tolerant. Space creeping phlox 12 inches apart and garden phlox 18 to 24 inches apart.

Growing Tips
Water new plants often enough to keep the roots moist but not wet. Established plants will need less frequent watering. Water them thoroughly whenever the top few inches of soil are moist and crumbly. Mulch the soil to conserve moisture and to suppress weeds. Established creeping phlox can tolerate drier soils. Minimal fertilization is needed.

Regional Advice and Care
Cut back creeping phlox halfway after flowering. This keeps the plants full and attractive and often encourages additional flowers later in the season. Deadhead garden phlox to extend the bloom time. Powdery mildew is the biggest problem of garden phlox. Select mildew-resistant cultivars such as 'David', 'Kathryn', 'Sherbert Cocktail', and 'Candy Floss' whenever possible. Remove one-third of the stems in spring to improve air circulation and reduce mildew problems. Remove and discard all infected leaves throughout the season. Fall cleanup will also help reduce mildew problems. Deer love phlox. Repellents, netting, and fencing can help reduce the damage. Vary controls and be persistent.

Companion Planting and Design
Use tall garden phlox for added color in the back of the perennial garden. Use creeping phlox as an edging plant, in rock gardens, or trailing over a wall. Both combine nicely with other perennials such as coreopsis, salvia, Russian sage, and ornamental grasses.

Try These
'Forever Pink' is hardy to Zone 4 and blooms between creeping and garden phlox. The pinkish purple flowers cover the plants for three weeks and repeat bloom into fall. Our native wild blue phlox, *Phlox divaricata*, creeps on the ground. It is 8 to 10 inches tall with blue flowers in spring.

Purple Coneflower

Echinacea purpurea

Botanical Pronunciation
eh-kih-NAY-shah per-per-EE-ah

Other Name Hedge coneflower

Bloom Period and Seasonal Color
Summer through fall blooms in purple and white

Mature Height × Spread
2 to 4 feet × 2 feet

Purple coneflower is as at home in its native environment as it is in the home landscape. A few coneflowers can create a mass of color in the fall garden or cutflower arrangements. Their large, daisy-like flowers will help attract butterflies, and the seedheads will attract birds to the landscape. Start small since one plant goes a long way. I learned this the hard way when my small city lot was soon overrun with the offspring of one purple coneflower. I still have purple coneflower in my yard; I just share or compost the offspring. You may recognize the name from the drugstore shelves. This plant has long been used to cure colds, scurvy, and snakebites. It is still used today to treat colds.

When, Where, and How to Plant

Sow seeds outdoors in fall or early spring. Spread seeds on prepared soils, rake to cover seeds, gently tamp, and water. These plants will bloom in several years. Plant container-grown purple coneflowers anytime during the growing season. See the chapter introduction for planting details. Grow purple coneflowers in full sun with well-drained soil. They will tolerate light shade, but excess shade will cause poor growth and flowering. Avoid rich soil and excess fertilizer that can cause the plants to topple and flower poorly. Space plants 24 inches apart.

Growing Tips

Established coneflowers are heat and drought tolerant. Water new plantings often enough to keep the soil slightly moist. Water established plants thoroughly during extended dry periods.

Regional Advice and Care

Purple coneflowers will grow and prosper with very little care. Encourage more compact growth by cutting the plants back halfway in mid-June. Pruning will reduce the plant size but also delay flowering. Try pruning just half of your plants to extend the bloom time with pruned and unpruned plants. Deadheading is not necessary but will give the plants and garden a neater appearance. Stop deadheading by early September to allow seedheads to form. Coneflowers suffer from leaf spot diseases, stem wilt, and aster yellows. Remove spotted leaves, prune out wilted stems, and remove aster yellow (green and distorted flowers) infested plants. Surrounding plants will quickly fill in the vacant area. Sanitation and proper care will keep most of these problems under control.

Companion Planting and Design

Combine coneflower with Russian sage, garden phlox, and ornamental or native grasses. The finer-textured plants help the coneflowers blend into the perennial or naturalized garden.

Try These

'PowWow Wildberry' is an All American Selections Winner with deep rose-purple blooms, on sturdy 1- to 3-foot stems. 'Burgundy Fireworks' is 18 inches tall with burgundy red stems and beet red quill-shaped ray flowers (petals). 'Hot Papaya' has striking orange-red double flowers. The 1998 Perennial Plant of the Year was 'Magnus' with large flowers and flat, dark purple petals.

Russian Sage

Perovskia atriplicifolia

Botanical Pronunciation
per-OV-skee-ah at-trih-pliss-ih-FOE-lee-ah

Other Name Azure sage

Bloom Period and Seasonal Color
Midsummer through fall blooms in blue

Mature Height × Spread
3 to 5 feet × 3 to 4 feet

Russian sage was a Perennial Plant of the Year. Its silvery stems and foliage make a nice backdrop or filler in the perennial garden. The foliage has a nice sage-like fragrance when crushed. The airy blue flowers appear in midsummer and last all season long with no deadheading needed. This drought-tolerant plant tolerates alkaline soil and appears to be deer resistant. Try using young plants and small cultivars as a vertical accent in container plantings. Bury the weatherproof container or move it into an unheated garage for winter. Or transplant the Russian sage into the garden to enjoy for seasons to come. Plus I bet you'll have a good excuse to go plant shopping for its replacement the following spring.

When, Where, and How to Plant
Plant dormant container and bare-root Russian sage in spring after the danger of severe weather has passed. Plant hardened-off container-grown and potted plants anytime during the growing season. Grow Russian sage in full sun and well-drained soil. Good drainage is essential for vigorous growth and winter survival. Plants will flop in wet soil and shade. Space plants 30 to 36 inches apart.

Growing Tips
Russian sage is a low-maintenance plant with no real problems. Once established, it is very drought tolerant. Water established plants thoroughly during extended droughts. Avoid high-nitrogen fertilizer and excess fertilization that can lead to floppy growth and poor flowering.

Regional Advice and Care
Leave the Russian sage plants standing for winter interest and increased hardiness. The silvery stems and some of the foliage will last throughout the winter. Prune in spring to remove the dead stems and encourage sturdy new growth. Cut the stems back to just above a healthy bud 4 to 6 inches above ground level. You'll enjoy the plant's fragrance as you do your spring pruning. Mature plants, even when pruned in spring, may topple. Surround these with other plants to provide some needed support. Pruning the plants early in the season will encourage more compact growth. Cut the plants back halfway when they are 12 inches tall. Or try one of the more compact cultivars that are less likely to flop.

Companion Planting and Design
Russian sage provides year-round interest in the landscape. Its fine leaves and flowers give it an airy texture, making it a good filler plant. Mix Russian sage with coarser-textured plants, such as purple coneflower and black-eyed Susan.

Try These
Peek-a-Blue® has all the same attributes as the species on 2 feet tall plants. 'Little Spire' is a bit larger at 30 to 36 inches. 'Longin' is narrower and more upright than the species. The leaves are silver but not as finely divided. Try growing 'Filigran' for a more compact, 30-inch-tall and finer-textured plant. 'Blue Spire' produces a profusion of violet-blue flowers on 4-foot plants.

Salvia

Salvia species

Botanical Pronunciation
SAL-vee-ah

Other Name Perennial sage

Bloom Period and Seasonal Color
Summer blooms in blue, violet, and rose-pink

Mature Height × Spread
2 to 3 feet × 3 to 4 feet

Salvia has been a standard plant in perennial gardens for years. The spikes of blue and pink flowers add charm to the garden and color to flower arrangements. Plant a few of these long-blooming perennials near the window or patio so you can enjoy the butterflies and hummingbirds that come to visit. This plant also has an interesting history outside the garden. People have used this for healing problems with the liver, stomach, and heart as well as controlling fever and plague. Its perennial cousin *Salvia officinalis* is the sage usually grown in the herb garden and used for cooking. I often use it in perennial gardens. The colorful leaves and interesting texture make it a nice edging or specimen plant.

When, Where, and How to Plant
Plant dormant container and bare-root salvias in spring after the danger of severe weather has passed. Plant hardened-off transplants anytime during the growing season. Grow salvia in full sun and moist soil with good drainage. Plants tend to flop in excess shade and rich soils. Space plants 18 inches apart.

Growing Tips
Perennial salvia performs best in moist, well-drained soil. Once established, the plants will tolerate dry conditions. They grow better and flower longer in cool temperatures and moist soil. Mulch the soil with a 1- to 2-inch layer of organic material such as twice-shredded bark, shredded leaves, or evergreen needles. Mulch helps to conserve moisture, keep soil cool, and reduce weed problems. Avoid excess fertilizer that can lead to floppy growth and poor flowering.

Regional Advice and Care
Deadhead salvia to extend the bloom time. Remove the faded flower stems back to the side buds and stems. Prune salvia back halfway after flowering. Some salvia become floppy and open in the center during flowering. In that case, skip the deadheading and prune plants back after the first flush of flowers. Keep the soil moist after pruning. Leave plants standing for winter to increase hardiness. The overwintering stems capture snow for mulch and are less likely than cut stems to collect water and freeze. Divide overgrown salvia in spring.

Companion Planting and Design
Use the taller species as background plants. Salvias are nice, long-blooming plants for the perennial garden. Combine them with threadleaf coreopsis, *Rudbeckia*, daylilies, and lamb's ears.

Try These
There are several species and hybrids called perennial sage. Select a cultivar that holds it shape and is best suited for your landscape. *Salvia nemorosa* 'Caradonna' has violet-blue flower spikes along dark purple on to two feet upright stems. 'Eveline' grows two feet tall with two-toned pink and purple flowers; it may re-bloom when cut back. 'May Night' ('Mainacht') is a long bloomer that stays nice and compact. It produces indigo-blue flowers on 18-inch-tall plants. 'East Friesland' is another compact form that grows 18 inches tall with dark violet flowers.

Sedum

Sedum species

Botanical Pronunciation
SEE-dum

Other Name Stonecrop

Bloom Period and Seasonal Color
Summer and fall blooms in yellow, pink, red, and white

Mature Height × Spread
2 to 24 inches × 2 to 24 inches

Sedums have long been known and used for their ability to grow in difficult locations. Low maintenance, heat and drought tolerant, and flowers with butterfly appeal make sedums a great choice for beginning, busy, or just about any gardener. *Sedum* × 'Autumn Joy' ('Herbstfreude') with its dependable and adaptable beauty seemed to bring renewed interest to this group of plants. Its thick, fleshy leaves are topped with large, flat flower clusters in late summer. They start out pale pink, deepen to a rosy red, and then turn a rust color after the first frost. The dried seedheads persist, adding interest to the winter landscape. New introductions have broadened our planting palette with colorful foliage and impressive attractive flowers on equally dependable plants.

When, Where, and How to Plant
Plant dormant container and bare-root sedums in the spring after the danger of severe weather has passed. Plant hardened-off transplants anytime during the growing season. Sedums tolerate a wide range of conditions, but grow best in full sun and well-drained soil. Some sedums can tolerate light shade, but they will become open and leggy in heavy shade. Sedums will tolerate heavy clay soil with drainage.

Growing Tips
Water new plants often enough to keep the soil moist but not wet. Established plants are very drought tolerant. Water these thoroughly during extended periods of drought. Avoid overwatering and overfertilization, which can lead to floppy growth and root rot.

Regional Advice and Care
Divide overgrown sedums anytime during the season. Dig, divide, and replant by September to help them get established before winter. Spring division will allow plants to recover from transplanting before summer and fall bloom. Some of the taller sedums like 'Autumn Joy' can become floppy. Grow in full sun with well-drained soil to avoid this problem. Control floppiness on problem plants with proper pruning. Pinch back 8-inch-tall stems to 4 inches in June. Let the plants stand for winter interest.

Companion Planting and Design
Use taller sedums like 'Autumn Joy' and 'Purple Emperor' (smoky purple-red foliage topped with dusty red flowers) as an edging plant in rose and perennial gardens or even a perennial hedge. Planted as a specimen or *en masse*, it gives an impressive fall flower display. Include low-growing sedums in rock gardens or use as groundcover. Combine sedums with roses, low-growing grasses, daylilies, and yucca.

Try These
If you like 'Autumn Joy', consider 'Autumn Fire' with the same good looks but sturdier stems and longer-lasting blooms. 'Pure Joy' forms a 12-inch-tall mound of blue-green leaves that mature to green with bubblegum pink flowers. 'Angelina' is a low grower (3 to 6 inches) with needle-like foliage that is a bright yellow in full sun, turning amber in fall, and persisting over winter. 'Voodoo' is low growing, forming mats of burgundy foliage and red flowers in late summer.

Shasta Daisy

Chrysanthemum × superbum

Botanical Pronunciation
kris-AN-theh-mum ex soo-PER-bum

Bloom Period and Seasonal Color
Summer until frost blooms in white with yellow center

Mature Height × Spread
1 to 3 feet × 1 foot

Hardiness Zones 4

Shasta daisies provide a profusion of white flowers from summer until frost. The large daisy-like flowers are good for cutting, attracting butterflies, or providing a long season of bloom in the garden. Originally named *Chrysanthemum × superbum*, it was one of the many members of the Chrysanthemum group to be renamed. Shasta daisy became *Leucanthemum × superbum*; however, the name change was appealed and the plant is once again *Chrysanthemum × superbum*. You may see it listed both ways. The common name Shasta daisy goes back to its place of origin. Luther Burbank, credited for its introduction, did much of his breeding and research in California near the white peaks of Mount Shasta. The white flowers of the daisy were reminiscent of that snow-covered mountain peak.

When, Where, and How to Plant

Plant seeds in spring on a properly prepared seedbed. Move dormant container and bare-root plants into the garden in spring after the danger of severe weather has passed. Plant hardened-off transplants in spring or early summer. Grow Shasta daisies in full sun and moist, well-drained soils. Good drainage is important for winter survival. Space plants 18 to 24 inches apart.

Growing Tips

Keep the soil moist, but not wet, throughout the growing season. Water established plants thoroughly whenever the top few inches of soil are crumbly and moist. Mulch the soil to conserve water, keep the roots cool, and suppress weeds. Keep Shasta daisies healthy with a light fertilization in spring.

Regional Advice and Care

Shasta daisies tend to be short-lived. They do great for several years, and then one spring they fail to return. Regular dividing seems to keep the plants vigorous and prolongs their life. Divide Shasta daisies in early spring every two to three years. Staking is often needed for the species and taller cultivars. Spring pruning will help encourage more compact growth. Pinch back tall cultivars to 6 inches in late May or early June. This will delay flowering by one to two weeks but eliminates the need for staking. Deadheading will prolong blooms. Cut faded flowers back to side buds. Prune back plants to the new growth once flowering has finished. This will encourage more leaf growth with some sporadic blooms throughout the remainder of the season.

Companion Planting and Design

Use them in cottage, perennial, and cutting gardens. They combine well with perennial salvia, veronicas, yarrow, coreopsis, beebalm, and ornamental grasses.

Try These

'Banana Cream' has large lemon yellow flowers on 18-inch plants with clean dark green foliage (Zone 5). 'Alaska' Shasta daisy is hardier and tends to be longer lived, but it benefits from staking or pruning. 'Becky' is even hardier (Zone 3) and grows 3 feet tall but doesn't need staking. 'Sante' and 'Aglaia' both have semi-double pompom flowers. 'Snow Lady' is an AAS winner that grows 10 to 18 inches tall with single flowers.

Siberian Bugloss

Brunnera macrophylla

Botanical Pronunciation
brun-ERR-ah mak-roe-FY-lah

Bloom Period and Seasonal Color
Forget-me-not–like blue flowers in early to late spring

Mature Height × Spread
12 to 18 inches × 18 inches

Brighten up the shade with this Perennial Plant of the Year, 'Jack Frost' *brunnera*. The heart-shaped leaves have silvery variegation that looks good all season long. The blue flowers resemble forget-me-nots and cover the plant in spring. Cultivars combine nicely with ferns, hostas, astilbes, and other shade tolerant perennials. *Brunneras* reseed readily providing lots of plants for you and your friends. Deadhead to eliminate the problem or add a few seedlings to container gardens or new shade gardens. Unfortunately they do not retain the ornamental qualities of their parents. Save the ones you like and compost the rest. No need to feel guilty; you are just using the composted seedlings in a different form in the garden.

When, Where, and How to Plant

Seeds may be hard to find and most will need a chill before planting. Follow planting directions on the package. Plant dormant container and bare-root plants in spring after severe weather has passed and the soil can be worked. Plant hardened-off potted and container-grown plants anytime during the growing season after the danger of frost has passed. Grow *brunnera* in part sun and part shade. They can tolerate morning sun in our northern gardens. Hot afternoon sun can cause leaf browning (scorch). Plant in moist, well-drained soils about 12 inches apart.

Growing Tips

Water new plantings thoroughly and often enough to keep the roots moist. Water established plants thoroughly whenever the top few inches of soil are crumbly and moist. Mulch the soil with shredded leaves, evergreen needles, or other organic material to keep roots cool and moist. Topdress with an inch of compost every other year. Follow soil test recommendations or use a low-nitrogen slow-release fertilizer in spring if the plants need a nutrient boost. Divide in spring when the center of the plant dies out or you want to start new plants.

Regional Advice and Care

Scorch is a problem in extreme heat, drought, and full sun. Slugs can be a problem in cool wet weather, though, I have had no problems. Perhaps they were too busy eating my hostas. The new iron phosphate slug baits are effective and nontoxic to people, wildlife, and the birds and toads that eat the slugs.

Companion Planting and Design

Combine with other shade lovers like hosta, astilbe, Solomon seal, and ferns. Use as a groundcover or in woodland gardens.

Try These

'Variegata' has creamy white variegation. 'Looking Glass' has silvery white leaves with green veins that tend to cup downward. 'King's Ransom' has creamy yellow margins that lighten to creamy white with a light frosting over all of the leaf. 'Emerald Mist' has silver bars of variegation that reminds me of variegated yellow archangel foliage. But this plant has blue flowers and is better behaved.

Turtlehead

Chelone species

Botanical Pronunciation
kee-LO-nay

Other Name Shellflower

Bloom Period and Seasonal Color
Pink and purple flowers in late summer to
early fall

Mature Height × Spread
3 feet × 2 feet

*C*helone rhymes with baloney and that is just the start of the fun. A close look at the flowers reveals the inspiration of its common names. You may see a turtle with its mouth open or perhaps a shell. Include this late blooming perennial in wet or damp spots in the garden. It tolerates full sun to part shade. Place it in the back of the garden as a green backdrop for other flowers. It will go unnoticed for most of the season. That is, until the pink and purple flowers appear and steal the show. They add a fresh splash of color to the garden as many other flowers are starting to fade. Or use this long blooming moisture-tolerant plant in rain gardens.

When, Where, and How to Plant
Start plants from seeds. They will need six weeks of cold treatment (stratification) to germinate. Follow planting directions on seed packet. Plant turtlehead throughout the growing season. See the chapter introduction for planting directions. Grow in full sun to partial shade in moist organic soils for best results. Water new plantings thoroughly and often enough to keep the roots moist. Space plants 18 to 24 inches apart.

Growing Tips
Water established plants thoroughly whenever the top few inches of soil are crumbly and slightly moist. Mulch the soil with shredded leaves or evergreen needles to keep the roots cool and moist, suppress weeds, and improve the soil as they decompose. Topdress soil with an inch of compost every other

year. Follow soil test recommendations or use a low-nitrogen slow-release fertilizer if the plants need a nutrient boost. Divide overgrown plants in spring or fall. Remove flowers when digging and dividing plants in fall. Turtlehead usually does not need staking. Plants growing in heavy shade may need support from a stake or sturdy neighbor.

Regional Advice and Care
Don't deadhead. Instead, leave the seedheads intact and plants stand for winter interest. Turtleheads are late to emerge so mark their location or leave a few stems intact until growth begins. Pinch plants in spring when they are about 6 inches tall to encourage fuller growth. They have no serious pest problems. Powdery mildew may be a problem in heavy shade or droughty conditions. If this is a continual problem increase watering, thin plantings, or move plants to a sunnier location.

Companion Planting and Design
Combine with other perennials for added fall color. Include in bogs, waterside plantings, and rain gardens with sedges, swamp milkweed, and other rain garden plants. Or use in containers alone or with ornamental grasses and other flowers.

Try These
'Hot Lips' leaves emerge bronzy green then turn to green. The 2- to 3-foot-tall plants have red stems and hot pink blooms. Our native white turtlehead, *Chelone glabra*, can be found on streambanks, and in meadows, forests, and woods.

Variegated Solomon's Seal

Polygonatum odoratum 'Variegatum'

Botanical Pronunciation
pol-ig-on-AY-tum oh-dor-AY-tum

Bloom Period and Seasonal Color
White flowers in early spring

Mature Height × Spread
18 to 36 inches × 18 to 36 inches

The 2- to 4-foot-tall upright arching burgundy stems of variegated Solomon's seal add a unique form to the shade garden. The white variegation on leaf edges brightens the shade all summer long then turns golden in fall. Use the foliage in flower arrangements. Selected as a Perennial Plant of the Year, this perennial has multi-season interest. Pairs of fragrant white bell-shaped flowers dangle from the stems. These are followed by bluish black berries. Do not eat the berries; they are poisonous. Young shoots can be boiled and eaten like asparagus and the roots can be added to stews or boiled and eaten like potatoes. Or let them grow and multiply so you have more to enjoy in the garden.

When, Where, and How to Plant
Sow seed in the fall in coldframes. Follow planting directions on the seed packet. Plant dormant container, bare-root, and rhizomes in spring after severe weather has passed and the soil is workable. Place rhizomes just below the soil surface. Plant hardened-off transplants anytime during the growing season and after the danger of frost has passed. Plant in part to full shade and moist well-drained soils for best results. Established plants can tolerate dry shade. Water new plantings thoroughly and often enough to keep the soil moist. Space 18 to 24 inches apart.

Growing Tips
Water established plants thoroughly whenever the top few inches of soil are crumbly and moist.

Mulch with shredded leaves or other organic matter. Topdress the soil with an inch of compost every other year. Properly sited plants growing in prepared soil need little if any additional fertilizer. Follow soil test results or use a low-nitrogen slow-release fertilizer if plants need a nutrient boost. Divide in spring or fall as needed. Plant so the rhizomes are just below soil surface.

Regional Advice and Care
Solomon seals are low maintenance with no real pest problems. I read about slug problems, but like my *brunnera*, I've have not encountered them in mine or others garden. Plants growing in moist shaded conditions will spread. Dig and divide as needed.

Companion Planting and Design
Use the upright arching branches for vertical interest in the shade garden. Include a few in containers as your thriller and season long foliage. It looks great growing among ferns and with some Canadian ginger growing at its feet.

Try These
'Prince Charming' has green leaves with bluish cast, vigorous forms dense colony, but only 12 inches tall. Its leathery leaves make it more sun tolerant. Our native Solomon's seal (*P. biflorum*) has greenish white tubular flowers dangling from zigzag stems. False Solomon's seal (*Smilacina racemosa*) has a plume-type flower at the end of its stem and red berries.

Veronica

Veronica species

Botanical Pronunciation ver-ON-ih-kah

Other Name Speedwell

Bloom Period and Seasonal Color
Late spring to summer blooms in blue, red, and white

Mature Height × Spread
4 to 36 inches × 6 to 24 inches

Veronicas are versatile plants that fit into many garden situations. Spike speedwell, *Veronica spicata*, grows 10 to 36 inches tall and has spikes of white, blue, or red flowers. They blend nicely with other perennials in both formal and informal settings. Look for varieties like 'Royal Candles' that have a long period of bloom on upright plants. Many of the low growing species and cultivars like 'Waterperry Blue' are fast growing, mat forming, and great as groundcovers. This particular cultivar is deer and drought proof and salt tolerant. A good choice near walks and drives. A few like *Veronica incana* 'Pure Silver' have hairy foliage giving it a gray, or in this case silver, hue; it looks nice with the blue flowers.

When, Where, and How to Plant
Plant dormant container and bare-root veronicas in spring after the danger of severe weather has passed. Plant hardened-off potted and container-grown perennials anytime during the growing season. Plants tend to flop open in the center when grown in heavy shade and poorly drained soils. Most veronicas prefer full to part sun but will tolerate partial shade. They all need well-drained soils, especially for winter. Space plants 18 to 24 inches apart.

Growing Tips
Water established plants thoroughly whenever the top few inches of soil are crumbly. Mulch to keep the well-drained soil moist and weed free. Use organic materials such as twice-shredded bark, shredded leaves, or evergreen needles. Proper soil preparation and topdressing with compost is usually enough to keep the plants healthy and attractive. Avoid excess nitrogen, which can increase floppy growth and decrease bloom.

Regional Advice and Care
The upright types of veronica tend to open in the center and flop. Select cultivars with sturdier stems that resist flopping. Staking will help keep taller cultivars upright and attractive during blooming. Deadhead to extend the flower display. Clip off faded flowers back to side buds or leaves. Prune back halfway after this second flush of flowers to encourage compact growth. Divide floppy and overgrown veronicas in the spring. Most cultivars benefit from being divided every two or three years.

Companion Planting and Design
The lower growing types are good edging plants and groundcovers. Use the mat type between steppers for added interest. The upright types add color to the cutting, butterfly, and perennial gardens. Combine with threadleaf coreopsis, rudbeckias, and ornamental grasses.

Try These
'Hocus Pocus' has large spikes of violet purple flowers on 16- to 20-inch-tall plants. 'Sweet Lullaby' is a shorter, 6-inch plant with spikes of pink flowers. *Veronica* × 'Royal Candles' has stiff upright stems topped with long-blooming rich violet-blue flowers that look like candles. The Perennial Plant of the Year for 1993 was *Veronica* 'Sunny Border Blue', selected for its long bloom and light blue, spike-like flowers.

Yarrow

Achillea filipendulina

Botanical Pronunciation
ah-KILL-lee-ah fil-ih-pend-yew-LEE-nah

Bloom Period and Seasonal Color
Summer blooms in yellow, white, cream, pink, red, orange, and salmon

Mature Height × Spread
1 to 4 feet × 3 feet and spreading

Include yarrow when looking for low maintenance, heat- and drought-tolerant plants good for attracting butterflies and to use in cut flower arrangements. Select your plant carefully as some are well mannered and others can take over the landscape. Fernleaf yarrow, *Achillea filipendulina*, grows 3 to 4 feet tall and seldom needs staking. This well-mannered yarrow has attractive fern-like foliage with a spicy aroma. The golden flowers are quite impressive in the garden or flower arrangements. Common yarrow, *Achillea millefolium*, is a plant you will see listed in weed books, wildflower books, and garden catalogues. It is native to some of our prairies but can become a weed in the landscape. Select a non-invasive red, yellow, white, and orange flowering cultivar to minimize your workload.

When, Where, and How to Plant

See chapter introduction for planting directions. Plant hardened-off transplants anytime during the growing season. Grow yarrow in full sun with well-drained soil. Yarrow is able to thrive in hot, dry locations where other plants are lucky to survive. Space plants 2 to 3 feet apart.

Growing Tips

Yarrow tends to flop when grown in shade, fertile soil, or overfertilized gardens. Water new plantings often enough to keep the soil moist but not wet. Established plants are drought tolerant. Water during extended drought when the top few inches of soil are dry. Mulching helps conserve moisture and suppress weeds. Avoid excess fertilization, which leads to floppy growth.

Regional Advice and Care

Deadhead yarrow to remove unattractive seedheads and to encourage longer blooming. This also reduces reseeding of the more invasive yarrow species. Prune plants back to fresh new growth after the final bloom. The foliage will continue to look attractive into the winter. Fernleaf yarrow grown in the proper conditions does not need staking. Common yarrow will become leggy and topple over without pruning. Prune plants back halfway in early June and after the first and second flush of flowers. This will also prevent seeding. Divide overgrown, leggy, or poorly flowering plants in the spring. Common yarrow benefits from division every two to three years.

Companion Planting and Design

Combine fernleaf yarrow with Shasta daisies, black-eyed Susans, garden phlox, salvia, veronicas, and ornamental grasses. Use them in the perennial, naturalized, and cutting gardens, or areas where nothing else will grow.

Try These

'Coronation Gold' is a 3-foot upright cultivar of fernleaf yarrow with yellow long-lasting flowers. 'Sunny Seduction' is more compact, 2 feet tall, with the same attractive foliage and flowers. *Achillea* × 'Moonshine' has bright yellow flowers and silvery gray feather-like foliage. 'Terracotta has peachy yellow blooms that mature to a coppery bronze on 2½- to 3-foot-tall plants. Use *Achillea millefolium* cultivars with caution. Many reseed, and it take years to eliminate unwanted seedlings.

Yucca

Yucca filamentosa

Botanical Pronunciation
YUK-ah fil-ah-men-TOE-sah

Other Name Adam's needle

Bloom Period and Seasonal Color
July blooms in white; evergreen foliage

Mature Height × Spread
2 to 3 feet (in foliage) × 3 feet (up to 12 feet tall in bloom)

Yucca generates visions of the desert, and those are the conditions it prefers: hot, dry areas where other plants fail to thrive. In fact, a walk by the yucca planting at the Minnesota Landscape Arboretum makes you feel like you were transported to the Southwest. They combined yucca with prickly pear cactus and threw in a few boulders as accents. Proper planning is important when introducing this strong architectural feature into the garden. The sword-shaped leaves, vertical growth habit, and the large cluster of bell-shaped flowers held on long stems 5 to 8 feet above the ground can be challenging to blend into a northern garden. Soften the strong features with airy plants like threadleaf coreopsis or complement them with other bold plants like allium.

When, Where, and How to Plant
Plant dormant container and bare-root yucca in spring after the danger of severe weather has passed. Plant hardened-off transplants anytime during the growing season. I prefer spring or early summer to give the plants time to get established before winter. Grow yucca in full sun and well-drained soil. Space plants 24 inches apart.

Growing Tips
New plantings benefit from regular watering until the root system becomes established. Once established, plants are very heat and drought tolerant. Water established plants during extended droughts whenever the top few inches of soil are dry. Proper soil preparation and topdressing with compost every other year will keep the plants healthy. Avoid high-nitrogen fertilizers and excess fetilization, which can prevent flowering.

Regional Advice and Care
Yuccas thrive and flower best during hot, dry summers. Clip off faded flowers for a neater appearance or allow the seedheads to develop. These as well as the evergreen leaves add interest to the winter interest. The new growth in the spring will mask the fading leaves. Or for a tidier look, remove older leaves as new leaves appear. Yucca will occasionally suffer from leaf spot diseases, mostly in cool wet seasons. Remove infected leaves to reduce the spread. Cleanup is usually an adequate control. Often listed as deer resistant, I have seen these critters make a meal of a yucca or two.

Companion Planting and Design
Use yucca as a vertical accent in the garden or shrub bed. The tall flower stalk is quite impressive and will temporarily steal attention from the rest of the landscape. Use the yellow-variegated variety with black-eyed Susans or threadleaf coreopsis for a bit of color echoing. Use any of the yuccas in the corner of the garden or with a boulder to create a focal point.

Try These
'Color Guard' has a bright yellow wide stripe down the middle of the leaves. 'Golden Sword' has a more muted yellow stripe. 'Bright Edge' has yellow along the edges of its green leaves.

SHRUBS
FOR MICHIGAN

Shrubs can provide year-round beauty, screen bad views, and create intimate spaces in your landscape. Select the right plant for the location to minimize maintenance and increase longevity. Make sure the shrubs you choose will fit the space when they're mature and will tolerate the growing conditions.

First Things First

Once you have a plan, call the free utility locating service at 811. They will send someone to mark the location of any underground utilities in the planting area. Give them three working days to complete the task. This is an important step for your safety and pocketbook.

While waiting for the utility marking crew, visit a nursery or garden center to select and buy your plants. Store your plants in a cool, shady location until they can be planted.

Dig a planting hole the same depth and two to three times wider than the rootball. Remove the shrub from its container by rolling the pot on its side or squeeze the container to make it easier to slide the plant out. Or reduce root damage by cutting off the bottom of the pot. Place the shrub, pot and all, in the hole so the area where the stem meets the roots will be even with the soil surface. Cut away the remainder of the container. Fill the hole with existing soil, and then water.

Creeping juniper, such as this example of *Juniperus chinensis procumbens nana*, can be both a design element and solve a landscape problem.

Be sure new plantings receive about an inch of water each week from rainfall, irrigation, or a combination of the two. Some shrubs are planted in soil-less mixes. The rootball of these shrubs will dry out faster than the surrounding soil. You will initially need to water the root system more frequently than the surrounding soil to keep both moist but not wet.

Water established plants thoroughly when the top 4 to 6 inches of soil begin to dry.

Mulch the soil to conserve moisture and reduce weed problems. Use a 2- to 3-inch layer of woodchips,

Oak leaf hydrangea provides outstanding fall color.

shredded bark, or other organic materials. These help improve the soil as they decompose. Don't bury the base of the shrub and do not use weed barrier fabrics under these organic mulches.

Wait a year to fertilize new shrub plantings. Follow your soil test recommendations for the type and amount of fertilizer to use. If this information is not available, use a low-nitrogen slow-release fertilizer according to label directions. Young shrubs can be fertilized in late fall after the plants are dormant or in early spring before growth begins. Established shrubs need little, if any, fertilizer.

Pruning Starts with a Plan

Have a plan before taking the pruning saw to your plants. Prune shrubs to remove diseased and damaged branches, encourage flowering, improve bark color, control size, and shape the plants. Spring-flowering plants like lilacs and forsythia should be pruned right after flowering. Others can be pruned anytime during the dormant season. Late winter or early spring is better for the plant and allows you to enjoy the plant's winter interest and to repair winter damage at the same time you do routine pruning. Avoid late summer pruning that can stimulate late season growth that can be winter killed.

Prune above outward-facing buds, where branches join other branches, or to ground level. These cuts will close more quickly to keep out pests and help maintain the plants appearance.

Renew suckering shrubs by removing about one-third of the older, thicker canes to ground level each year for several years. You can also reduce the height of the remaining stems by one-third.

Shrubs are often sheared for a formal look. It's hard on the health of the shrubs as it leaves stubs that make perfect entryways for disease and insects. Hedge plants should be pruned so the top is several inches narrower than the bottom. This allows light to reach all parts of the plants and helps keep leaves on the bottom of the shrub.

With proper selection and care, your shrubs will give you years of enjoyment.

Arborvitae

Thuja occidentalis

Botanical Pronunciation
THOO-yah ox-ee-den-TAL-is

Other Name White cedar

Bloom Period and Seasonal Color
Evergreen foliage

Mature Height × Spread
3 to 40 feet × 4 to 15 feet

Arborvitaes are a favorite evergreen of deer and gardeners alike. This native can be found growing in our northern forests. Though not a true cedar, *Cedrus*, it is often called white cedar by northern gardeners. The scaly foliage is soft, flattened, and reminds me of fans. You will find it used as a screen, foundation plant, or tall evergreen hedge. Be aware that the American arborvitae is a tall plant reaching a height of 40 feet or more. Many homeowners found this out the hard way as the arborvitae quickly outgrew its spot in the landscape. American arborvitae also tends to turn a bit yellow-brown in the winter. Select a cultivar that is right for your climate and landscape and holds its green color throughout the year.

When, Where, and How to Plant

Plant balled-and-burlapped arborvitae as soon as possible after they are purchased. Plant container-grown plants by October 1 for best results. Plants grown in heavy shade tend to become loose and open. Avoid open areas and those exposed to drying northwest winter winds. Arborvitaes prefer moist, well-drained soil. Native arborvitae will grow in both wet and dry soil, but the cultivated plants are not as tolerant of these extremes. Plant shrubs the same depth they were growing in the nursery or container. Fill the hole with existing soil, and then water.

Growing Tips

Water plants thoroughly whenever the top 4 to 6 inches of soil are crumbly and moist. Mulch the soil to help conserve moisture and reduce weed problems. Wait at least one year to fertilize new plantings according to soil test recommendations. Once established, arborvitaes need little, if any, fertilizer.

Regional Advice and Care

Arborvitaes need minimal pruning if the right size cultivar is selected. Prune in the spring before growth begins, or in midsummer during their semi-dormant period. You can shear the sides and top of the plants to control their size. Overgrown specimens can be topped but will be more subject to damage from heavy snow loads. Reshape the topped shrub as new growth fills in. Multistemmed arborvitae tend to split apart under the weight of heavy snow. Prevent the problem by loosely tying the upright stems together in the fall. Arborvitae foliage often browns during the winter. Reduce the damage by keeping plants properly watered and growing in protected areas. Try repelling deer with repellents, scare tactics, and fencing.

Companion Planting and Design

This plant is commonly used in long rows as a hedge or screen. Use small clusters of arborvitae to block views and provide shelter. Mix them with deciduous shrubs for added interest.

Try These

'Technito' is a new introduction from Johnson's and Bailey's nurseries. This smaller form of 'Techny' has dense, dark growth that resists winter burn and does not need shearing. Western arborvitae, hardy in Zone 5 is more deer resistant. Variegated varieties also exist.

Blue Spirea

Caryopteris × clandonensis

Botanical Pronunciation
kare-ee-OP-ter-iss ex klan-don-EN-sis

Other Name Bluebeard

Bloom Period and Seasonal Color
Late summer through frost with blue flowers

Mature Height × Spread
3 feet × 3 feet

You'll see this plant listed as only hardy to Zones 5 or 6. Being a typical northern gardener with "Zone envy" I had to give it a try. My plant has not only survived a difficult planting location for fifteen years, it also rewarded me with offspring to enhance my landscape and share with other gardeners. I have seen this plant growing throughout Zone 4 gardens. The top often dies back, so treat it like butterfly bush and Russian sage. The blue-gray foliage is a nice addition to the perennial border. The silver-gray foliage is topped with true blue flowers and can't be beat for a late summer through fall display. Bees love this plant but won't bother you or others that pass by the plants.

When, Where and How to Plant
Plant container-grown plants in spring through early summer to get them established before our harsh winter. These can be short-lived plants in the north, so use them in an area with easy access—just in case. Grow in full sun to partial shade in moist, well-drained soils. They tolerate most soils, but good drainage, especially in winter, is important for survival. Carefully slide the plant out of the pot. Set it in a hole the same depth as but wider than the rootball. Loosen circling roots, backfill with existing soil, and water. Keep soil around new plantings moist but not wet. Space 2½ to 3 feet apart.

Growing Tips
Water established plants whenever the top 4 to 6 inches are moist but crumbly. Apply an organic mulch to help conserve moisture and reduce weed problems. Wait a year to fertilize new plantings. Avoid excess fertilization that stimulates growth more likely to be winter killed. Consider using slow-release, low-nitrogen fertilizers.

Regional Advice and Care
Winter kill is the only real problem. Proper siting and care will help with this plant's longevity. Let the plants stand for winter. This will add winter beauty to the landscape and increase winter survival. Prune blue spirea down to 6 inches in late winter or early spring. The plant will quickly reach its full size and begin flowering in late summer.

Companion Planting and Design
The gray foliage combines nicely with a wide range of shrubs and flowers. Combine with shrub roses or dwarf conifers, and skirt with low growing annuals and perennials like Rozanne geranium, perennial verbena, or *Corydalis lutea* for season-long interest.

Try These
I have 'Blue Mist' growing in my yard. I like the powder blue flowers. I cut the plant back in late winter, and it usually grows to 2½ to 3 feet tall and wide each summer. 'Dark Knight' is similar in size with deep purple flowers. 'Sunshine Blue' (*Caryopteris incana* 'Jason') has yellow foliage with blue flowers, *C. divaricata* 'Snow Fairy' has green and white leaves and blue flowers, and is rated Zone 5.

Boxwood

Buxus microphylla

Botanical Pronunciation
BUKS-us my-kro-FY-lah

Other Name Littleleaf boxwood

Bloom Period and Seasonal Color
Spring blooms in white; evergreen foliage

Mature Height × Spread
3 feet × 3 feet

Hardiness Zones Hardy to Zone 4

These broadleaf evergreens have long been used as sheared hedges in the formal landscapes of Europe and the southern United States. The large-leafed boxwood, *Buxus sempervirens*, is not hardy in our area. Winter damage is the biggest concern with boxwood. Northern gardeners need to select hardier, small-leafed boxwood cultivars bred to be more tolerant of our winters. Consider adding a few boxwoods to your shade garden or shrub bed. Left to grow naturally, they blend well with a variety of perennials and shrubs in more informal garden designs. Take a close look at boxwoods in the spring. They produce small, white flowers that are hard to see. Their fragrance, however, makes a second look, or should I say sniff, worthwhile.

When, Where, and How to Plant

Plant balled-and-burlapped plants soon after they are purchased. Remove any twine and cut away burlap on balled-and-burlapped plants. Plant container-grown boxwood in the spring and early summer. Follow planting directions at the introduction to this chapter. Grow boxwood in protected locations sheltered from winter wind and winter sun for best results. Space plants 2½ to 3 feet apart.

Growing Tips

Water thoroughly whenever the top 4 to 6 inches of soil are moist and crumbly. Proper placement and watering throughout the season will help decrease winter browning. Mulch with woodchips, shredded bark, or another organic material to keep the roots cool and moist, reduce weed problems, and improve the soil as they decompose. Keep cultivators and

tillers away from boxwoods and their roots. Water new and established plants thoroughly in the fall before the ground freezes. Wait a year to fertilize new plantings, following soil test recommendations for the type and amount of fertilizer.

Regional Advice and Care

Non-sheared boxwoods require very little pruning. Cut long branches back to a side branch in midsummer. Remove winter damage and do more severe pruning or shearing in early spring before new growth appears. A burlap wrap, decorative wind break, or cylinder of hardware cloth filled with evergreen boughs or straw can reduce winter damage on more tender cultivars or plants exposed to winter wind and sun.

Companion Planting and Design

Use them as a hedge, edging plant, or as part of a formal garden. They are naturally compact, dense growers with a round growth habit, but too often they are sheared beyond recognition. Use them as the framework of your mixed border or evergreen foil in a shady rock garden.

Try These

The following are among the hardiest boxwood: 'Wintergreen' grows 3 to 4 feet tall, 'Winter Gem' is 2 feet tall and wide, and 'Green Velvet' is probably the hardiest. This compact grower maintains its evergreen color. 'Green Velvet' has small, dark green leaves and grows 3 feet tall and wide. 'Green Gem' is a slow growing to 2 feet tall and wide. 'Chicagoland Green' (*Buxus* 'Glencoe') stays green in winter.

Bush-Honeysuckle

Diervilla lonicera

Botanical Pronunciation
dy-er-VIL-ah lon-ISS-ER-ah

Other Name Northern bush-honeysuckle

Bloom Period and Seasonal Color
June to July, yellow

Mature Height × Spread
2 to 3 feet × 2 to 3 feet (and wider), suckering

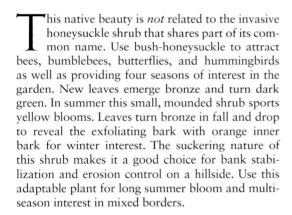

This native beauty is *not* related to the invasive honeysuckle shrub that shares part of its common name. Use bush-honeysuckle to attract bees, bumblebees, butterflies, and hummingbirds as well as providing four seasons of interest in the garden. New leaves emerge bronze and turn dark green. In summer this small, mounded shrub sports yellow blooms. Leaves turn bronze in fall and drop to reveal the exfoliating bark with orange inner bark for winter interest. The suckering nature of this shrub makes it a good choice for bank stabilization and erosion control on a hillside. Use this adaptable plant for long summer bloom and multi-season interest in mixed borders.

When, Where, and How to Plant
Purchase from local garden centers and nurseries specializing in native plants. Plant container-grown bush-honeysuckle spring through fall. Grow bush-honeysuckle in full to part sun. They are shade tolerant but grow and flower best in part to full sun. These adaptable plants tolerate a wide range of soils including poor rocky soils to clay. Dig a hole the same depth and two to three times wider than the rootball. Slide the plant out of the container and loosen any girdling roots. Backfill the hole with existing soil and water.

Growing Tips
Water new plantings thoroughly and often enough to keep the rootball and surrounding soil moist but not wet. Spread a 2- to 3-inch layer of shredded bark, woodchips, or other organic mulch on the soil surrounding the plants. Be careful not to bury the stems. Mulching conserves moisture, suppresses weeds, and improves the soil as it decomposes. Wait a year to fertilize new plantings. Follow soil test results or use a low-nitrogen slow-release fertilizer. Established plants need minimal fertilizer.

Regional Advice and Care
Bush-honeysuckle is basically pest free. Prune, if needed, in late winter or early spring before growth begins. Remove larger, older stems to the ground to encourage new growth at the base of the plant. Reduce the height as needed. Make these cuts above a healthy bud or where a branch joins another branch.

Companion Planting and Design
Use in natural plantings, mixed borders, and shrub beds. Use on a hillside or raised beds. The variegated cultivar 'Cool Splash' brightens up the shade.

Try These
D. sessilifolia 'Cool Splash' has green-and-white variegated leaves and yellow flowers. It is a good substitute for variegated dogwood, which is susceptible to leaf spot. Visit the University of Minnesota landscape arboretum or Energy Park at the Wisconsin State Fairgrounds to see a planting of these. 'Butterfly' southern bush-honeysuckle has deep yellow flowers, good fall color, and grows 3 to 5 feet tall.

Butterfly Bush

Buddleja davidii

Botanical Pronunciation
BUD-lee-ah dah-VID-ee-eye

Other Name Summer lilac

Bloom Period and Seasonal Color
July through frost blooms in purple, white, pink, and yellow

Mature Height × Spread
5 to 8 feet × 5 to 8 feet

Give butterfly bush a try, or maybe it's your second or third attempt. The fragrant flowers that appear summer through fall, along with the butterflies and hummingbirds it attracts, makes butterfly bush worth the risk. I hope you, like me, feel you get your investment back after just one season of enjoyment. A quick pruning job in late winter is all the maintenance needed. New growth bursts from the ground and quickly grows to its mature size. Be patient; the plants are slow to emerge in cool springs. Even with a late start the plants will quickly reach mature full size and bloom in midsummer and continue through frost. The flowers are 6 to 12 inches long and resemble lilac flowers.

When, Where, and How to Plant
Plant container-grown butterfly bushes in the spring and early summer. Grow butterfly bush in full sun or light shade with moist, well-drained soil. Remove plants from the pot and loosen potbound roots. Plant the shrub at the same depth it was growing in the nursery, backfill, and water. Space plants 4 to 5 feet apart.

Growing Tips
Water thoroughly whenever the top 4 to 6 inches are crumbly and moist. Mulch the soil to help conserve water and reduce weed problems. Wait a year to fertilize newly planted butterfly bushes. Follow soil test recommendations for the amount and type of fertilizer to use. Or use a low-nitrogen slow-release fertilizer in spring. Butterfly bush benefits from regular fertilizing.

Regional Advice and Care
Let the plants stand for winter. The seedheads and plant form add to your landscape's winter interest and increase hardiness. Some gardeners add a layer of woodchips or other winter mulch for added insulation. Prune the plants back to 4 to 6 inches above ground level in late winter or early spring. Make your cuts at a slight angle above a bud. These plants are not long lived in the landscape. They may die out after an extremely harsh winter. But don't give up on your plants too soon. Wait until the soil warms to make sure it is dead before removing it from the garden. My first planting lasted five years, my second one made it for ten, and my third one is thriving! Consider growing them in containers and overwintering in an unheated garage or sheltered location to increase overwintering success.

Companion Planting and Design
This large shrub can be used alone or grouped in shrub beds and perennial gardens. Plant it where you can sit and watch the butterflies and hummingbirds that visit.

Try These
Lo and Behold® grows less than 3 feet and is non-invasive. Lavender Veil™ is a low growing cultivar with a cascading growth habit perfect for containers and hanging baskets. The large lavender flowers have a white eye and cover the plant throughout much of the growing season.

Chokeberry

Aronia melanocarpa

Botanical Pronunciation
ah-ROE-nee-ah mel-an-oh-KAR-pah

Other Name Glossy chokeberry

Bloom Period and Seasonal Color
White flowers in spring

Mature Height × Spread
3 to 5 feet × 5 feet or more

As northern gardeners, we need to make the most of all four seasons. Chokeberries white spring flowers greet the new season. The glossy green foliage is a nice addition to shrub beds, foundation plantings, and mixed borders. Its fall color is a beautiful wine to red. The black fruit persists through much of the winter, adding beauty to the landscape and food for the birds. This beautiful shrub is also tough. It can tolerate wet and dry soils and full sun to partial shade. Include these adaptable plants in rain gardens as well. You will get the best fall color and flowering in full sun, though they perform pretty well in partial shade. All this *and* it is hardy to Zone 3.

When, Where, and How to Plant

Plant container-grown plants anytime during the growing season. Grow chokeberry in full sun to partially shaded locations. They tolerate a wide range of soil, including wet and dry, but prefer moist, well-drained soils. Carefully slide the plant out of the pot. Set it in a hole the same depth as, but wider than, the rootball. Loosen circling roots, backfill with existing soil, and water. Keep soil around new plantings moist but not wet. Space plants 2½ to 3 feet apart.

Growing Tips

Water established plants thoroughly whenever the top 4 to 6 inches of soil are moist and crumbly. Wait a year to fertilize new plantings. Avoid excess nitrogen, which can limit flowering and fall color.

Regional Advice and Care

Chokeberries may be slow to start but eventually sucker and can form a colony. Give them plenty of space to take advantage of this growth habit. Remove older canes to ground level in late winter. This encourages new growth at the base. Regular renewal pruning controls the overall size. This is a fairly pest-free plant that tolerates a wide range of growing conditions. You may see problems with leaf spot or powdery mildew in wet seasons when diseases are prevalent. Rake and destroy infested leaves as they drop.

Companion Planting and Design

Use this as an accent plant with evergreens. The flowers, fruit, and fall color add life to evergreen screens and hedges. Add a few to the mixed border as part of the framework and for seasonal interest.

Try These

Several dwarf cultivars are available. 'Autumn Magic', 'Morton', and 'Viking' are about one-half to two-thirds the size of the straight species. All have good fall color. 'Viking' blooms a bit earlier and produces larger fruit that is great for attracting wildlife. The red chokeberry, *Aronia arbutifolia*, is a bit larger, growing 6 to 10 feet tall and 3 to 5 feet wide, than the black fruited, glossy chokeberry with the same seasonal appeal. Its cultivar 'Brilliantissima' produces an abundance of fruit, exceptional scarlet fall color, and almost waxy leaves.

Dogwood

Cornus species

Botanical Pronunciation
KOR-nus

Bloom Period and Seasonal Color
Spring to summer blooms in white, yellow, and pink; fall foliage in red, orange, and yellow

Mature Height × Spread
5 to 15 feet × 5 to 15 feet

Our native dogwoods are prominent members of our landscapes. They can be used in natural settings, informal landscapes, or formal gardens. The flower show may not compare with the flowering dogwood of the South, but our dogwoods make up for it by providing food and shelter for the birds and year-round interest in the landscape. Our native (redosier) dogwood, *Cornus sericea*, has bright red stems and can be found in natural areas and landscapes. Redosier dogwoods are spreading shrubs that tolerate moist to wet sites. Gray dogwoods, *Cornus racemosa*, are larger plants that can quickly form a dense colony. The gray bark, red tinged new growth, white fruit for the birds, and good fall color provide year-round interest.

When, Where, and How to Plant
Most prefer moist soil, and many tolerate wet sites. Grow in full sun with moist soil or shaded locations. Plant bare-root dogwoods in the spring before growth begins and container-grown plants throughout the season. Follow planting directions at the chapter introduction. Be sure to loosen girding roots and fill the planting hole with the existing soil and water well. Spacing varies with variety.

Growing Tips
Water new plants thoroughly and often enough to keep the rootball and surrounding soil moist but not wet. Thoroughly water established plants whenever the top 4 to 6 inches of soil feel crumbly and moist. Mulch to help conserve water and reduce weed problems. Wait a year to fertilize new plantings. Regular fertilization will encourage rapid growth on young shrubs. Established shrubs need minimal fertilization.

Regional Advice and Care
Prune established shrubs in late winter or early spring if needed. Remove old, diseased, or damaged canes on redtwig, gray, and variegated dogwoods at ground level. Color coded for pruning, the older stems of redosier turn brown. Renewal pruning helps stimulate new brightly colored stems. You can prune back overgrown shrubs by one-third. Stressed plants can suffer from scale insects and drought-induced cankers. Proper watering and regular pruning of the discolored, cankered stems will reduce these problems. Disinfect tools between cuts on diseased plants.

Companion Planting and Design
Use redtwig dogwood for bank stabilization, along streams, and in natural settings. Gray dogwood makes a great hedge and screen. Give it plenty of room to grow.

Try These
Cornus hesseyii 'Garden Glow' has brilliant lime green foliage, burgundy red fall color, and bright red stems. The beautiful flowering dogwood, *Cornus florida*, is native to southern Michigan. The plants are hardy but flower buds can be killed in a cold winter. Select a northern grown plant to increase your flowering success. Kousa dogwood, *Cornus kousa*, performs better. Rated hardy for Zone 5, a few gardeners grow it successfully in Zone 4 with flowers and fruit.

Elderberry

Sambucus species

Botanical Pronunciation
sam-BOO-kus

Other Name Elder

Bloom Period and Seasonal Color
June to July in white

Mature Height × Spread
5 to 20 feet × 5 to 20 feet

The purplish black berries of the native American elderberry have long been used for jelly, pies, and, of course, wine. You'll find these plants growing in moist soils along roadsides, streams, and ditches. Their tiny cream-colored flowers are in lacy clusters that adorn the plants in summer. Many of the newer, more ornamental, cultivars of European elderberry are equally adaptive, growing in sun to part shade and wet to dry soils. Most are hardy in Zones 4 and 5. The colorful foliage, fragrant flowers, and fruit make them a great addition to landscapes and containers. The flowers of elderberry attract butterflies and bees, adding color to the landscape. And leave some fruit on the plants to encourage birds to visit your landscape.

When, Where, and How to Plant
Grow elderberries in full sun to part shade. They will tolerate shaded locations, but flowering, fruiting, and foliage color may suffer. These adaptable plants prefer moist soil but will tolerate drier conditions once established. This makes them well suited to rain gardens. Plant container-grown plants throughout the growing season. Carefully remove the plant from the pot and loosen any girdling roots. Set the plant in a hole the same depth and at least twice as wide as the rootball. Backfill with existing soil and water thoroughly.

Growing Tips
Water new plantings thoroughly and often enough to keep the rootball and surrounding soil moist but not waterlogged. Once established, water thoroughly whenever the top 4 inches of soil are slightly moist and crumbly. Mulch the soil surrounding the plants with a 2- to 3-inch layer of shredded bark or woodchips. Wait a year to fertilize new plantings. Follow soil test recommendations or use a low-nitrogen slow-release fertilizer in spring according to label directions.

Regional Advice and Care
Elderberries are basically pest free. Allow plants to sucker and form dense thickets when naturalizing. Prune established plants to maintain a more refined growth habit. Occasionally remove older and larger stems to ground level on suckering plants. Reduce height by as much as one-third pruning back to a healthy bud or side branch.

Companion Planting and Design
Use these adaptable plants in rain gardens, moist areas, and natural plantings. Use these hardy plants in large containers. Select companion plants that complement the ornamental features of the elderberry you are growing. 'Black Lace' combines nicely with ornamental grasses, shrub roses, and butterfly bush.

Try These
Sambucus nigra 'Black Lace'™ has dark purple, nearly black, finely dissected leaves, pinkish flowers, and blackish red fruit. With a bit of pruning 'Black Lace' makes a hardy substitute for Japanese maple, which struggles to survive in most of our gardens. *Sambucus racemosa* 'Sutherland Gold' has golden yellow finely cut foliage, and has performed well at the University of Minnesota Landscape Arboretum.

Forsythia

Forsythia hybrids

Botanical Pronunciation
for-SITH-ee-ah

Bloom Period and Seasonal Color
Early spring blooms in yellow

Mature Height × Spread
1 to 10 feet × 4 to 10 feet

The bright yellow flowers of forsythia signal the start of spring. Unfortunately for northern gardeners, the floral display may not live up to the catalogue descriptions. Though the plant may be hardy and thriving in your garden, the flower buds are frequently killed in our winters. The common forsythia usually have great flowering after a mild winter or from the snow line down. Snow provides the perfect insulation protecting them from the cold winter temperatures. Fortunately, there are varieties with hardy flower buds that will flower in spring despite our cold winter temperatures. Select hardy types bred for reliable flowering and varieties that fit the available space in your landscape. Enjoy the bright yellow flowers in the garden or cut and added to your spring arrangements.

When, Where, and How to Plant
Plant bare-root forsythia in the spring before growth begins and, container-grown plants throughout the season. Forsythia prefers full sun and well-drained soil. They will tolerate a wide range of pH, as well as urban conditions. Follow planting directions in the chapter introduction. Space depends on the size and spread of the cultivar grown.

Growing Tips
Water established plants thoroughly whenever the top 4 to 6 inches are moist and crumbly. Mulch the soil to help conserve moisture and reduce weed problems. Wait a year to fertilize young plants according to soil test recommendations. Once established, shrubs need little, if any, fertilizer.

Regional Advice and Care
Prune established shrubs in the spring after flowering to preserve blooms and control size. Remove one-third of the older stems at ground level. You can then cut the remaining stems by one-third. Or cut all the stems back to several inches above ground level. Regrowth from severe pruning may be overly robust and require more pruning. Lack of flowers is the major problem on forsythia; this is caused by cold temperatures, poorly timed pruning, excess nitrogen, and too much shade. Avoid excess fertilization and grow in full sun for best results. Bring a bit of spring indoors by forcing a few forsythia branches. Select stems with lots of plump flower buds. Submerge the stems in water overnight. The next morning place the stems in fresh water and store at 60 to 70 degrees Fahrenheit until blooming starts in about two weeks.

Companion Planting and Design
Plant in shrub beds, add a few to the mixed border, or use as a bank cover in areas where the spring floral display can be enjoyed. It's a nice backdrop for early blooming tulip or daffodil varieties that complement yellow forsythia blooms.

Try These
Grow cultivars with hardy flowerbuds. 'Sunrise' grows 5 feet tall and wide and is hardy in Zone 4b. 'Meadowlark' grows up to 9 feet tall and is hardy throughout Michigan and has the added benefit of purplish fall color. 'Northern Gold' is 6 to 8 feet tall.

Fothergilla

Fothergilla gardenii

Botanical Pronunciation
fah-ther-GILL-ah gar-DEN-ee-eye

Other Name Dwarf fothergilla

Bloom Period and Seasonal Color
White flowers in April to May, blue-green leaves
become yellow to orange to scarlet in fall

Mature Height × Spread
2 to 3 feet × 2 to 3 feet

A cousin to our native witchhazel, fothergilla is much smaller with low, dense bushy
growth. Include fothergilla for multiple
seasons of interest in your landscape. The fragrant
white flowers usually appear before the leaves
emerge and look like small bottlebrushes. The dark
green to blue-green leaves look good all season and
turn yellow to orange to scarlet in fall. You'll get
the best flowers and fall color in full sun, but it still
performs well in partial shade. Native to southeastern United States, this plant is found in pine savan-
nas, and near ponds and boggy depressions. Use
this big impact, low-maintenance plant in shaded
areas, moist spaces, cottage gardens, mixed borders, or shrub beds. And the deer tend to leave this
plant alone.

When, Where, and How to Plant
Grow fothergilla in full sun to partly shaded location. Native to moist acidic soils, this plant does
best in moist acidic soil, though I have had good
luck growing it in well-drained alkaline soils. Plant
balled-and-burlapped plants soon after they are purchased. Remove any twine and cut away burlap on
balled-and-burlapped plants once they're set in the
hole. Plant container-grown fothergilla throughout
the growing season. Dig a hole as deep and twice as
wide as the rootball. Slide the plant out of the container and loosen any girdling roots. Set in the hole,
fill with existing soil, and water thoroughly.

Growing Tips
Water new plantings thoroughly and often enough
to keep the rootball and surrounding soil moist but

not wet. Once established, water thoroughly when
the top 4 to 6 inches of soil are crumbly and moist.
Mulch the soil with a 2- to 3-inch layer of shredded bark or woodchips. Wait a year to fertilize new
plantings. Established plants need minimal fertilization. Follow soil test recommendations or use
a low-nitrogen, slow-release fertilizer if a nutrient
boost is needed.

Regional Advice and Care
It's basically pest free, but this plant needs minimal pruning. Wait until the flowers fade but before
growth begins to do any pruning. Remove any dead
or damaged branches. Prune out crossed and rubbing branches. Make cuts just above a healthy bud
or where a branch joins another branch.

Companion Planting and Design
Place fothergilla in an area where you can enjoy
the fragrant flowers. Grow a few in front of
evergreens to create a backdrop that maximizes
the impact of the spring flowers and fall color.
Include fothergilla in foundation plantings and
natural and shade gardens. Use as a specimen or
as a hedge.

Try These
'Blue Mist' has blue-green leaves all season but less
spectacular fall color. *Fothergilla major* 'Mt. Airy'
is upright growing to 5 to 6 feet tall. It produces
lots of flowers and has consistently good fall color;
Fothergilla × intermedia 'Blue Shadow' grows 4 to
6 feet tall with powder blue leaves and outstanding
fall color.

Hydrangea

Hydrangea species

Botanical Pronunciation
hy-DRAIN-jah

Other Name Snowball bush

Bloom Period and Seasonal Color
Summer blooms in white

Mature Height × Spread
3 to 15 feet × 10 to 15 feet

Hydrangeas are among the few shrubs that can put on a dramatic floral display even in the shade. Cultivars of smooth hydrangeas, *Hydrangea arborescens*, often called snowball bush, are the most shade tolerant. They are covered with large white flowers that fade to beige. Leave them on the plants for added winter interest. Cultivars of panicle hydrangea, *Hydrangea paniculata* (shown), are larger, hardier and bloom later. Its large, white, cone-shaped flowers develop a hint of pink color as they pass their peak. The explosion of panicle hydrangea cultivars with unique flowers or size has increased the use of this plant in our landscapes. You can't make these white hydrangeas pink or blue without the use of floral dyes and paint.

When, Where, and How to Plant

Plant container-grown hydrangeas throughout the growing season. Less hardy species and cultivars should be planted in spring to increase winter survival. Grow these shrubs in partial shade for best results. They will tolerate full sun as long as the soil is kept moist. Hydrangeas tolerate a wide range of growing conditions but prefer moist, well-drained soil. Some hydrangeas do become ratty in drought conditions. Spacing depends on the type of hydrangea grown.

Growing Tips

Water thoroughly whenever the top 4 to 6 inches of soil feel crumbly and moist. Mulch the soil to help conserve moisture and reduce weed problems. Wait a year to fertilize new plantings. Some hydrangeas benefit from a light fertilization in the spring before growth begins. Use a low-nitrogen, slow-release

fertilizer like Milorganite to avoid overfertilization and improve flowering. Research found using Milorgante helps release some of the phosphorous (good for flowering) and potassium bound in the soil.

Regional Advice and Care

Prune snowball-type hydrangeas to 12 inches above ground level every spring. Panicle hydrangea requires very little pruning. Remove older stems to the ground or adjoining branches or cut them back above the bud to maintain the desired size and shape. Improve flowering by pruning them back to their woody framework annually. Lack of flowers is the biggest problem on the blue and pink flowering hydrangeas. These plants (*Hydrangea macrophylla*) typically bloom on old wood so when they die back or are pruned to the ground over winter, the plants fail to bloom. 'Endless Summer', 'Blushing Bride', and 'Twist'n Shout' bloom on both old and new wood. Keep soil moist and fertilize with Milorganite in spring to promote flowering. The big leaf hydrangea flowers are blue in acidic soil and pink in alkaline soils.

Companion Planting and Design

The panicle hydrangeas make a nice focal point or combine nicely with ornamental grasses and perennials. Use the smaller scale hydrangeas in shade garden, mixed borders, and foundation plantings.

Try These

Oakleaf hydrangea, *Hydrangea quercifolia*, is a four-season shade-tolerant hydrangea with orange exfoliating bark, creamy white flowers, and outstanding fall color. Hardy in Zone 5.

Juniper

Juniperus species

Botanical Pronunciation
joo-NIP-er-us

Other Name Red cedar

Bloom Period and Seasonal Color
Evergreen foliage

Mature Height × Spread
20 feet × 10 feet

Its wide variety of sizes, shapes, and foliage colors make juniper a valuable landscape plant. These tough evergreens can be used as windbreaks, groundcovers, screens, hedges, or rock garden plants. Use them alone as specimens or in groups for a mass display. There are hundreds of juniper species and cultivars available. They come in upright forms, spreading types, and low-growing ground huggers. Many junipers can spread to 20 feet wide. Save yourself a lot of work and frustration by selecting the juniper that fits the space available. Use the hardiest, most disease-resistant cultivars available. And don't forget to enjoy the fruit display. The blue, berry-like fruit add winter interest, feed the birds, and flavors gin (which explains its slightly "evergreen" aroma.)

When, Where, and How to Plant

Plant balled-and-burlapped plants as soon as possible after they are purchased and container-grown junipers spring through September. Planting by October 1 gives the plants time to put down roots before winter. Grow junipers in well-drained soil. They tolerate a variety of soil conditions from sandy to clay. These tough plants grow in urban areas, dry soil, and windy locations. Be sure to wear long sleeves and gloves when planting this prickly evergreen. Follow planting guidelines in the chapter introduction.

Growing Tips

Water thoroughly whenever the top 4 to 6 inches start to dry. Established plantings are drought tolerant. Increase overwintering success and decrease winter damage by mulching and watering junipers and other evergreens in the fall before the

ground freezes. Wait a year to fertilize new plantings according to soil test recommendations or use a low-nitrogen slow-release fertilizer. Once established, junipers need little, if any, fertilizer.

Regional Advice and Care

Reduce snow and ice damage on upright junipers by loosely tying the stems in fall. Prune junipers in the spring before growth begins or in midsummer during their semi-dormant period. Wear long sleeves and gloves. When properly sited and spaced, junipers need little pruning. You can top overgrown junipers and reshape, but it is not the best practice. Prune spreading and creeping junipers by selectively removing the longest branches. Cut these back to a side branch or main stem. Phomopsis blight is a fungal disease that causes tip dieback. Prune infected branches back to healthy side shoots with disinfected tools. Cedar rust is a common problem on red cedar, *Juniperus virginiana*. Rust won't kill the plant but looks bad when the galls sprout their slimy orange tendrils in spring. Juniper may experience some browning after extremely cold winters. Prune out the damaged foliage.

Companion Planting and Design

Use low growing junipers as groundcovers, trailers over walls, or *en masse* on a bank. Upright forms make nice backdrops, screens, and vertical accents in the mixed border.

Try These

Select the most disease resistant cultivar that is the size and form that best fits your landscape design.

Lilac

Syringa species and cultivars

Botanical Pronunciation
sih-RIN-gah

Other Name Syringa

Bloom Period and Seasonal Color
Spring blooms in white, blue, purple, pink, and magenta

Mature Height × Spread
4 to 15 feet × 4 to 15 feet

Add a lilac or two to your landscape and enjoy beautiful spring flowers, fragrance, and the butterflies and hummingbirds they attract. For those who don't like its aroma, less fragrant cultivars are available. That way everyone can enjoy a bouquet of freshly cut lilacs. There are hundreds of common lilacs, *Syringa vulgaris*, on the market. They grow up to 15 feet tall with white, blue, or purple flowers. The new repeat blooming 'Bloomerang®' is perfect for those of us that can't get enough lilac flowers and fragrance. This 4- to 5-feet-tall and wide plant produces fragrant blooms in spring, rests during the heat of the summer, then flowers again. Mine has performed well for several years in a container on my patio.

When, Where, and How to Plant
Plant balled-and-burlapped lilacs as soon as possible after they are purchased, and container-grown plants throughout the season. Grow lilacs in full sun and moist well-drained soil. Follow planting instructions at the beginning of this chapter. Spacing varies with species grown.

Growing Tips
Water thoroughly whenever the top 4 to 6 inches of soil are moist and crumbly. Mulch the soil to help conserve moisture and reduce weed problems. Wait a year to fertilize new plantings. Avoid high-nitrogen fertilizers that can prevent flowering. Established lilacs need little, if any, fertilizer.

Regional Advice and Care
Remove old flower heads to encourage good flowering the following season. Lilacs bloom on the previous season's growth. Prune established lilacs in spring after flowering so you won't interfere with next year's blooms. Remove one-third of the older canes to ground level. You can also prune remaining stems by one-third. Regular pruning will reduce pest problems and control plant growth, while improving the overall appearance. Powdery mildew is the most common disease. Grow lilacs in full sun with good air circulation to reduce this problem. Proper pruning allows air and light in, reducing mildew problems. Bacterial blight and scale insects are usually controlled with proper pruning. These pests attack older, stressed stems. Regular pruning removes the susceptible stems and infected growth.

Companion Planting and Design
Lilacs can be used as hedges, screens, or as a backdrop for other plantings. Add a few specimen plantings to the mixed border as a spring accent. Grafted tree forms of 'Miss Kim' give the look of a tree on a smaller scale. Use them in a formal garden, as an open screen, or near a patio.

Try These
Palabin lilac, *Syringa meyeri* 'Palabin', is a smaller plant, growing 4 to 5 feet tall and up to 7 feet wide. This easy-to-grow lilac is disease resistant. Miss Kim lilac, *Syringa patula* 'Miss Kim', grows up to 6 feet tall and 4 feet wide. It produces fragrant, icy-blue flowers and has purple fall color. It is disease resistant and hardy. 'Dappled Dawn' has cream-mottled leathery leaves and mauve flowers.

Ninebark

Physocarpus opulifolius

Botanical Pronunciation
fy-so-KAR-pus op-yew-lih-FOE-lee-us

Other Name Eastern ninebark

Bloom Period and Seasonal Color
Spring with white or pinkish flowers

Mature Height × Spread
5 to 10 feet × 5 to 10 feet

Ninebark is a big bold plant that offers a dramatic silhouette against the winter sky. Often overlooked for more ornamental shrubs; ninebark's drought tolerance, adaptability, and many of the new colorful cultivars, like 'Diablo', brought renewed interest to this group of plants. Many new and colorful cultivars have been added. The straight species has pinkish white flowers in spring. The fruit is an eye-catching angular dried capsule that starts out red, eventually turning brown. The stout peeling stems are attractive, though masked by the leaves in summer and tangled stems in winter. Regular pruning will help you get the most out of the winter show. This hardy native has been used for medicinal purposes by Native Americans and in our landscapes since 1879.

When, Where, and How to Plant
Ninebark is usually sold as a container-grown plant. It responds well to transplanting and can be planted throughout the season. Grow this adaptable plant in full sun to partial shade location. This plant has the adaptability and toughness of the spirea. It tolerates acid to alkaline soils as well as drought. Follow planting directions in the chapter introduction. Space them 5 to 6 feet apart.

Growing Tips
Water established plants when the top 4 to 6 inches of soil begin to dry. They are drought tolerant. Organic mulch will help conserve moisture and reduce weed problems. Wait a year to fertilize new plantings. Follow soil test recommendations or use

a low-nitrogen slow-release fertilizer. Established plants need little, if any, fertilizer.

Regional Advice and Care
Minimal care is needed for these tough plants. Regular pruning will improve their appearance. Prune a few of the old (larger) stems to the ground every year. The total height can be reduced by one-third. Older and overgrown plants can be pruned back to ground level but regrowth can be vigorous and need additional pruning the following year. Powdery mildew is a problem on 'Diablo' and a few other cultivars. Grow in full sun, avoid overhead irrigation, and properly prune to reduce this problem. I occasionally see borers. Remove infested stems as discovered and use regular pruning to manage this pest.

Companion Planting and Design
When looking for a purple-leafed plant, use a purple-leaf ninebark cultivar instead of the pest-ridden purple-leaf sand cherries and Newport plums. Use these with ornamental grasses and silver and chartreuse flowers and foliage. Include ninebark in natural plantings and in mixed borders or use as a hedge.

Try These
'Diablo' grows 8 to 10 feet, and retains its purple color throughout the season. 'Summer Wine' is 5 to 6 feet with purple leaves, and 'Little Devil' has smaller leaves and grows 3 to 4 feet tall and wide. 'Amber Jubilee' is 5 to 6 feet tall with orange, yellow, and gold leaves that turn red to purple in fall.

Potentilla

Potentilla fruticosa

Botanical Pronunciation
poe-ten-TIL-lah froo-ti-KOH-sa

Other Name Bush cinquefoil

Bloom Period and Seasonal Color
Summer blooms in yellow

Mature Height × Spread
1 to 4 feet × 4 feet

Potentilla's bright yellow blossoms add color to the summer landscape. Its color, dense growth habit, and pest-free nature make it a popular landscape plant. And just like with any tough plant, we gardeners push it beyond its limits. Proper cultivar and site selection and correct pruning will keep potentillas looking good in the landscape. Select the cultivar with the flower color and plant size that best suits the location. This is one of the few woody plants native throughout most of the Northern Hemisphere. You will find plants throughout the United States (including our area), and pretty much the rest of the Northern Hemisphere. The botanical name *Potentilla* is from the Latin word *potens* meaning "powerful." It refers to its medicinal properties.

When, Where, and How to Plant
Potentillas are usually sold as container-grown plants at nurseries and garden centers. Plant them anytime during the growing season. Grow potentillas in full sun and well-drained soil for best results. See the planting directions in the chapter introduction. Space plants 2½ to 3 feet apart.

Growing Tips
Water thoroughly whenever the top 4 to 6 inches of soil are crumbly and moist. Established potentillas can tolerate dry conditions. Mulch the soil to help conserve moisture and reduce weed problems. Wait a year to fertilize new plantings according to soil test recommendations or use a low-nitrogen slow-release fertilizer. Avoid high-nitrogen fertilizers that can prevent flowering and encourage floppy growth. Established shrubs need little, if any, fertilizer.

Regional Advice and Care
Potentilla needs regular pruning to remain attractive. Prune overgrown and floppy potentillas in late winter or early spring before growth begins. Cut the plants back halfway to the ground. Remove about one-third to one-half of the larger stems to ground level. Or prune all the stems back to just above ground level. This rejuvenation pruning can be done every second or third year as needed. Potentillas pruned this way are often more floppy.

Companion Planting and Design
These shrubs are used in a shrub border, for mass plantings, mixed with perennials, or as a low hedge. They combine nicely with other sun-loving, drought tolerant plants.

Try These
'Dakota Goldrush'™ grows 3 to 3½ feet with deep blue-green leaves. 'Dakota Sunspot'™ with bright green leaves grows 2½ to 3 feet; both are long blooming with yellow flowers. 'Goldfinger' has large, bright yellow flowers, dark green leaves, and grows 3 to 4 feet tall. The white flowers and smaller size of 'Frosty' make it a good addition to perennial and rock gardens. Or use it in front of shrub borders. A larger white cultivar is 'Abbotswood', with blue-green foliage and outstanding white flowers growing 3 feet tall. 'McKay's White', developed in Wisconsin, has more of a creamy white flower with yellow-green leaves. Red and pink varieties tend to fade to yellow in our hot summers.

Rhododendron

Rhododendron species

Botanical Pronunciation
roe-doe-DEN-dron

Other Name Azalea

Bloom Period and Seasonal Color
Spring blooms in all colors

Mature Height × Spread
5 feet × 3 to 5 feet

Rhododendrons like cool, moist, acidic soil and milder winters than we usually have. So why are so many of us trying to grow them? The large, beautiful, and often fragrant flowers cannot be duplicated by another spring flowering plant. Their unique beauty has driven gardeners to expend time and money amending the soil and providing winter protection. This interest has encouraged plant breeders to develop more northern-hardy cultivars. There are over 900 species of rhododendrons and many more cultivars. So is it a rhododendron or an azalea? There is no clear distinction between them. In general, rhododendrons are evergreen, have bell-shaped flowers with ten or more stamens. Azaleas are usually deciduous with funnel-form flowers and five stamens.

When, Where, and How to Plant
Plant balled-and-burlapped plants as soon as possible after purchasing. Plant container-grown plants in spring or early summer so they establish before winter. Grow rhododendrons in moist, acidic soil (though I have seen plants survive in alkaline clay). Rhododendrons prefer full sun in summer if the soil is kept moist. Avoid planting where the leaves will be subject to drying by winter wind and sun. An east-facing location works well. Add several inches organic matter to the top 12 inches of soil prior to planting to improve the drainage in heavy clay soil and the water-holding capacity of sandy soil. Alkaline soil may require adding granular sulfur or some other acidifying material prior to planting. See the chapter introduction for planting guidelines. Space them about 3 feet apart.

Growing Tips
Established rhododendrons prefer moist soil. Water thoroughly whenever the top few inches of soil are moist but crumbly. Mulch the soil with shredded leaves, evergreen needles, or other organic material to conserve moisture, improve the soil, and reduce weed problems. Wait a year to fertilize new plantings.

Regional Advice and Care
Rhododendrons require little pruning. Remove any winter damage and thin out overcrowded branches in the spring after flowering, or when they should have flowered. Winter injury is the biggest problem facing rhododendrons. Water them thoroughly in the fall before the ground freezes. Mulching insulates the roots. Young plants and those growing in exposed sites benefit from additional winter protection. Wrap them in burlap or surround with a hardware cloth cylinder filled with straw or evergreen boughs.

Companion Planting and Design
Rhododendrons are nice as a focal point in the spring garden or as an understory plant in woodland gardens.

Try These
The University of Minnesota developed 'Northern Lights' azaleas and the 'PJM' cultivar rhododendrons for hardiness. The 'Northern Lights' azaleas are hardy to Zone 3b. These compact plants grow up to 5 feet tall and have fragrant pink, orange, yellow, or white flowers. 'PJM' rhododendron is evergreen in our area. 'Roseum Elegans' rhododendron has rosy-lilac flowers that fade to pink.

Rose-of-Sharon

Hibiscus syriacus

Botanical Pronunciation
hi-BIS-kus seer-ee-AY-kus

Bloom Period and Seasonal Color
Summer to fall blooms in blue, lavender, and white

Mature Height × Spread
8 feet × 5 feet

Hardiness Zones Hardy to 5

Add some late season color and bring in the hummingbirds and butterflies with this traditional garden favorite. Rose-of-Sharon starts to brighten the landscape in summer long after most trees and shrubs have stopped flowering. Their beautiful hibiscus flowers continue into fall and are followed by brown fruit capsules that persist, adding some interest to the winter landscape. Many of the newer cultivars have larger and longer lasting flowers. This shrub has been enjoyed by American gardeners since colonial times and in England for two hundred years prior to that. Its former botannical name is *Althaea*. The plant was originally discovered in Syria and thought to be native to that country, thus the species name, *syriacus*. Later it was discovered that the plant had been introduced to Syria from China.

When, Where, and How to Plant
Plant container-grown plants in the spring or early summer to get them established before winter. Grow these plants in full sun to part shade. They tolerate a wide range of soil conditions but do best in moist, well-drained soil. Space plants 4 to 6 feet apart.

Growing Tips
Established plants perform best in moist soil. Water thoroughly whenever the top 4 to 6 inches of soil are crumbly and moist. Mulch the soil to help conserve water and reduce weed problems. Slower growing rose-of-Sharon plants tend to have a greater rate of winter survival. Wait a year or two to fertilize new plantings. Avoid excess fertilization and high-nitrogen fertilizers.

Regional Advice and Care
Prune established plants yearly to remove dead wood and increase flower size. Prune the main branches and shorten side shoots to two or three buds for an impressive flower display. Rose-of-Sharon can be severely damaged or killed in extremely cold winters. Rated hardy to Zone 5, I have seen gardeners grow this in Zone 4. New plantings are often slow to leaf out in the spring. Give them plenty of time to leaf out before declaring them dead and replacing them. Established plants seem to have a better chance of survival. Provide winter protection the first couple of years for increased success. Wrap with burlap or hardware cloth filled with evergreen boughs.

Companion Planting and Design
The late season bloom is this plant's greatest asset. Use it as a small specimen or in the shrub border where this feature can be enjoyed. It combines nicely with a wide variety of annuals and perennials. The old-fashioned feel of this plant looks nice against a stone house or mixed with other heirloom plants.

Try These
'Blue Bird' is a favorite of many gardeners but sometimes lacks vigor. It has 3-inch, sky blue flowers with red centers. 'Aphrodite' has dark pink flowers with a reddish purple throat; 'Minerva' has 4- to 5-inch-diameter lavender flowers that are tinged with pink; and 'Helene' has white flowers with reddish purple throats. These grow about 6 to 8 feet tall.

Shrub Rose

Rosa species and hybrids

Botanical Pronunciation
ROE-sah

Other Name Hardy rose

Bloom Period and Seasonal Color
Early summer blooms (some repeating throughout) in variety of colors

Mature Height × Spread
2 to 8 feet × 2 to 8 feet

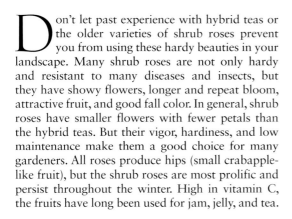

Don't let past experience with hybrid teas or the older varieties of shrub roses prevent you from using these hardy beauties in your landscape. Many shrub roses are not only hardy and resistant to many diseases and insects, but they have showy flowers, longer and repeat bloom, attractive fruit, and good fall color. In general, shrub roses have smaller flowers with fewer petals than the hybrid teas. But their vigor, hardiness, and low maintenance make them a good choice for many gardeners. All roses produce hips (small crabapple-like fruit), but the shrub roses are most prolific and persist throughout the winter. High in vitamin C, the fruits have long been used for jam, jelly, and tea.

When, Where, and How to Plant
Shrub roses are usually sold as container plants; however, small plants may be available bare root. Plant bare-root roses in the spring while they are still dormant. Container plants can be planted anytime the ground is not frozen. I prefer to plant in the spring and early summer, giving the rose time to get established before winter. These hardier roses are much more tolerant of late-season planting than the hybrid teas. Grow shrub roses in full sun and moist, well-drained soil. Their size and growth habit will help determine their suitability for use as climbers, hedges, specimens, borders, and for winter interest. Plant shrub roses so their crown, the place where roots meet stems, is even with the soil surface.

Growing Tips
Don't deadhead single-blooming shrub roses. Allow the fruit (rose hips) to develop and provide interest from summer through winter. Stop deadheading repeat bloomers in the late summer to allow their colorful fruit to develop.

Regional Advice and Care
Shrub roses require much less care and less pruning. Fertilize as needed in the spring after new growth has developed. Follow soil test recommendations or use a low-nitrogen slow-release fertilizer. Mulch the soil to conserve moisture and reduce weed problems. Remove dead and crowded stems in the spring before growth begins. Prune a few older stems back to ground level to control overall size and encourage new growth at the base of the plant. Shrub roses are generally resistant to insects and disease, and do not need winter protection. Japanese beetles, however, can be a problem. Select one that's hardy for your area.

Companion Planting and Design
Use shrub roses in perennial gardens, mixed borders or foundation plantings. Chicago Botanical Gardens used Russian sage (*Perovskia atriplicifolia*) with a lower growing, repeat blooming shrub roses for year-round appeal. Or try 'Black Lace' elderberry with Rainbow Knock Out®.

Try These
The 'Knock Out®' series was bred for low maintenance, pest resistance, and hardiness by Bill Radler of Wisconsin. 'The Fairy' has clusters of small pink flowers, and 'Starry Nights' white flowers brighten up the landscape.

Spirea

Spiraea species

Botanical Pronunciation
spy-REE-ah

Other Name Bridal wreath

Bloom Period and Seasonal Color
Spring or summer blooms in white, pink, and rose

Mature Height × Spread
2 to 8 feet × 2 to 8 feet

Spireas are adaptable, colorful plants that have been used extensively in the landscape. Many cultivars of the summer-blooming spireas are filling our landscapes. These shrubs require little maintenance and tolerate the stresses of urban landscapes. Let the plants stand for winter. The chestnut brown stems and dried seedheads can add to your winter landscape. Vanhoutte spirea, *Spiraea × vanhouttei*, is one of several species called bridal wreath spirea by gardeners. It is a large, arching shrub with long branches covered with white flowers in the spring. Snowmound spirea is a bit tidier in appearance and may be a good substitute for bridal wreath. It has similar white flowers in late May, dark blue-green leaves, a dense habit, and is only 3 to 5 feet tall and wide.

When, Where, and How to Plant
Plant balled-and-burlapped shrubs as soon as possible after they are purchased, and container-grown plants throughout the season. Spireas tolerate a wide range of soils, except for wet sites. Follow planting directions in the chapter introduction. Spacing varies with species grown.

Growing Tips
Most established spirea plants are drought tolerant. Water thoroughly whenever the top 4 to 6 inches feel slightly dry. Mulch to conserve moisture and reduce weed problems. Wait at least a year to fertilize new plantings. Follow soil test recommendations or use a low-nitrogen slow-release fertilizer. Spireas are fast growers and need minimal fertilizer when young and very little, if any, once they are established.

Regional Advice and Care
Spring-blooming spireas flower on the previous season's growth. Prune them just after flowering. Pruning at any other time will eliminate the flowers. Summer-blooming spireas flower on new growth. Prune in late winter before growth begins. Prune overgrown and floppy spireas back halfway to the ground. Remove about one-third to one-half of the older stems to ground level. Or prune all the stems back to ground level. This method is quick and easy, but the plants tend to be a bit more relaxed in their growth habit. Lightly shear summer-blooming spireas as the flowers fade to encourage a second and even third flush of flowers.

Companion Planting and Design
Bridal wreath spirea works well in heirloom landscapes and near older homes. Give it room to show off its natural form. All spireas can be used in mass plantings, as filler plants, and as bank cover. The smaller-scale spireas work nicely in rock gardens and the mixed border.

Try These
'Firegold' has growth habit and white flowers like bridal wreath but chartreuse foliage in summer. 'Golden Glitter' is compact with white flowers and yellow speckled foliage. 'Magic Carpet' spirea puts on a show with its foliage and flowers. The new growth is red maturing to gold and turning russet in fall. Pink flowers provide additional summer color. 'Neon Flash' has neon red flowers and bright green leaves that turn dark burgundy in fall.

Viburnum

Viburnum species

Botanical Pronunciation
vy-BURN-um

Other Name Cranberrybush viburnum

Bloom Period and Seasonal Color
Spring blooms in white

Mature Height × Spread
2 to 15 feet × 2 to 10 feet

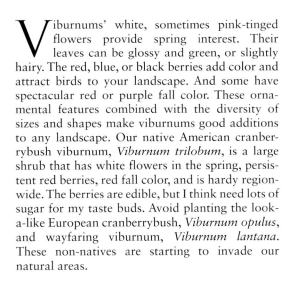

Viburnums' white, sometimes pink-tinged flowers provide spring interest. Their leaves can be glossy and green, or slightly hairy. The red, blue, or black berries add color and attract birds to your landscape. And some have spectacular red or purple fall color. These ornamental features combined with the diversity of sizes and shapes make viburnums good additions to any landscape. Our native American cranberrybush viburnum, *Viburnum trilobum*, is a large shrub that has white flowers in the spring, persistent red berries, red fall color, and is hardy region-wide. The berries are edible, but I think need lots of sugar for my taste buds. Avoid planting the look-a-like European cranberrybush, *Viburnum opulus*, and wayfaring viburnum, *Viburnum lantana*. These non-natives are starting to invade our natural areas.

When, Where, and How to Plant
Plant tender viburnums in spring or early summer to give them time to get established before winter. Viburnum species vary slightly in their light and soil requirements. Most tolerate full sun to partial shade. They prefer moist soil, but some species are drought tolerant. See the chapter introduction for planting information. Spacing varies with the species.

Growing Tips
Established viburnum species that require moist soil should be watered during dry periods. Water thoroughly whenever the top 4 to 6 inches are moist but crumbly. Mulch the soil to conserve moisture and reduce weed problems. Wait a year to fertilize new plantings. Established shrubs need little, if any, fertilizer.

Regional Advice and Care
Slow-growing viburnums need little pruning. Remove dead, damaged, and unwanted branches back to an adjoining branch or main stem. For fast-growing suckering types, prune out old wood to ground level in the spring after flowering. You can prune the remaining stems by one-third. Viburnum borers are the most deadly pest, killing viburnum stems. Regular pruning and proper care will reduce the risk. Prune out and destroy infected stems as soon as they are discovered.

Companion Planting and Design
Use viburnums as screens, hedges, backdrops, specimen plants, and wildlife plants. Most work well in formal, informal, or natural settings.

Try These
'Spice Island™' and 'Sugar 'n' Spice™' are compact heavy flowering cultivars of the fragrant Koreanspice viburnum. Our native arrowwood viburnum, *Viburnum dentatum*, has white spring flowers, blue fruit the birds love, and excellent fall color. It is resistant to viburnum borers. 'Emerald Triumph' was developed by the University of Minnesota and selected for its hardiness and pest resistance. 'Blue Muffin' was selected for its abundance of blue fruit and Red Feather® has new red foliage that turns red as it matures and a maroon fall color; it's rated hardy in Zone 3.

Weigela

Weigela florida

Botanical Pronunciation
wy-JEE-lah FLOOR-ih-dah

Bloom Period and Seasonal Color
Spring through summer blooms in pink, red, white, and purplish red

Mature Height × Spread
Up to 6 feet × 9 to 12 feet

Bring in the birds, butterflies, and hummingbirds with this traditional garden favorite. The large arching growth habit makes it a perfect fit in heirloom landscapes, natural plantings, and wildlife gardens. The many new cultivars have colorful foliage, intense flowers, and more compact growth habit, expanding their use in both small and large landscapes. Weigela flowers in spring and sporadically throughout the summer and into fall. I have even found a few stray weigela blossoms in November. You may see hummingbirds nectaring on the flowers and other birds feeding on the seeds. The leaves can be green, bronze, or variegated, adding to the shrubs summer appeal. The dried seed capsules may look messy to some, but they do add a bit of winter interest.

When, Where, and How to Plant
Plant bare-root weigela in the spring before growth begins, and container-grown plants throughout the season. Planting in the spring or early summer gives the plants time to get established before winter. Grow weigela in full sun with well-drained soil. Good drainage is key to good performance and survival. Follow planting instructions in the chapter introduction. Space plants 3 to 4 feet apart.

Growing Tips
Water established plants thoroughly whenever the top 4 to 6 inches of soil are starting to dry. Older weigelas tend to be drought hardy. Mulch the soil to help conserve moisture and reduce weed problems. Wait a year before fertilizing new plantings. Follow soil test recommendations or use a low-nitrogen slow-release fertilizer. Established shrubs need little, if any, fertilizer.

Regional Advice and Care
Young weigelas need very little pruning. Remove any dead wood as it is discovered. Prune established shrubs in early summer after the first flush of flowers. Reduce the overall shrub size by cutting back long flowering stems to older upright growth. Remove several older stems to ground level each season. You can prune overgrown weigela back to ground level. Weigelas frequently suffer winter injury, especially those in poorly drained soils. Extensive damage will require major pruning. The plants will survive, but you will lose the first and largest flush of flowers.

Companion Planting and Design
Weigela works best when used for massing, in the shrub border, or combined with other plants. The small size and dark burgundy foliage of 'Midnight Wine' fits in my small yard and combines nicely with annuals, perennials, and my dwarf conifer garden.

Try These
'Wine and Roses' has burgundy foliage and pink flowers on a 4- to 5-foot plant. 'Pink Poppet' produces pale pink blooms on a 2-foot-tall plant. 'Dark Horse' has bronze leaves with lime green venation that make an eyecatching backdrop for its magenta pink flowers. 'My Monet' series has attractive variegated foliage on 18- to 24-inch plants. 'Carnaval' has white, pink, and red flowers on 3- to 5-foot plants.

Winterberry

Ilex verticillata

Botanical Pronunciation
EYE-leks ver-tih-sih-LAY-tah

Other Name Michigan holly

Bloom Period and Seasonal Color
Brilliant red berry-like fruit that ripen in fall and persist into winter

Mature Height × Spread
6 to10 feet × 6 to 10 feet

Add bright red berries to the winter landscape and bring in the birds with this deciduous holly. Hardy throughout our region, this native holly provides nectar for the bees as well as food and habitat for the birds. Combine Michigan holly with dwarf conifers, ornamental grasses and perennials to create a beautiful garden. Use these adaptable plants in damp areas where other plants have failed. You'll need one male for every five females for pollination and fruit set. (Many nurseries include both in the same pot, which is great until one of the plants dies.) Cut a few stems to enjoy in indoor arrangements and outdoor containers.

When, Where, and How to Plant
Grow winterberry in full sun to light shade for the best fruit display. Plants will tolerate partial shade and damp soils. These, like most hollies, prefer moist organic soils. Add organic matter to the planting bed, not just the planting hole, to create better growing conditions. I have seen winterberry growing successfully in alkaline (high pH) soils even though they prefer acidic conditions, but the leaves may turn pale green or yellow and plants struggle if pushed beyond their limits into very alkaline soil. Use an acidifying fertilizer or plant in a container or move it to more suitable location. Plant balled-and-burlapped plants as soon as possible after purchase and container-grown plants throughout the growing season. Follow planting directions in the chapter introduction. Space plants 3 to 4 feet apart.

Growing Tips
Water new plantings thoroughly and often enough to keep the rootball and surrounding soil moist. Once established, continue to water thoroughly whenever the top few inches of soil are crumbly but still moist. Mulch the soil surface with shredded leaves, evergreen needles, shredded bark, or woodchips. This keeps the soil moist and helps suppress weeds. Wait a year before fertilizing new plantings. Follow soil test recommendations or use a low-nitrogen slow-release fertilizer in early spring. Established plants need little if any fertilizer.

Regional Advice and Care
Winterberry need minimal pruning. Remove any damaged, dead, or rubbing branches. This plant is low maintenance when grown in the right conditions. Fruit may drop during drought.

Companion Planting and Design
Locate these moisture lovers in damp areas and near waterways and ponds. Include some in natural spaces, wildlife gardens and mixed borders. Back winterberry with evergreens or ornamental grasses for great impact.

Try These
'Red Sprite' grows 3 to 5 feet tall with bright red berries. Winter Red® produces lots of fruit that maintain their color throughout the winter and keep for months indoors if not placed in water. 'Berry Nice' drops its leaves early in fall to better expose the vivid red fruit suitable for cutting. 'Jim Dandy' is a suitable pollinator for most northern winterberry cultivars.

Witchhazel

Hamamelis virginiana

Botanical Pronunciation
ham-ah-MAY-lis ver-jin-ee-AH-nah

Other Name Common witchhazel

Bloom Period and Seasonal Color
Fall blooms in yellow

Mature Height × Spread
10 to 15 feet × 10 to 15 feet

Look for this native plant growing in shaded areas along the banks of streams in our forests. In the landscape, it can tolerate a wider range of conditions. Its fragrant, yellow flowers are the last of the season. They open in mid-October or November as the leaves turn yellow and drop from the plant. Witchhazel fruits are dried capsules that form in November or December and persist for a year. The seeds ripen in twelve months and are literally shot out of the capsule. It is fun to listen to this unique seed-dispersal technique. Witchhazel also has an interesting and useful history. Divining rods made out of witchhazel are used to locate water. The witchhazel extract my grandma used to cure everything is still available.

When, Where, and How to Plant
Plant balled-and-burlapped shrubs as soon as possible after purchasing. You can plant container-grown plants throughout the season. I prefer getting them in the ground in spring or early summer so they establish before winter. Witchhazel grows well in sun or shade and performs best in moist soil, though it will tolerate some extremes. Avoid growing witchhazel in very alkaline soil. Dig a hole the same depth, but at least twice as wide, as the rootball. Cut away the burlap and twine once the shrub is set in place. For container-grown plants, remove the shrub from its container so the crown (where the stem meets the roots) will be even with the soil surface. Fill the hole with existing soil and water. Space at least 5 to 6 feet apart.

Growing Tips
Water established plants thoroughly whenever the top 4 to 6 inches of soil are crumbly but moist. Mulch to help conserve moisture and reduce weed problems. Wait at least a year before fertilizing new plantings. Follow soil test recommendations or use a low-nitrogen slow-release fertilizer. Avoid high-nitrogen fertilizers that may inhibit flowering. Witchhazel leaves may yellow in alkaline soil. Use acidifying fertilizers, such as ammonium sulfate, to minimize the problem. Established shrubs need little, if any, fertilizer.

Regional Advice and Care
Keep pruning to a minimum. They are slow growing and respond slowly to pruning. Remove dead, damaged, or wayward branches in the spring. Prune them back to young healthy growth. Extensive feeding by rabbits will kill the plant. Fencing is the most effective way to protect these plants.

Companion Planting and Design
This large shrub is excellent for naturalizing large areas. It can also be included in shrub borders or near large buildings. I have seen it pruned up into a small tree and used in more formal settings. Place the plant where its fall color and fall flowers can be enjoyed.

Try These
Vernal witchhazel, *Hamamelis vernalis* (shown), blooms in late winter instead of fall. The flowers are yellow to red, appear in late February or March.

Yew

Taxus species

Botanical Pronunciation
TAKS-us

Bloom Period and Seasonal Color
Evergreen foliage

Mature Height × Spread
20 feet × 10 feet

Evergreen yews can be found in most Midwest landscapes. Canadian yew, *Taxus canadensis*, is native and hardy but is not well suited to most landscape situations. But the wide variety of shapes and sizes available, along with the yew's ability to grow in sun or shade, make the cultivated yew adaptable to many landscape situations. The soft, dark green needles add texture to the landscape while the red fruit and bark provide additional interest. They're pretty to look at, but don't eat. The red fruit consists of a single seed covered by a fleshy red cup. It has a sweet but unpleasant taste that usually makes curious children spit it out. The red portion is not toxic, but the seeds, bark, and foliage are.

When, Where, and How to Plant
Yews transplant best as balled-and-burlapped plants and should be planted as soon as possible after purchasing. Some nurseries and garden centers dig yews and place them in pots for easy handling. Others sell container-grown yews. Plant evergreens by October 1 to give them time to get established before winter. Avoid areas with drying winter winds to minimize the risk of winter burn. Good drainage is essential; plants grown in poorly drained soils will eventually die. See the chapter introduction for planting tips. Spacing varies with type.

Growing Tips
Water thoroughly whenever the top 4 to 6 inches of soil are moist and crumbly. Be sure to water all evergreen plantings thoroughly in the fall before the ground freezes. Mulch the soil to help conserve moisture, insulate the roots, and reduce weed problems. Wait at least a year to fertilize new plantings. Established yews need little, if any, fertilizer.

Regional Advice and Care
Yews are traditionally sheared into hedges, rectangles, and gumdrops but are quite attractive and healthier when grown in their natural form. They also require very little pruning if the right-sized plant is selected for the location. Prune yews, if needed, in the spring before growth begins, or lightly in midsummer when they are semi-dormant. Maintain the yew's natural form by pruning branches back to a healthy bud, where the branch joins another branch, or back to the main trunk. Yews will also tolerate severe pruning, but be patient—it takes time for the plants to recover. Prune out any browning caused by winter damage or disease.

Companion Planting and Design
Yews are used as foundation plants, screens, and hedges. Combine yews with deciduous shrubs like chokeberry, serviceberry, and dogwoods for added beauty. The dark green foliage is a nice backdrop for perennial and annual flower gardens.

Try These
Emerald Spreader® Japanese yew has dark green needles in an unique arrangement and grows 30 inches tall and spreads to 8 to 10 feet. There are hundreds of cultivars of yews on the market. Look for the cultivar with the best size and shape for your landscape.

TREES
FOR MICHIGAN

Magnolia underplanted with *Paeonia liliiflora*.

Add year-round structure and beauty to your landscape with trees. Select the right tree for the growing conditions, available space, desired function, and your landscape design for decades of beauty and enjoyment.

Step One

Locate the planting site and call 811, a *free* utility locating service, at least three business days prior to planting. They will mark the location of any underground utility in the planting area. Digging into a utility line can be an expensive, even deadly, decision.

Purchase your trees from a quality nursery or garden center. Trees may be available bare-root, balled-and-burlapped, and most often as container grown. Choose a tree with a straight trunk, good structure, and no signs of insect or disease problems. Smaller trees are easier to handle and recover more quickly from transplanting.

Give your tree a safe ride home. Cover the top of the tree to prevent wind damage and cover the roots of bare-root trees to prevent drying. Use a towel to wrap the trunk where it will rest on the vehicle. And always move the tree by the rootball, *not* the trunk, to prevent damage. Or have the tree delivered to make sure your investment arrives home safely.

Tree Planting Tips

Plant the tree with the root flare (the bell-shaped area where the roots angle away from the trunk) at or slightly above the soil line. Dig a shallow planting hole the same depth as and three to five times wider than the root system. Roughen the sides of the planting hole to make it easier for the roots to enter the surrounding soil. Remove container-grown plants from the pot. Loosen or slice potbound and girdling roots. Remove the tags, twine, and metal baskets and cut away the burlap on balled-and-burlapped trees.

Fill the hole with existing soil. Do not amend the backfill. The tree roots need to adjust to their new environment, and amended soils encourage roots to stay in the planting hole instead of moving out into the landscape. Water and mulch. Only stake trees with large canopies and a small root system, those exposed to high winds, or bare-root plants. Use a soft strap rather than wire around the tree trunk and secure the stakes in undisturbed soil. Remove the stakes one or two years after planting. (See the planting diagram on page 224.)

Only remove broken and damaged branches at planting time. Prune young established trees to create a strong framework, keeping the plant's growth habit in mind. Start by removing crossed, rubbing, and parallel branches. Select branches with wide crotch angles, the angle between the trunk and branch, to form the framework. Create a framework of branches that spiral upward around one trunk. Prune out competing central leaders. Do not apply pruning paint.

Water the area near the trunk to beyond the planting hole. Thoroughly moisten the top 12 inches often enough to keep the rootball and surrounding soil moist but not wet.

Mulch the soil to conserve moisture, reduce competition from grass, and prevent weeds. It also keeps the tree-damaging mowers and weed whip away from the tree trunk. Apply a 3-inch layer of woodchips or shredded bark on the soil surface at least a couple of inches away from the tree trunk.

Wait a year to fertilizer new planting. Use the amount recommended by soil test results or a low-nitrogen slow-release fertilizer in spring. Established trees do not need routine fertilization. They usually get plenty of nutrients from the fertilizers applied to surrounding lawns and gardens. Overfertilization can reduce flowering, increase risk of certain diseases and insects, damage tree roots, and actually reduce the plant's health and vigor. Proper watering and mulching is the best care you can give your plants.

In Case of Problems

Despite your best efforts, problems may arise. Contact the local University Extension Office or a certified arborist (tree care professional). Visit www. treesaregood.com to find an International Society of Arboriculture certified arborists in your area.

Trees add a restful feel to many landscape settings.

Beech

Fagus species

Botanical Pronunciation
FAY-gus

Bloom Period and Seasonal Color
Golden bronze foliage in fall

Mature Height × Spread
50 or more feet × 35 or more feet

The beech tree is one of the majestic trees of the woods and landscape. These slow-growing trees carefully build a strong framework that lasts for many years. The smooth gray bark provides beauty and interest in all four seasons. Watch with great anticipation as the bronze leaves unfurl in the spring. Soon, they turn green for the summer and develop a rich brown hue in the fall. Some of the leaves persist on the tree through the winter to provide sound, color, and movement. The fruit on mature beeches is quickly devoured by a variety of birds. The word *beech* refers to the ancient practice of using beech wood for writing boards. Unfortunately, lovers and graffiti artists have continued the practice on these trees.

When, Where, and How to Plant

Plant young trees in early spring. European beeches adapt better to transplanting and are more readily available. Beeches must have moist, well-drained soil and grow best in full sun but tolerate partial shade. The European beech tends to be a little more tolerant of varied and urban conditions. Locate the tree's root flare. Dig a shallow planting hole the same depth as, and three to five times wider than, the root system. Plant the tree with the root flare at or slightly above the soil line. Remove the container, twine, and metal baskets. Cut away the burlap and fill the hole with existing soil. Water to settle the soil, then mulch.

Growing Tips

Water thoroughly whenever the top 4 to 6 inches are crumbly and moist. Mulch the soil under these

trees to conserve moisture, reduce weeds, and protect the shallow roots. Wait a year to fertilize new plantings. Be patient as it may take a couple years for the trees to get growing.

Regional Advice and Care

If planted in the proper location, beech trees are low maintenance and have no real problems, but remember this is a slow growing plant. Prune young trees to establish a framework.

Companion Planting and Design

Use American beeches as specimen plants or for naturalizing. The European beech also makes a nice specimen plant. It can be trimmed into a hedge, although it is difficult for many gardeners, including me, to severely prune such a lovely, sometimes hard-to-find, and expensive tree. Both the American and European beech trees will eventually grow into large shade trees. The beech tree is shallow rooted, making it nearly impossible to grow grass beneath its canopy. So give up the losing battle and mulch the area under the tree. Or, better yet, leave the beech branched to the ground. This is an attractive way to grow this large tree.

Try These

The American beech, *Fagus grandifolia*, is native to parts of our area. Consider these European beech cultivars: 'Purpurea' ('Atropunicea'), the most common of the purple-leaf cultivars, and 'Roseomarginata' ('Purpurea Tricolor') with purple, pinkish white, and rose-colored leaves.

Birch

Betula species

Botanical Pronunciation
BET-choo-lah

Other Name Paper birch

Bloom Period and Seasonal Color
Early spring not significant; yellow fall color

Mature Height × Spread
40 to 50 feet × 20 to 25 feet

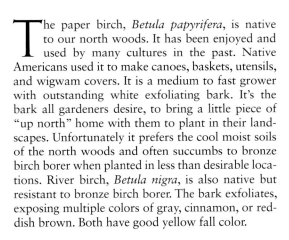

The paper birch, *Betula papyrifera*, is native to our north woods. It has been enjoyed and used by many cultures in the past. Native Americans used it to make canoes, baskets, utensils, and wigwam covers. It is a medium to fast grower with outstanding white exfoliating bark. It's the bark all gardeners desire, to bring a little piece of "up north" home with them to plant in their landscapes. Unfortunately it prefers the cool moist soils of the north woods and often succumbs to bronze birch borer when planted in less than desirable locations. River birch, *Betula nigra*, is also native but resistant to bronze birch borer. The bark exfoliates, exposing multiple colors of gray, cinnamon, or reddish brown. Both have good yellow fall color.

When, Where, and How to Plant
Plant birch trees in the spring so this slow-to-establish plant has time to root before winter. Grow birches in full sun to partial shade with moist, well-drained soil. This is especially critical for hot dry locations such as urban settings and warmer parts of our region. Follow the planting directions in the chapter introduction.

Growing Tips
Birches need cool, moist soil. Mulch or plant groundcovers under the trees to create this environment. Water trees thoroughly whenever the top few inches are moist and crumbly. Wait a year to fertilize new plantings. Fertilizer is often included with insecticides used to treat leafminer and borer. Check labels before adding more nutrients. River birch prefers a slightly acidic soil. Use fertilizers like ammonium sulfate or Milorganite that don't increase the soil pH.

Regional Advice and Care
Leafminers feed between the upper and lower leaf surface, causing the leaves to brown. Treat leafminer to reduce plant stress and borer problems. And this is a favorite of Japanese beetles. Treat these to minimize the stress and risk of borers. Bronze birch borer is the biggest killer of white birch. Plant species resistant to this pest or minimize plant stress to prevent problems. Consult a certified tree care professional for effective control. Birch trees will "bleed" when pruned in the spring. It won't hurt the plant; it just makes for a messy job.

Companion Planting and Design
Birches prefer woodland-type settings. Plant them *en masse* to create a northern woodland in your backyard or include birches in planting beds. Plant the tree where you can enjoy the attractive bark year-round. Place it in front of an evergreen for an even better show. Keep the roots cool and moist by growing perennial groundcovers or low-growing shrubs under your birches. Use river birch in groves or planted near water features.

Try These
'Prairie Dream' and 'Renaissance Reflection' paper birches have white bark, yellow fall color, and resist the bronze birch borer. 'Dura Heat®' river birch has all the beauty and more heat tolerance. 'Little King' is a compact river birch growing 10 feet tall after twenty years.

Blackgum

Nyssa sylvatica

Botanical Pronunciation
NISS-uh sill-VAT-ih-kuh

Other Name Sour gum

Bloom Period and Seasonal Color
Yellow to orange to scarlet to purple fall color

Mature Height × Spread
30 to 50 feet × 20 to 30 feet

Hardiness Zones 4 and 5

This underutilized shade tree deserves a place in more landscapes. Add this to your wish list if the soils in your area are moist and acidic. The blackgum's fall color is its most striking attribute. The glossy green summer leaves consistently turn bright yellow, orange, red, or purple. The small, greenish yellow spring flowers are missed by most gardeners but not the bees, which enjoy the nectar. Trees may produce a small or large crop of ½-inch blue-black fruit in late summer. The fruit is edible but quite sour. The birds and other wildlife don't seem to mind as they clean the fruit off the tree. As the leaves drop, they reveal a furrowed bark that adds interest to the winter landscape.

When, Where, and How to Plant

Blackgum is a slow grower, but give it room to reach its mature size and show off its beauty. In nature it can be found growing in upland dry-lands and swampy woods. But in the landscape it is more particular. Grow blackgum in full sun to light shade for the best fall color. Make sure it has moist, well-drained acidic soil and is sheltered from the wind. Purchase and plant young trees in spring to increase transplant success. Trees are sold balled-and-burlapped and container-grown. See the planting instructions at the beginning of this chapter.

Growing Tips

Water trees thoroughly whenever the top 4 inches of soil are crumbly and moist. Mulch the soil surrounding the trees with a 3-inch layer of shredded bark or woodchips. This helps conserve moisture, keep roots cool and moist, suppress weeds, and improves soil as it decomposes. Chlorosis (yellowing leaves, plant decline and eventual death) is a problem when these acid lovers are grown on very alkaline (high pH) soils.

Regional Advice and Care

Blackgum is native to central and southern parts of Michigan's lower peninsula. Several sources list blackgum as hardy in zone 3. I'm a bit skeptical so I recommend those gardening in northern parts of Zone 4 to proceed cautiously. Talk to your local nursery or garden center to see if they can help. Local nature centers may also have a list of growers that specialize in native plants.

Companion Planting and Design

Blackgum is an alternative to many of the invasive trees that overpopulate our landscapes. Grow this tree where its year-round beauty can be enjoyed. Use as a specimen plant or part of a naturalized or wildlife garden.

Try These

The leaves on the new shoots of 'Wildfire' are reddish purple to bronze-red and persist into summer. Red Rage® has glossy, dark green leaves and bright red fall color.

Crabapple

Malus hybrids

Botanical Pronunciation
MAY-lus

Other Name Flowering crab

Bloom Period and Seasonal Color
Spring blooms in white, pink, and red

Mature Height × Spread
40 to 60 feet × 20 to 40 feet

Stop! Don't turn the page! If you have an old crabapple tree, you may be wondering whatever possessed me to recommend this plant. Many of you may have suffered through the mess of summer leaf drop and fallen fruit. Fortunately, there are many new disease-resistant crabapples with small, persistent fruit, eliminating the litter problem. Select crabapples for their year-round features. The colorful white, pink, or red flowers provide several weeks of beauty in the spring. The fruit, however, will give you months of enjoyment and bring in the birds. Look for persistent fruit in many shades of yellow, orange, and red. The trees can be small and mounded, spreading, weeping, or upright. There are hundreds of crabapples in cultivation from which to choose.

When, Where, and How to Plant
Crabapples respond best to spring planting. Grow crabapples in full sun with moist, well-drained soil. See the chapter introduction for planting directions.

Growing Tips
Water established plants thoroughly whenever the top 4 to 6 inches of soil are moist and crumbly. Wait a year before fertilizing new plantings. Follow soil test recommendations or use a low-nitrogen slow-release fertilizer. Avoid excess fertilization, which can encourage disease problems and eliminate flowering and fruit.

Regional Advice and Care
Prune only to establish and maintain the tree's structural framework. Excessive pruning will encourage water sprouts. Prune crabapple trees in late winter for quick wound closure that reduces the risk of disease. Select disease-resistant cultivars to avoid major problems. Fireblight is a bacterial disease that can eventually kill the tree. Prune out infected branches 12 inches beneath the canker (sunken area) to control the disease. Disinfect tools with alcohol or with a bleach-and-water solution between cuts. Apple scab causes leaf spotting and dropping. Rake and destroy fallen leaves to reduce the source of infection. Several applications of a fungicide in early spring will help control this disease. Unfortunately, even some scab-resistant cultivars are showing signs of disease. Talk to your University Extension agent for the most current recommendations. Crabapples are a favorite food for tent caterpillars. Physically remove the caterpillar-filled tent to control this pest.

Companion Planting and Design
Use them as specimen plants or in small groupings. The weeping cultivars complement water features, and the spreading types blend well in Japanese gardens. Include some of the smaller types in your perennial gardens. They can provide structure and year-round interest in large flower gardens.

Try These
'Louisa' is a small scale, weeping form that fits into small yards, accents patios, and serves as a focal point for a mixed border. 'Firebird'® is a cultivar of Sergeant crabapple with fragrant snow-white flowers and small, red persistent fruit. 'Dolgo' has fragrant white flowers and large fruit suitable for making jelly.

Douglasfir

Pseudotsuga menziesii

Botanical Pronunciation
soo-doe-SOO-gah men-ZEEZ-ee-eye

Bloom Period and Seasonal Color
Evergreen foliage

Mature Height × Spread
70 feet × 20 feet

Douglasfir's majestic appearance is striking. Its green to bluish green needles have a camphor aroma when crushed. It grows at a medium rate, adding 12 to 15 feet over a ten-year period. Like the Colorado blue spruce, this tree will outgrow most small city lots if it's not properly placed. You will then face the tough decision of cutting down the overgrown tree, limbing it up and ruining its appearance, or crawling under it to get to your front door. Douglasfir is native to the Rocky Mountains and the Pacific Coast. Plants from the Rocky Mountains tend to be shorter, tougher plants that do not live as long as those on the coast. They are, however, the best choice for our area.

When, Where, and How to Plant

Plant balled-and-burlapped Douglasfir as soon as possible after it is purchased. They recover and adapt quicker from transplanting than container-grown plants. You can plant container-grown trees throughout the growing season. Plant evergreens before October 1 for best results. Grow these evergreens in full sun with moist, well-drained soil. Douglasfir will not tolerate high winds or dry, rocky soil. Plant the tree with its root flare at or slightly above the soil line. Dig a shallow planting hole at the same depth as, and three to five times wider than, the root system. Place the tree in the planting hole. Remove the container, twine, and metal baskets. Cut away the burlap. Remove the pot and loosen girdling roots on container-grown plants. Set in place. Fill the hole with existing soil, water, then mulch.

Growing Tips

Douglasfir needs very little care if it's planted in the proper location. Water established plants during periods of drought. Water the whole area under the tree thoroughly, wetting the top 12 inches of the soil whenever the top 4 to 6 inches are moist and crumbly. Mulching will also help keep the roots cool and moist. Wait a year before fertilizing new plantings. Follow soil test recommendations or use a slow-release low-nitrogen fertilizer. Evaluate tree health before fertilizing established plantings.

Regional Advice and Care

A variety of insects and diseases can attack. Proper watering and mulching will keep Douglasfirs healthy and better able to tolerate pest problems. Contact a certified arborist or your local University Extension Service when arise.

Companion Planting and Design

Consider using this tree where a large vertical accent is needed. Don't use these trees as windbreaks. Take advantage of their form and stature by planting them as a specimen tree or en masse. Give Douglasfir plenty of room to grow and show off its beauty.

Try These

Pseudotsuga menziesii glauca has reliably blue-green needles. It is more compact than the species. 'Fastigiata' is a narrow, upright form. Several dwarf variteties are available for use in smaller landscapes or dwarf conifer gardens.

Elm

Ulmus species and hybrids

Botanical Pronunciation
UL-mus

Bloom Period and Seasonal Color
Many with yellow fall color

Mature Height × Spread
30 to 80 feet × 40 feet

D o you remember the beautiful elm-lined streets of the 1950s and early 1960s? Maybe you only saw the pictures. But the overuse of this tree followed by the advent of Dutch Elm Disease (DED) changed the urban forest and our memories forever. In the 1960s, the air was filled with the sound of dropping elms. The remaining American elms are still subject to an early death from this disease. Look for DED-resistant elms when adding them to your landscape. 'Princeton' is an American elm with the typical habit, large leathery leaves, is resistant to bark beetle, and has good resistance to DED. Triumph™ hybrid elm has good DED, disease and insect resistance, and yellow fall color.

When, Where, and How to Plant

Elms adapt well to transplanting. Plant balled-and-burlapped trees as soon as possible after purchasing. Plant container-grown plants throughout the growing season. Grow elms in full sun with moist soil, but many will tolerate wet soil and even temporary flooding. Follow planting directions in the chapter introduction. Water new plantings enough to keep the soil around the tree and beyond the planting hole moist.

Growing Tips

Water established trees thoroughly when the top 4 to 6 inches of soil are moist and crumbly. Mulch the soil around the tree with a 2- to 3-inch layer of shredded bark, woodchips, or other organic maters. This conserves moisture, reduces weeds, and eliminates grass competition. Wait a year to fertilize new plantings. Follow soil test recommendation or use a low-nitrogen slow-release fertilizer. Well-cared-for, established trees need minimal fertilization.

Regional Advice and Care

Elms tend to be fast growers and weak wooded. Proper pruning throughout the tree's life will help reduce storm damage. American and red elms are susceptible to Dutch Elm Disease (DED). Avoid adding these disease-susceptible plants to your landscape. The red elm is often called slippery elm, *Ulmus rubra*, for its moist slimy inner bark. Pioneers used to chew the bark to quench their thirst. (You can still buy slippery elm throat lozenges.) Plant resistant species and hybrids to avoid DED. Use a preventative fungicide treatment to protect valuable trees. Lightly infected (5 percent or less) trees have been successfully treated. Contact a certified arborist for proper diagnosis and treatment.

Companion Planting and Design

Large elms make good shade trees. Some species have been sheared into hedges. An elm relative, hackberry, *Celtis occidentalis*, has been used as an elm replacement. This large shade tree has a similar growth habit, is urban tolerant with textured bark, and DED resistance.

Try These

The Chinese or lacebark elm, *Ulmus parvifolia*, is a tough tree that can tolerate a wide range of conditions. It is resistant to DED, elm leaf, and Japanese beetle. The small leaves and beautiful bark make this an attractive and useful shade tree (borderline hardy in Zone 4).

Fir

Abies species

Botanical Pronunciation
A-beez

Bloom Period and Seasonal Color
Evergreen needles

Mature Height × Spread
70 feet × 30 feet

If you like the look of a blue spruce but are tired of fighting the pests, I have the tree for you. The white fir, *Abies concolor*, has blue-green needles and a pyramidal shape similar to the Colorado blue spruce. The broader, flat needles and growth habit of white fir give it a softer appearance, making it easier to blend with other plants. White fir is the best fir for home landscape situations. It prefers ideal growing conditions but is more tolerant of heat, drought, and urban conditions than other firs. Its name *concolor* means "same color," referring to the needles that are blue-green on both the upper and lower surfaces. Our native balsam fir is not as tolerant or well suited to landscape conditions.

When, Where, and How to Plant

For best results, plant balled-and-burlapped trees in the spring. Plant container-grown trees before October 1 so the plants will have time to root before the harsh winter. Grow firs in full sun or light shade. They prefer moist, well-drained soil in cool, humid locations. Firs do not tolerate hot, dry conditions. The white fir prefers ideal conditions but is more tolerant of dry soil and city conditions than other firs. See the chapter introduction for planting directions.

Growing Tips

Proper site selection is critical for growing success. A well-placed fir will require little maintenance. Mulch the soil with woodchips or another organic material to keep the roots cool and moist. Water thoroughly whenever the top 4 to 6 inches of soil are crumbly and moist. Wait one year to fertilize new plantings. Properly watered and mulched firs need little, if any, fertilizer once established.

Regional Advice and Care

Healthy fir trees suffer few pest problems and require very little pruning. Give this large tree plenty of room to grow so you won't be fighting to keep a large tree in a small space.

Companion Planting and Design

Use the white fir individually as a specimen plant or in small groupings. They make a nice backdrop to deciduous trees and shrubs. A flowerbed with a group of white firs in the background is quite impressive.

Try These

The introduction of new dwarf cultivars is allowing greater use of these finicky trees. Most gardeners can find the perfect microclimate for a small scale tree but not always for their full-sized counterparts. 'Candicans' is a narrow, upright cultivar that grows 5 feet tall in ten years, eventually growing to 15 feet. 'Gable's Weeping' is a slow growing mounding concolor fir. The dwarf balsam fir, *Abies balsamea* 'Nana', can be carefully sited and enjoyed in a dwarf conifer or perennial garden. Or include 'Tyler Blue' balsam fir with blue foliage to color up the shade. A favorite is the 'Silberlocke' Korean fir, *Abies koreana* 'Silberlocke'. The curved needles show off the silver undersides of the needles. Protect it from the hot afternoon sun.

Fringetree

Chionanthus virginicus

Botanical Pronunciation
ki-oh-NAN-thus ver-JIN-ih-kus

Other Name White fringetree

Bloom Period and Seasonal Color
White flowers in May to June

Mature Height × Spread
12 to 20 feet × 12 to 20 feet

Add some fragrance and spring blooms to any size landscape. Use this slow grower as a large shrub or small multi-stemmed tree. The white, lightly fragrant and frilly flowers give this southeastern native its common name, fringetree. The flowers bring in the butterflies and beneficial insects. Once pollinated the flowers give way to blue fruit that is often masked by the foliage. The birds, however, seem to have no trouble finding the fruit. Fall color can vary from a poor yellow or brown to a bright or golden yellow. Fringetree can be found in moist stream banks, limestone glades, hillsides from southern New Jersey to Florida and west to Texas. Though native to the South, gardeners are successfully growing this plant in our area.

When, Where, and How to Plant

Grow fringetree in moist but well-drained acidic soils for best results. These plants are pretty adaptable but not tolerant of very alkaline soils and drought. Check with local nurseries and garden centers for availability. Plant balled-and-burlapped or container-grown plants in early spring. Plant the tree with the root flare at or slightly above the soil line. Dig a shallow planting hole the same depth as and three to five times wider than the root system. Roughen the sides of the planting hole to make it easier for the roots to enter the surrounding soil. Remove container-grown plants from the pot. Loosen or slice potbound and girdling roots. Remove the tags, twine, and metal baskets and cut away the burlap on balled-and-burlapped trees. Fill the hole with existing soil. Water and spread a 2- to 3-inch layer of shredded bark or woodchips over the surrounding soil.

Growing Tips

Wait a year to fertilize following soil test recommendations or use a low-nitrogen slow-release product. Established trees need little if any fertilizer. Avoid high-nitrogen fertilizer that can interfere with flowering and fruiting. These plants are low maintenance and fairly pest free. They need minimal pruning though some gardeners do a bit of thinning to improve the flower and fruit display.

Regional Advice and Care

This southeastern native is hardy in Zones 4 and 5. Place in a sheltered location free from late spring frosts to increase growing success. Fringetree is late to leaf out so don't be alarmed when nearby plants are fully leafed before this starts showing signs of growth.

Companion Planting and Design

Use these plants in natural areas and wildlife gardens, as specimen plants or grouping for greater impact. Include a few in plants near patios, decks, or entryways where you can enjoy their fragrance and the butterflies and birds that visit.

Try These

Check with specialty nurseries or online for cultivars. 'Emerald Knight' has dark green foliage, all male large flowers, and no fruit. This cultivar tends to be more tree-like.

Ginkgo

Ginkgo biloba

Botanical Pronunciation
GINK-oh by-LO-bah

Other Name Maidenhair tree

Bloom Period and Seasonal Color
Fall foliage in yellow

Mature Height × Spread
50 or more feet × 30 or more feet

Ginkgoes are often called living fossils. They have been growing on the earth for over 150 million years. You may recognize the name from the ginkgo leaf extract sold to improve your memory. The ginkgo is also a beautiful landscape tree. The attractive, fan-shaped leaves add to the overall uniqueness of this plant. Its irregular shape and open appearance can make it difficult to blend in small landscapes. Mature specimens are breathtaking, especially in the fall. The leaves turn a clear yellow and, best of all, they all drop from the tree at the same time, making cleanup easier. Female ginkgo trees produce smelly, messy fruit with edible seeds inside. Plant male clones to avoid the problem. Otherwise, rake and compost the fruit.

When, Where, and How to Plant

Ginkgo trees adapt easily to transplanting. Plant balled-and-burlapped trees as soon as possible after they are purchased. Plant container-grown plants throughout the growing season. Ginkgo is a tough tree that seems to thrive anywhere. It prefers full sun with slightly moist, well-drained soil. It is very tolerant of salt, pollution, and other urban conditions. It does surprisingly well in the hostile environment of sidewalk plantings in downtown areas. Follow planting directions in the chapter introduction.

Growing Tips

Ginkgos require patience, adding about 10 to 15 feet of growth in ten to twelve years. You can speed things up by providing adequate, but not too much, water and fertilizer. Water the tree thoroughly whenever the top 4 to 6 inches of soil are moist and crumbly. Mulch to conserve moisture, suppress weeds, and eliminate competition from nearby grass. Wait a year to fertilize new plantings. Use moderate amounts of slow-release nitrogen fertilizer (see chapter introduction) to encourage faster growth on young trees. Established plants need little, if any, fertilization.

Regional Advice and Care

Ginkgo trees have no real pest problems and tolerate a wide range of growing conditions. The slow growth and open habit eliminate the need for regular pruning.

Companion Planting and Design

Remember, this slow grower will eventually get big, so give it room. Ginkgo trees have an open growth habit. The light colored bark and interesting habit against the sky make it a nice addition to the winter landscape. Plant them where their fall color and winter interest can be appreciated. Seek out local foragers if your female tree is creating a mess. They will be thrilled to harvest the ginkgo fruit, called silver apricots, to use in Oriental cooking.

Try These

Select male clones or cultivars like one of these to avoid problems with messy fruit. *Ginkgo biloba* 'Fastigiata' and 'Princeton Sentry' are upright, male forms of ginkgo. 'Pendula' has strong, horizontal branching. Sold as a weeper, it actually spreads horizontally, creating an interesting look. 'Tuberiformis' is a dwarf male ginkgo with unique leaves that emerge rounded like a tube curled upward.

Hawthorn

Crataegus species

Botanical Pronunciation
krah-TEE-gus

Other Name Thornapple

Bloom Period and Seasonal Color
May blooms in white

Mature Height × Spread
20 to 30 feet × 20 to 30 feet

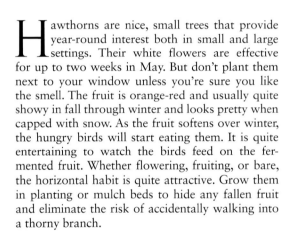

Hawthorns are nice, small trees that provide year-round interest both in small and large settings. Their white flowers are effective for up to two weeks in May. But don't plant them next to your window unless you're sure you like the smell. The fruit is orange-red and usually quite showy in fall through winter and looks pretty when capped with snow. As the fruit softens over winter, the hungry birds will start eating them. It is quite entertaining to watch the birds feed on the fermented fruit. Whether flowering, fruiting, or bare, the horizontal habit is quite attractive. Grow them in planting or mulch beds to hide any fallen fruit and eliminate the risk of accidentally walking into a thorny branch.

When, Where, and How to Plant
Plant small balled-and-burlapped trees in the spring. Plant container-grown plants throughout the growing season, but they do best when planted spring through early summer. Hawthorns prefer full sun and will tolerate a variety of soils as long as they are well drained (see the chapter introduction).

Growing Tips
Water established plants thoroughly whenever the top 4 to 6 inches of soil are starting to dry. Most are drought tolerant once established. Wait a year to fertilize new plantings. Follow soil test results or use a low-nitrogen slow-release fertilizer. Avoid excess fertilization and fast-release, high-nitrogen fertilizers that can reduce flowering and fruiting and increase the risk of disease.

Regional Advice and Care
Prune hawthorns in late winter when the pruning cuts will close quickly and minimize the risk of disease. Hawthorns are susceptible to several major diseases including fireblight, scab, and rust. See crabapples for more details on scab and fireblight. Select the least susceptible species whenever possible. Rust is the most common disease. It causes leaves and fruit to develop orange spots and drop prematurely. Rust is usually harmless but looks bad. Rake and destroy infected leaves and fruit as they fall. Avoid planting red cedar, *Juniperus virginiana*, the alternate host for rust, in the same area. Falling fruit from the large fruited hawthorns can create a mess. Groundcovers will allow it to compost out of sight. Avoid the area until the fruit rots and the German yellow jackets are done feeding.

Companion Planting and Design
Hawthorn's strong, horizontal branching helps anchor large buildings to the landscape. I have seen hawthorns used for screening, hedging, and as barrier plants. Avoid using these thorny plants next to entrances, walkways, and play areas.

Try These
Washington hawthorn, *Crataegus phaenopyrum*, and *Crataegus viridis* 'Winter King' hawthorn are finer textured with smaller fruit. Heavy snow loads may cause damage. I prefer Washington's fall color but the 'Winter King' has fewer thorns. Cockspur hawthorn, *Crataegus crusgalli*, is native, has glossy green leaves, ½-inch red fruit, and long, sharp thorns. The variety *inermis* is thornless.

Hemlock

Tsuga canadensis

Botanical Pronunciation
SOO-gah kan-ah-DEN-sis

Bloom Period and Seasonal Color
Evergreen foliage

Mature Height × Spread
75 feet or more × 25 feet or more

Hemlock is a graceful beauty that is often overlooked for landscape use. Its shade tolerance extends the use of evergreens in the landscape. This native evergreen tree is pyramidal when young. With age, hemlock maintains its pyramidal shape, but the branches begin to weep, giving it a soft and graceful silhouette. The straight species is large and best suited for sizable landscapes. Many dwarf and uniquely shaped cultivars have recently been introduced, making hemlock an option for those with a small yard. This evergreen will tolerate pruning and can be used as a hedge. Before you reach for the shears, take a look at its beautiful shape. Maybe an informal hedge will work just as well. **Note:** this not the infamous poison hemlock, *Conium maculatum*.

When, Where, and How to Plant
Plant balled-and-burlapped trees as soon as possible after purchasing. Plant container-grown trees by October 1 to allow root establishment before winter. Hemlocks are particular about their growing location. They are one of the few evergreens that prefer shade. Grow hemlocks in a sheltered location out of wind, drought, pollution, and waterlogged soil. Winter winds and sun can be especially damaging. Follow the planting directions in the chapter introduction.

Growing Tips
Moisture and mulch are the keys to growing healthy, long-lived hemlocks. Water established trees thoroughly whenever the top 4 to 6 inches are crumbly and moist. Mulch the roots to keep the soil cool and moist. Wait a year to fertilize new plantings with a low-nitrogen slow-release fertilizer. Avoid fertilizing stressed trees. This can stimulate new growth instead of allowing the plant to focus its energy on repair. Established trees, especially those growing in shade, require little if any fertilizer. They also require little if any pruning.

Regional Advice and Care
Stressed trees are susceptible to quite a few pests. Brown needles and branch dieback can occur when the plants are exposed to temperatures over 95 degrees Fahrenheit, drying winter winds, or drought. Prune out damaged branches, eliminate the stress, or move the plants to a more suitable location.

Companion Planting and Design
Hemlocks are attractive grown individually or in small groups. Dwarf cultivars are nice additions to small landscapes and perennial gardens. They provide structure and year-round interest. Use them as specimens, accents, screens, or transition plants on the woodland's edge. Their light, airy texture can soften surrounding plants and landscape structures.

Try These
'Gentsch White' is a dwarf cultivar that only grows to 3 feet in ten years. The new growth has white tips. Prune this rounded plant for more compact growth habit. 'Cole's Prostrate' is a ground-hugging plant that grows 8 inches tall and up to 7 feet wide. Use it as a groundcover or rock garden plant in protected locations. There are several interesting weeping forms including 'Sargentii' and 'Pendula'.

Honey Locust

Gleditsia triacanthos var. *inermis*

Botanical Pronunciation
gled-IT-see-ah try-ah-KAN-thos ih-NER-miss

Bloom Period and Seasonal Color
Fall foliage in yellow

Mature Height × Spread
40 feet × 30 feet

Honey locust is a popular tree in the home landscape. This fast-growing tree provides fine texture and interesting form in both summer and winter. The small green leaves (actually leaflets) provide shade while allowing the sun to reach the grass below. The leaves turn a nice yellow in the fall. The flowers aren't showy, but they do provide a pleasant fragrance in early June. If you have a honey locust, take good care of it and keep it healthy; mature specimens are quite impressive. The honey locust's fruit is a long brown pod. Whether you like the winter interest or not, there is no debate about the mess they create. Fortunately many podless cultivars have been introduced to alleviate this problem.

When, Where, and How to Plant
Plant balled-and-burlapped trees as soon as possible after purchasing. Plant container-grown plants throughout the growing season. Grow honey locust in moist, well-drained soil. This tough plant tolerates a wide range of conditions including drought, salt, and high pH. Handle with care and avoid damage when transporting and planting. Wounds create an opening for life-threatening diseases like nectria canker. Follow planting directions in the chapter introduction.

Growing Tips
Water established trees thoroughly whenever the top 4 to 6 inches of soil are crumbly and moist. Mulch the soil under trees to conserve moisture, suppress weeds, eliminate grass competition, and prevent damage from mowers and weed whips.

Regional Advice and Care
In spring, honey locusts are often attacked by plant bugs and leafhoppers. The insects won't kill the tree, but heavy populations can delay leaf development and cause twig dieback. The biggest problem is nectria canker. It causes sunken and discolored areas to develop on the branches and trunk, eventually killing them. Prevention is the best defense. Select healthy, disease-free trees and avoid injuries to the trunk and branches during transplanting and maintenance. Prune in early spring before growth begins so the wounds will close quickly and the disease organism is less active. Honey locusts also produce lots of sprouts off the main trunk. Remove these at the same time to maintain the tree's structure and appearance. Wait for cool dry weather if you must prune during the growing season.

Companion Planting and Design
Honey locusts are frequently used in difficult growing spots. They are often used to shade patios, decks, and lawn areas. The filtered shade is cooling but not detrimental to the grass.

Try These
Almost all the honey locusts sold are the variety *inermis*, thornless. Their long thin thorns were once used by Civil War soldiers as pins to fasten their coats. Today they create a painful nuisance when caring for the tree. Select podless cultivars to avoid the mess. 'Shademaster' and 'Skyline' have similar upright habits. The new growth on 'Sunburst' (shown) emerges yellow before turning green.

Horsechestnut

Aesculus hippocastanum

Botanical Pronunciation
ESS-kew-lus hip-oh-kass-TAY-num

Bloom Period and Seasonal Color
Late spring blooms in white with yellow and pink blotch at base

Mature Height × Spread
50 or more feet × 40 feet

Hardiness Zones 4

Flowering horsechestnuts steal the show in late spring. Their large, cone-shaped blossoms make them a popular choice for gardeners as well as bees and hummingbirds. The horsechestnut's coarse texture, attractive platy bark, and large size make it a good fit in park-like settings. Horsechestnut trees produce light brown, spiny fruits that look like the spiked metal head of a mace. Inside are dark brown nuts with a light blotch. The falling fruit and seeds can create a mess. These are not the holiday chestnuts that are roasted on an open fire. Those edible chestnuts are from the American chestnut, *Castanea dentata*. The nuts and twigs of horsechestnut are poisonous. Select a fruitless cultivar, like the long-blooming 'Baumanii', to avoid the mess.

When, Where, and How to Plant

Horsechestnuts respond best to spring transplanting, though container-grown plants can be planted throughout the growing season. Plant balled-and-burlapped trees as soon as possible after purchasing. Horsechestnuts prefer moist, well-drained soil, although I have seen them growing in clay soil. See the chapter introduction for planting directions.

Growing Tips

Water established trees thoroughly whenever the top 4 to 6 inches of soil are crumbly and moist. Mulch the soil to conserve moisture, suppress weeds, and eliminate competition from grass. Wait a year to fertilize new plantings. Avoid excess fertilizing and fast-release, high-nitrogen fertilizers that can interfere with flowering. Established trees need little, if any, fertilizer.

Regional Advice and Care

Leaf blotch, anthracnose, and powdery mildew can all cause leaves to discolor and drop prematurely. Rake and destroy infected leaves as soon as they fall to reduce future infection. Healthy trees can tolerate these diseases. It's too late to treat the disease once symptoms appear.

Companion Planting and Design

Horsechestnuts are massive trees that need room to showcase their beauty. Place them where their late spring bloom can be enjoyed. Use them as a shade or large specimen tree in expansive lawn areas or on a woodland edge. Avoid planting these over sidewalks where falling fruit can create a messy hazard. Use mulch or groundcovers under fruiting trees to minimize cleanup. Use fruitless varieties where you don't want to attract squirrels or provide ammunition for children.

Try These

Ohio buckeye, *Aesculus glabra*, is a shorter, 20 to 40 feet, cousin to the horsechestnut. Its smaller size and fall color make it a better fit for most home landscapes. A close look at the horsechestnut-like nuts reveals the source of its common name. 'Autumn Splendor' Ohio buckeye is a small- to medium-sized tree with very showy flowers in late spring. This tough cultivar is winter-hardy and tolerant of deicing salts. The yellow buckeye is a large, beautiful tree with a cleaner appearance and pumpkin fall color. Ruby horsechestnut, *Aesculus × carnea* 'Briotii', has deep red flowers and is borderline hardy in Zone 5.

Ironwood

Ostrya virginiana

Botanical Pronunciation
OSS-tri-ah ver-jin-ee-AY-nah

Other Name Hophornbeam

Bloom Period and Seasonal Color
Spring flowers in greenish yellow with good, yellow fall color

Mature Height × Spread
30 feet × 20 or more feet

The underutilized ironwood is a native understory tree that can be found on dry wooded slopes. The slow growth rate, 10 to 15 feet in fifteen years, and shade tolerance make it an appropriate tree for small settings and city lots. It is somewhat pyramidal when young, becoming more rounded with age. The fine, horizontal branches, and finely shredded bark ensure year-round interest. Ironwood flowers in the early spring. It produces a subtle show providing a glimpse of other spring blooms yet to come. The long, narrow flowers (catkins) droop from the fine branches. The pale green female flowers later develop into small, hop-like fruit, thus the other common name, hophornbeam. The extremely hard and dense wood is source of the other common name, ironwood.

When, Where, and How to Plant
Ironwood may be a little difficult to find. Start by checking with nurseries and garden centers that specialize in native plants. Plant balled-and-burlapped or container-grown trees in the early spring, in full sun or partial shade. They prefer moist, well-drained soil but can tolerate the dry, gravelly and sandy soils found in our region. Dig a shallow planting hole the same depth as, and three to five times wider than, the root system. Plant ironwood trees with the root flare at or slightly above the soil line. Remove the container, twine, and metal baskets. Cut away the burlap. Backfill with existing soil then water and mulch. See the chapter introduction for more detailed directions.

Growing Tips
Though tolerant of dry soil, ironwoods do best when watered during extended drought periods. Water established trees thoroughly whenever the top 4 to 6 inches of soil begin to dry. Maintain a 2- to 3-inch layer of mulch around the tree to conserve moisture, suppress weeds, and reduce completion from grass. Wait a year to fertilize new plantings with a low-nitrogen slow-release fertilizer. Though slow to get started, this tree will grow a bit faster once it's established. Properly watered and mulched established trees need little, if any, fertilizer.

Regional Advice and Care
Ironwood has no serious pests. The wood is hard and durable, helping the plant resist wind and ice damage. It has been used for wedges, levers, and other tools.

Companion Planting and Design
These small trees are a good fit in small landscapes. Plant them in groupings for a bigger impact in larger settings. Ironwood's graceful growth habit helps soften vertical elements in the landscape. Take advantage of ironwood's shade tolerance. Use it in woodland gardens or as an understory plant for your larger shade trees. This native tree is at home in both natural and manicured landscapes.

Try These
Hornbeam or blue beech, *Carpinus caroliniana*, is often called ironwood. It is another small, slow growing tree with a similar growth habit. See the musclewood entry for more on this tree.

Katsuratree

Cercidiphyllum japonicum

Botanical Pronunciation
sir-sid-ih-FIL-um jah-PON-ih-kum

Bloom Period and Seasonal Color
Yellow to apricot fall color

Mature Height × Spread
40 to 60 feet × 20 to 60 feet

Enjoy the seasonal changes of this delicate beauty. The leaves emerge reddish purple and change to a blue-green for summer. In fall they again change, this time, a clear yellow or apricot. The heart-shaped leaves are held by long petioles (leaf stems) that allow them to "quake" like aspens in the wind. And once the leaves are fully colored, take a whiff. You'll notice a brown sugar/cinnamon smell. The bark is slightly shaggy, somewhat like but more refined than a shagbark hickory. Native to China and Japan, katsuratree is medium to fast grower. It is pyramidal when young, but the mature shape can vary from tree to tree. Some trees retain their pyramidal shape, others, are more upright, and some are widespreading.

When, Where, and How to Plant

Plant balled-and-burlapped and container-grown trees in early spring so they have more time to establish before winter. Grow in rich moist well-drain soils for best results. Katsuratrees are adaptable to both acidic and alkaline soils. Plants prefer full sun and need ample moisture throughout their lives. Dig a shallow planting hole the same depth as and three to five times wider than the root system. Plant katsuratrees with the root flare at or slightly above the soil line. Remove the container and loosen any girdling roots. Set balled-and-burlapped plants in the planting hole. Remove twine, metal baskets and cut away the burlap. Backfill with existing soil then water and mulch. See the chapter introduction for more detailed directions.

Growing Tips

Wait a year to fertilize new plantings. Follow soil test recommendations or use a low-nitrogen slow-release fertilizer. Established trees need little if any fertilizer. These plants need even moisture. Water thoroughly whenever the top 4 to 6 inches of soil are slightly moist but crumbly. Make sure to water these trees during drought. Mulch the soil surrounding the tree with 2 to 3 inches of shredded bark or woodchips. This will help keep the roots evenly moist. Mulch also moderates soil temperature, suppresses weeds, and improves the soil as it decomposes.

Regional Advice and Care

Getting this plant through the first few years seems to be the challenge. Once established, specimens can be fairly long lived. Boerner Botanical Gardens has a fifty plus-year-old multi-stemmed tree. And there is good news for northern gardeners. The University of Minnesota continues to develop landscape plants hardy to Zones 3 and 4. They are screening seedlings of the katsuratree, corneliancherry dogwood, bald cypress, and lacebark elm looking for plants with exceptional cold hardiness.

Companion Planting and Design

Weeping forms look nice next to entryways and water features. Use as a specimen plant or small shade tree. Place in areas where the fall color, fragrance, and quaking leaves can be enjoyed

Try These

'Pendulum' is a weeping form that grows to 15 to 25 feet tall and wide or wider.

Kentucky Coffeetree

Gymnocladus dioicus

Botanical Pronunciation
jim-NOK-lad-us dy-oh-EYE-kas

Bloom Period and Seasonal Color
Early June creamy flowers and yellow fall color

Mature Height × Spread
75 feet × 40 feet

Hardiness Zones 3b

Kentucky coffeetree is native to our region and makes an excellent landscape plant. It is a close relative to the honey locust but with fewer pests. Use the large Kentucky coffeetree to provide shade in the summer and an interesting silhouette in winter. Give it time, young plants look quite homely, and space to grow. This versatile plant tolerates a wide range of conditions while blending into formal and informal landscape designs. Early Kentucky settlers used the seeds as a coffee substitute. It is thought that the roasting helped eliminate the toxic properties. I hear the taste isn't that great—I think I'll stick to the real thing.

When, Where, and How to Plant
Spring planting is best, though container-grown plants can be planted throughout the season. Plant balled-and-burlapped trees as soon as possible after purchasing. Kentucky coffeetrees prefer full sun and moist, well-drained soil but will tolerate wet and dry locations. Follow planting directions in the chapter introduction. Once planted, water the tree and cover the surrounding soil with a 2- to 3-inch layer of shredded bark or woodchips.

Growing Tips
Kentucky coffeetree is a low-maintenance plant. Water established plants thoroughly whenever the top few inches of soil begin to dry. Wait a year before fertilizing new plantings. Follow soil test recommendations or use a low-nitrogen slow-release fertilizer. Established trees that are properly watered and mulched require little, if any, fertilizer.

Regional Advice and Care
There are no serious pests. The limited number in the landscape and fewer pest problems make this a superior choice to honeylocust. The fruit and leaves, however, can be messy. Fall leaves tend to drop over a long period of time. The small leaflets can easily be chopped with the mower. The long leaf stem (rachis) is what causes the mess. More meticulous gardeners (that's not me) may be annoyed by this extended fall cleanup.

Companion Planting and Design
This tough tree is a great choice for windy sites and urban areas. Use Kentucky coffeetrees as specimen plants. Their large compound leaves can reach 36 inches in length and 24 inches in width. They are made up of many small, blue-green leaflets that are only 1½ to 3 inches long. The feathery leaves help soften the coarse features of this plant. Once the leaves drop, the brown pods, scaly bark, and thick, stark branches stand out against the winter sky. Olbrich Botanical Garden in Madison, Wisconsin, prunes these into tropical lookalikes for the gardens around their Thai Pavillion.

Try These
Kentucky coffeetree may be hard to locate, so pick up the phone before you hop in the car. 'Espresso' is a fruitless (male) cultivar. It is smaller, with an elm-like growth habit.

Korean Sun Pear

Pyrus fauriei 'Westwood'

Botanical Pronunciation
PY-rus FAR-ee-eye

Bloom Period and Seasonal Color
White flowers in spring; bright reddish orange fall color

Mature Height × Spread
12 feet × 15 feet

This small-scale tree is a good alternative for the invasive Callery pear and the popular crabapple. It is hardier with stronger branching than other pears. The small scale and finer features make it a good choice for small landscapes or planted in masse in larger landscape. I first saw this tree when the crown was covered with glossy green leaves and a blanket of white blooms. I visited the tree throughout the year. Small pea-sized black fruit appeared in late summer and persisted through fall. The leaves turned a brilliant combination of yellow, orange, and red several weeks before the Callery pear. This reduces the risk of fall foliage display being lost to an early fall frost.

When, Where, and How to Plant

Check with local garden centers and nurseries for this relatively new ornamental tree. Grow this adaptable plant in full sun for the best flowering and fruiting. It prefers moist well-drained soil but is very adaptable and seems to tolerate clay soil and somewhat poorly drained soils. Plant balled-and-burlapped or container-grown plants in spring or early summer to allow plants time to adapt before winter. Follow planting instructions in the chapter introduction.

Growing Tips

Wait a year to fertilize new plantings. Follow soil test recommendations or use a low-nitrogen slow-release fertilizer. Avoid high-nitrogen fast-release fertilizer that can inhibit flowering and fall color and increase the risk of disease. Mulch the soil to conserve moisture, suppress weeds, reduce competition from grass and improve the soil as it decomposes. Prune young trees to establish a strong framework. This ornamental pear tends to be widely branched so minimal pruning will be needed.

Regional Advice and Care

This tree has been successfully grown in northern regions including Fargo, North Dakota. No disease or insect problems have been reported, but fireblight on pears is always a threat. Don't overfertilize or use high-nitrogen fertilizer that promotes lush succulent growth that is more susceptible to this disease. The trees tend to produce small quantities of fruit, and gardeners have been monitoring and not finding offspring of this plant

Companion Planting and Design

A nice specimen plant especially for small yards. Include in mixed borders as an accent or for vertical interest. Use *en masse* as a screen, backdrop, or hedge. This plant is tolerant of urban conditions and pollution, making it a good choice for city gardens.

Try These

If you are looking for other small-scale trees for your landscape, check out crabapple, hawthorn, ironwood, musclewood, and pagoda dogwood profiles in this book. Also consider some of the dwarf cultivars of deciduous and evergreen plants. Be sure to check the tag for the plant's mature size. Dwarf just means smaller than the species, and it may grow much bigger than you expect or your space allows.

Larch

Larix species

Botanical Pronunciation
LAIR-iks

Other Name Tamarack

Bloom Period and Seasonal Color
Fall foliage in yellow

Mature Height × Spread
75 feet × 40 feet

On your next road trip through our region, watch for a grove of our native larch trees. The American larch, *Larix laricina*, is also called tamarack and is a tall pyramidal plant. They are most noticeable in the fall when their needles turn a beautiful golden yellow. Look for them in wet, soggy locations. This adaptability is what makes tamarack wood so rot resistant. Larches are deciduous conifers. The needles fall to the ground after their beautiful golden fall display. The tree silhouette is quite effective in the winter landscape. In the landscape, you are more likely to see the European or Japanese larch. These beautiful trees are less tolerant of wet soil but are more adapted to transplanting than our American larch.

When, Where, and How to Plant
Plant balled-and-burlapped trees in the spring when the plants are dormant. Plant container-grown plants throughout the growing season in moist, well-drained soil. Though our native larch tolerates wet, soggy soils in the wild, it performs best in landscapes with moist, well-drained soil. Avoid dry soil and polluted locations. Plant larch with the root flare at or slightly above the soil line. Remove containers, twine, and metal baskets; cut away burlap at time of planting. Backfill the hole with existing soil, then water and mulch. See the chapter introduction for more planting details.

Growing Tips
Mulch to keep the roots cool and moist. Water established plants thoroughly whenever the top 4 to 6 inches of soil are crumbly and moist. Wait a year to fertilize young trees. Established trees need very little fertilizer.

Regional Advice and Care
Properly placed larch trees need little maintenance. Insect and disease problems are few and infrequent. Healthy plants properly watered and mulched usually resist and tolerate any damage. I have had several distraught homeowners call panicked because their evergreen's needles turned yellow and dropped in fall. I even know of a building manager who cut down several healthy trees because of this. I'm glad I didn't have to tell him or his boss this was an unnecessary loss of a healthy tree.

Companion Planting and Design
Consider using one of these graceful plants near a pond or water feature. Larches are good plants for large landscapes and new dwarf cultivars are making them useful in small-scale yards. The European and Japanese larches make attractive specimen plants. Plant individually or *en masse*. Groupings of larch make effective screens. Create a grove using a grouping of these plants.

Try These
You may have trouble finding the American larch. Check with local nurseries specializing in native plants. The Japanese larch, *Larix kaempferi*, and European larch, *Larix decidua*, are the most ornamental, but both need lots of space to grow and show their beauty. *Larix kaempferi* 'Pendula' is just one of many dwarf cultivars now available.

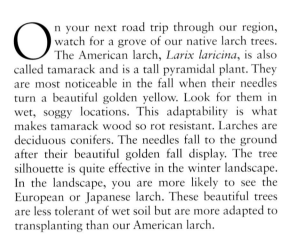

Linden

Tilia species

Botanical Pronunciation
TIL-ee-ah

Other Name Basswood

Bloom Period and Seasonal Color
Late June to early July in yellow; yellow
fall foliage

Mature Height × Spread
Up to 75 feet × 40 feet

Lindens are a useful group of plants and provide several seasons of interest. Watch for the fragrant yellow flowers in late June or early July. You will probably smell them and hear the buzz of bees before you see the flowers. In fact, the honey they make from these flowers is supposed to be some of the best. The fall color is usually a good yellow. All lindens have attractive forms, adding year-round interest. American linden, *Tilia americana*, is a large, irregularly shaped, upright native tree with large leaves. It's a good plant for large, informal yards and naturalized landscapes. The popular littleleaf linden, *Tilia cordata*, has small, glossy, heart-shaped leaves. Its smaller size and pyramidal shape make it suitable for landscapes.

When, Where, and How to Plant
Lindens adapt well to transplanting. Plant balled-and-burlapped trees as soon as possible after purchasing. Plant container-grown plants throughout the growing season. Grow lindens in full sun with moist, well-drained soil. Most lindens tolerate heavy clay soil (see the chapter introduction for planting details).

Growing Tips
Lindens require minimal maintenance. Water established trees thoroughly whenever the top 4 to 6 inches of soil are moist and crumbly. Mulch to conserve moisture, suppress weeds, and eliminate competition from grass. Wait a year before fertilizing new plantings. Properly watered and mulched lindens usually need minimal fertilization.

Regional Advice and Care
Recent droughts and environmental stresses have increased problems with linden borer. Mulch and proper watering, especially during drought, will help reduce the risk. Littleleaf lindens produce lots of side branches very close together. These will need to be thinned to prevent future problems with rubbing branches. There are a few diseases and insects that attack lindens. A few holes chewed in their leaves is not uncommon and does not require treatment. This is not the case if Japanese beetles have invaded your landscape. Healthy trees will survive. Drought-stressed and specimen trees may benefit from control. Watch for nectria canker on littleleaf lindens. Avoid damage when transporting, planting, and caring for this tree. (See honey locust profile.)

Companion Planting and Design
All lindens make good shade trees. American linden is good for naturalized settings or woodland areas. The littleleaf linden is the most frequently used in the landscape for street trees, planters, and planting beds. Use littleleaf lindens to line a driveway or a wide walkway. Or you can trim them into a large hedge.

Try These
'American Sentry' American linden has a uniform pyramidal shape and is reported to be the most Japanse beetle resistant of the lindens. 'Glenleven' littleleaf linden is fast growing, more open, and fewer problems with Japanese beetles. Silver linden, *Tilia tomentosa*, has dark green leaves with silver undersides. Hardy to Zone 5 and tolerant of heat and drought conditions.

Magnolia

Magnolia species

Botanical Pronunciation
mag-NO-lee-ah

Bloom Period and Seasonal Color
Early spring blooms in pink and white

Mature Height × Spread
15 to 40 feet × 30 feet

When you hear the word *magnolia* you may think of the South and its trees with large fragrant flowers and huge, glossy, evergreen leaves. Or maybe the flowers conjure up visions of Chinese art. They were the first to grow these plants. They used the buds for flavoring rice and medicine. Many northern gardeners would also like to enjoy these beautiful plants. We can't enjoy the same species as our southern gardening friends, but we can enjoy magnolias. Select hardy types, plant them in the right location, and provide proper care. Look for late-blooming varieties that escape our late spring frost and repeat blooming types for greater enjoyment. The smooth, gray bark is beautiful year-round. When the blooms appear, they are spectacular.

When, Where, and How to Plant

Magnolias do not respond well to transplanting. Plant balled-and-burlapped and container-grown plants in the early spring. Grow them in moist, well-drained soil. They will not tolerate wet or dry conditions. Avoid low spots and other areas subject to late spring frosts that can destroy the spring floral display. See the chapter introduction for planting directions.

Growing Tips

Mulch the soil to keep roots cool and moist. Keep mulch several inches away from the tree trunk. Water established trees thoroughly whenever the top 4 to 6 inches of soil are moist but crumbly. Wait a year to fertilize new plantings. Avoid excess fertilization and fast-release, high-nitrogen fertilizers.

Regional Advice and Care

Pests are generally not a problem. Plants grown in poorly drained soil are subject to yellow leaves, poor growth, and even death. Magnolias are subject to snow and ice damage. Reduce the risk with proper training and pruning. Very little pruning is needed once the framework is established on young trees. Prune magnolias after flowering. Finish the job by early summer so you don't interfere with the next season's bloom.

Companion Planting and Design

Small magnolias can be used as an accent, a flowering specimen, or as a mass display in small or large yards. Include smaller trees near the house and patio or as part of a mixed border. Save the larger magnolias for bigger settings.

Try These

The small star magnolia, *Magnolia stellata*, and long-time favorite saucer magnolia, *Magnolia × soulangiana*, are rated hardy to Zone 4. Their early blooms are often damaged by spring frosts. The Little Girl series (Ann, Betty, Jane, Judy, Pinki, Randy, Ricki and Susan) are hybrids of the star and saucer magnolias. Hardy and flowering 2 to 4 weeks later and some repeat bloom. *Magnolia × loebneri* 'Merrill' has large white flowers, grows 25 to 30 feet tall, and has performed well in Zone 4. The cucumber magnolia, *Magnolia acuminata* (Zone 3), has less ornamental flowers but large leaves reminiscent of the southern magnolia. 'Butterflies' magnolia is one of the best and hardiest (Zone 4) yellow-flowering magnolias.

Maple

Acer species

Botanical Pronunciation
AY-sir

Bloom Period and Seasonal Color
Early spring flowers in red or yellow, with yellow-orange and red fall color

Mature Height × Spread
Up to 75 feet × 40 feet

Maple is one of the most widely used landscape plants. You may remember throwing maple seeds (we called them helicopters) in the air as a child. The colorful yellow, orange, and red fall leaves of the sugar maple, *Acer saccharum*, can be found decorating elementary schools' fall bulletin boards. Sugar maple sap is also used to make maple syrup. You need 40 gallons of sap for 1 gallon of syrup. These native trees grow best in moist, rich soil. They do not tolerate heat, drought, or salt. Use them as shade trees in lawn areas and other park-like settings. The true red maple, *Acer rubrum*, is native, has brilliant red fall color, and tolerates wet conditions but requires acidic soils.

When, Where, and How to Plant
Plant balled-and-burlapped trees as soon as possible after they are purchased. Plant container-grown plants throughout the growing season. Red and free-man maples respond best to spring planting. Grow maples in full sun with moist, well-drained soil. Some species tolerate wet, dry, or other difficult conditions. See the chapter introduction for planting directions.

Growing Tips
Water established trees when the top 4 to 6 inches of soil are moist and crumbly. Mulch around maple trees. Avoid excess fertilization that can hinder fall color.

Regional Advice and Care
Avoid planting invasive Norway and Amur maples. Their seedlings are finding their way into

and upsetting the balance in our natural spaces. Prune young trees to establish a central leader and sturdy framework. Maple trees will bleed when pruned in the spring. It won't hurt the plant but makes most gardeners wince. Verticillium wilt can be deadly. Prune out infected branches, disinfecting tools between cuts. Do not replace trees killed by Verticillium wilt with other susceptible plants. Anthracnose, tar spot, petiole borer, cottony maple scale, aphids, and galls are a few of the maples' pests. Healthy trees will tolerate all these pests. Rake and destroy spotted leaves as they fall to reduce future disease problems. Galls are just benign, colorful, and uniquely shaped bumps on leaves caused by insect feeding. They are harmless.

Companion Planting and Design
Maples are shallow-rooted trees that make it difficult to grow and maintain grass. Eliminate this frustration by mulching the roots or growing shade-tolerant groundcovers under the tree. Do *not* cut or bury the roots. This can eventually kill the tree.

Try These
Select the species and cultivars appropriate for your growing conditions and landscape design. Freeman maple is a hybrid of red and silver maples; it's fast growing and more tolerant of alkaline soil. 'Sienna' (Sienna Glen®) freeman maple grows 50 feet tall has good fall color, resists frost crack, and is hardier and drought tolerant. *Acer miyabei* 'Morton (State Street®) grows 40 feet tall, has yellow fall color, is urban and salt tolerant, and non-invasive.

Mountainash

Sorbus species

Botanical Pronunciation
SOR-bus

Other Name Rowan

Bloom Period and Seasonal Color
Spring blooms in white

Mature Height × Spread
30 feet × 20 feet

The European mountainash, *Sorbus aucuparia*, has long been a favorite tree for our gardens, providing seasonal interest. It has white flowers in the spring followed by showy orange-red fruit in the fall. The flower show is good, but not spectacular, and just a bit smelly. The fall color is often a good reddish purple, and the fruit display is excellent and attractive to birds. In fact, the botanical name *aucuparia* comes from the Latin words *avis* meaning "bird" and *capere* meaning "to catch." Our native mountain ashes, American mountainash (*Sorbus americana*) and showy mountainash (*Sorbus decora*), are similar in appearance and bird appeal. All of these trees are small-scale ornamental trees that do best with cool moist soils.

When, Where, and How to Plant
Plant balled-and-burlapped trees as soon as possible after they are purchased. Plant container-grown trees throughout the growing season, preferably spring and early summer so the plants have time to adapt before winter. Plant mountainash in areas with cool, moist, but well-drained soil. They will not tolerate heat, drought, pollution, or compacted soil. Grow in full sun for best flowering, fruiting, and fall color. But keep specimens away from heat-reflecting structures and pavement. Follow planting directions in the chapter introduction.

Growing Tips
Plant mountain ash in the right location to minimize maintenance. Mulch the roots with wood-chips or another organic material to keep them cool and moist. Water thoroughly whenever the top 4 to 6 inches are crumbly and moist. Wait a year after planting to fertilize. Avoid using fast-release and high-nitrogen fertilizers that can increase the risk of fireblight and interfere with flowering and fruiting.

Regional Advice and Care
Mountainash trees are susceptible to quite a few disease and insect problems. The shiny, smooth bark is susceptible to sunscald and frost cracking. The leaves often spot and drop from scab. Rake and destroy fallen leaves to reduce future risk. Fireblight can kill the tree one branch at a time or very quickly in one season. Remove wilted branches well below the canker (sunken discolored area), disinfecting your tools between cuts. Stressed trees can be finished off by borers. Proper watering and mulch will keep the trees healthy and borer resistant.

Companion Planting and Design
Plant them on the east or cool side of your home in a spot where they can be enjoyed. They make a nice ornamental tree for small yards or for a mixed planting bed and wildlife garden. The fruit is edible but too acidic to be eaten fresh. Instead use it to make jams and jellies.

Try These
Korean mountain ash, *Sorbus alnifolia*, shown above, has simple leaves like a beech and puts on a better flower and fruit display than the European mountain ash. It tolerates our climate and is considered the best of the introduced mountainash trees.

Musclewood

Carpinus caroliniana

Botanical Pronunciation
kar-PYE-nus kair-oh-lin-ee-AY-nuh

Other Name American hornbeam

Bloom Period and Seasonal Color
Fall foliage in yellow, orange, and red

Mature Height × Spread
Up to 30 feet × 30 feet

Musclewood is a beautiful native tree often overlooked for use in the home landscape. It tolerates moist soil, even temporary flooding, and shade. The fine texture and smooth, gray bark give this tree year-round appeal. The elm-like leaves turn yellow, orange, or red in the fall. The flowers are not very effective, but the papery fruit can persist and add winter interest. Musclewood goes by several common names. The slate gray, fluted bark looks like flexed muscles. That's how it got the name musclewood. The bark also resembles that of a beech, thus blue or water beech. And like the other ironwood, *Ostrya virginiana*, this tree has very hard and durable wood. It's worth the effort it may take to find one for your yard.

When, Where, and How to Plant
Musclewood trees do not respond well to transplanting. Plant balled-and-burlapped and container-grown trees in the spring. Musclewood is native to our forests. It prefers partial shade and moist soil in the landscape but will tolerate heavy shade and temporary flooding. Locate the tree's root flare. That is the bell-shaped area where the roots angle away from the trunk. Plant the tree with the root flare at or slightly above the soil line in a hole as deep as and three to five times wider than the root system. See the chapter introduction for more planting details.

Growing Tips
Patience is the key to care. New trees take time to adjust to their new location. The slow-growing musclewood averages less than 1 foot of growth each year. Mulch the roots to keep the soil cool and moist. This also suppresses weeds and keeps away competitive grass that can further slow development. Water established trees thoroughly whenever the top 4 to 6 inches of soil are crumbly and moist. Wait a year to fertilize new plantings. Follow soil test recommendations or use a low-nitrogen slow-release fertilizer. Established trees need little, if any, fertilization.

Regional Advice and Care
Once established, musclewood requires little maintenance. Although trees are subject to damage from ice storms, properly trained trees will be less susceptible. Prune young trees to establish a structurally sound framework. Minimal pruning should be done after this. No serious pests when plants are properly planted and maintained.

Companion Planting and Design
Musclewood works equally well in a naturalized area or a more formal landscape. Its shade tolerance makes it a good choice for an understory tree in woodland settings or shady yards. The attractive bark, fine texture, and growth habit make them specimen-quality plants.

Try These
Firespire™ is a narrow upright cultivar (20 feet tall × 20 feet wide) with outstanding orange-red fall color. 'Ball O' Fire' is 15 feet tall and wide with same excellent fall color. 'J.N. Strain' transplants readily, and has similar growth habit as the species, with orange, red, and some yellow fall color.

Oak

Quercus species

Botanical Pronunciation
KWER-kus

Bloom Period and Seasonal Color
Fall foliage in yellow, brown, or red

Mature Height × Spread
50 to 80 feet × 50 to 80 feet

Oaks are the majestic trees of nature, and they bring the same feeling of majesty to large landscapes. Oak trees are becoming more readily available thanks in part to an increased interest in native plants and greater transplanting success. These large trees are medium to slow growing but can still be enjoyed in our lifetime. Some oaks have good fall color. Many hold their leaves over the winter, adding subtle interest and sound to the winter landscape. The nuts are ornamental and provide food for a variety of wildlife. Plus their coarse texture and dramatic silhouette provide year-round beauty. Members of the red or black oak group have leaves with pointed lobes, while members of the white oak group have rounded leaves.

When, Where, and How to Plant
Most oaks are difficult to transplant. Plant balled-and-burlapped trees in the spring soon after purchasing. In general, oaks prefer moist, well-drained soil. Some require acidic soil while others will tolerate alkaline soil. Select species adapted to your soil conditions.

Growing Tips
Most established oaks are drought tolerant. Water them thoroughly during extended dry periods. Mulch to conserve moisture, suppress weeds, and eliminate the frustration of trying to grow grass under their dense canopies. Wait for one year after planting to fertilize.

Regional Advice and Care
Prune oaks during the dormant season to minimize the risk of oak wilt infection. Oak wilt is a deadly disease that enters through wounds, such as pruning cuts. The upper leaves wilt then turn brown and drop from oak wilt-infected trees. Apply pruning paint to oaks pruned during the growing season. This is the only time you should use a pruning paint. Anthracnose and galls are common problems on oaks but are not harmful. (See the maples entry.) Several oaks are very intolerant of alkaline (high pH) soil. They develop chlorosis, a yellowing of leaves. Avoid planting acid-loving oaks in alkaline soils.

Companion Planting and Design
Plant these trees for future shade, specimen plants, and the next generation. Give them plenty of room; they will eventually need it.

Try These
White oak, *Quercus alba*, is a native tree with beautiful red fall color. It is hardy to Zone 4b but not tolerant of alkaline and compacted soils. The red oak, *Quercus rubra*, is a little faster growing than most oaks and a good choice for urban areas. The native swamp white oak, *Quercus bicolor*, tolerates moist, even wet, soil conditions. It is a good choice for urban areas, and the exfoliating bark is an added ornamental feature. Bur oak, *Quercus macrocarpa*, of our native oak-savannas will tolerate wet to dry soil. The coarse texture and furrowed bark provide year-round interest. Pin oak, *Quercus palustris*, is often used in home landscapes as it fast growing, finer textured, hardy to Zone 4b, but requires acidic soil.

Ornamental Plum and Cherry

Prunus species

Botanical Pronunciation
PREW-nus

Bloom Period and Seasonal Color
Spring blooms in white or pink

Mature Height × Spread
Up to 30 feet × 30 feet

Ornamental plums and cherries are grown for their impressive flowers or decorative foliage. These small trees can add early spring interest to both large and small landscapes. Many have decorative bark, nectar for attracting hummingbirds, fruit for the wildlife, and interesting form. After a mild winter and spring with no flower-killing frosts, we will have a beautiful spring floral display and a run on these plants at the garden center. Over time they fade away until the next glorious spring bloom. So treat these as short-lived plants in the landscape. Select the most pest-resistant varieties suited to your growing conditions and landscape design. The native cherries and plums are often considered less ornamental but are more suited to our soils and climate.

When, Where, and How to Plant

Plant bare-root, balled-and-burlapped, and container-grown trees in the spring. Proper siting will help extend the life of these short-lived plants. Grow them in moist, well-drained soil, avoiding the heavy clay soils found in many areas of our region and newer housing developments. Plant them in a protected site or on the east side of your home in full sun. That will reduce the risk of winter injury and flower damage from a late spring frost. Follow planting directions in the introduction.

Growing Tips

Water established trees thoroughly whenever the top 4 to 6 inches of soil are moist and crumbly. Mulch the roots to keep them cool and moist. Wait a year to fertilize new plantings. Avoid excess fertilization that can interfere with flowering.

Regional Advice and Care

These ornamental plants have many insect and disease problems. Healthy plants are the best defense against these problems. Plant trees in protected areas with well-drained soil. Reduce problems by avoiding injuries caused by mowers, weed whips, or other items. Prune these trees during dry weather to avoid the spread of disease. These trees tend to be short-lived and also sucker freely. You will discover little trees throughout your lawn. Cut them off below ground level to discourage resprouting. Treating the sprouts with total vegetation killers will kill the parent tree too.

Companion Planting and Design

Use these ornamental trees as a ten- to twenty-year specimen or accent plant. They also work well in patio and Japanese gardens.

Try These

Schubert cherry, *Prunus virginiana* 'Schubert', or its branch sport 'Canada Red' are the best of the purple-leafed prunus. The leaves emerge green and turn a deep purple for the season. White flowers in spring are followed by red fruit the birds like and can be used for jams, jellies, and wine. These are hardy throughout the region. Amur chokecherry, *Prunus maackii*, is fast growing, a reliable bloomer with shiny, amber-colored exfoliating bark. Moist well-drained soil is a must. Dwarf Russian almond, *Prunus tenella*, is a low suckering shrub, hardy to Zone 2, with fair drought tolerance.

Pagoda Dogwood

Cornus alternifolia

Botanical Pronunciation
KOR-nus all-ter-nih-FOE-lee-ah

Other Name Alternate leaf dogwood

Bloom Period and Seasonal Color
Creamy fragrant flowers in May to June

Mature Height × Spread
15 to 25 feet × 25 to 35 feet

Shade tolerant, four seasons of interest, *and* native. This combination is hard to beat. Include this small-scape tree in shade gardens or formal plantings. The pagoda dogwood's horizontal branching provides year round interest in its natural habitat and the landscape. Fragrant cream-colored flowers appear with the leaves in late spring. You will find bees visiting these blooms. The flowers give way to bluish black fruit the birds love. Fortunately they leave the red fruit stalks behind that persist and add color throughout the remainder of the season. The leaves turn a reddish purple that is attractive but not always outstanding. A close look may find the larvae of the spring azure butterflies feeding on these plants in spring through early summer.

When, Where, and How to Plant
Grow pagoda dogwood in partially shaded, slightly acidic, cool moist soils for best results. A bit of shade from the hot afternoon sun is ideal. These plants will tolerate full sun as long as the roots are kept cool and moist. Purchase young balled-and-burlapped or container-grown plants. See the chapter introduction for planting instructions.

Growing Tips
Wait a year to fertilize new plantings according to soil test recommendation or use a low-nitrogen slow-release fertilizer. Once established, these trees need little if any fertilizer. Water plants thoroughly and often enough to keep the soil evenly moist. Mulch to keep the roots cool and moist. Be patient; pagoda dogwood can be slow to start. It spends the first few years putting down roots before adding top growth. Once started it grows more quickly.

Regional Advice and Care
Pagoda dogwood is native to our area, but urban heat islands and warmer summers can be stressful on this plant. Golden canker is a common problem seen on heat-stressed dogwoods, especially this one. The stems turn a bright golden color and eventually die. Prune out and destroy diseased branches at least 6 to 9 inches below the canker (sunken discolored area) or back to a healthy branch. Disinfect tools with a 70 percent denatured alcohol or 10 percent bleach solution between cuts. Proper siting, watering, and mulch will help prevent this problem. Leaf spot is an occasional but not life-threatening problem.

Companion Planting and Design
Pagoda dogwoods make a nice accent on the shady corner of a house. They complement formal and Japanese garden styles as well as an informal mixed border. Use them at the water's edge, in natural settings, shade gardens, or anywhere their horizontal branching will be highlighted.

Try These
'Argentea' has white variegated leaves that help brighten up shaded areas. It tends to be a bit shrubbier than the species. Gold Bullion™ has golden yellow foliage in spring that turns more chartreuse in summer and contrasts nicely with surrounding greenery. The leaves may turn green in the heat of the summer.

Pine

Pinus species

Botanical Pronunciation
PY-nus

Bloom Period and Seasonal Color
Evergreen needles

Mature Height × Spread
Up to 75 feet × 40 feet

Pines have long been used in our landscapes as windbreaks, screens, and wildlife habitats. Planted in the right location with sufficient space, pines provide years of beauty. Michigan's state tree, the white pine, *Pinus strobus*, is native and was an important lumber tree because it is easy to work and finishes nicely. Landscapers like this beautiful tree because of its soft wispy texture. It starts out pyramidal and becomes picturesque with age. It is hardy statewide but will not tolerate salt, pollution, and alkaline soils. The red pine, *Pinus resinosa*, is a tough native used for windbreaks. Considered more of a workhorse than a beauty in the landscape, it has attractive red bark and green needles that turn yellow-green over the winter.

When, Where, and How to Plant

Plant balled-and-burlapped trees as soon as possible after they are purchased. Plant container-grown plants by October 1 to allow the plants to adjust before winter. Pines prefer full sun and moist, well-drained soil. Most pines can tolerate dry conditions once established. Follow planting direction in the chapter introduction.

Growing Tips

Water established plants thoroughly whenever the top 4 to 6 inches of soil are crumbly and moist. Mulch to conserve moisture and suppress weeds since grass won't usually grow beneath these trees. Wait a year to fertilize new plantings. Properly managed trees need minimal fertilization.

Regional Advice and Care

Pines need minimal pruning. Prune out dead and damaged branches and maintain a central leader. Pines can be pruned to limit growth. This is done in the spring as the new growth elongates. This tight, new growth is called a candle. Cut off one-half or two-thirds of the candles to shorten and thicken the new growth. There are several fungal diseases and insect problems that can be damaging. Contact your local University Extension Office or a certified arborist for diagnosis and treatment.

Companion Planting and Design

Use these evergreens for windbreaks, screens, specimen plants, and winter color. Remember, these nice, small "Christmas" trees will grow into large, spreading trees sooner than you think. Use them as specimen plants or as a nice backdrop for deciduous plants. The dark green needles make the colorful bark of birches, dogwoods, and red maples stand out.

Try These

Swiss stone pine, *Pinus cembra*, is a good choice for small areas. It is a slow grower with a narrow upright growth habit. Many dwarf pines are now available. 'Blue Mound' Swiss stone pine has excellent blue color and grows 3 feet in ten years. The dwarf limber pine, *Pinus flexilis* 'Vanderwolf's Pyramid', has blue-green needles, pyramidal habit, grows to 6 feet in ten years and is hardy to Zone 4. Limit the use of Austrian pine, *Pinus nigra*. Once the workhorse of the landscape, it has recently been besieged by multiple pest problems.

Redbud

Cercis canadensis

Botanical Pronunciation
SIR-sis kan-ah-DEN-sis

Other Name Eastern redbud

Bloom Period and Seasonal Color
Early spring blooms in rosy pink; fall foliage
in yellow

Mature Height × Spread
Up to 30 feet × 30 feet

The redbud is one of the most beautiful trees when it is in bud and bloom. The dark branches and trunk are covered with reddish purple buds in early spring. The buds open into rosy pink flowers and put on quite a show. The flowers are edible as well as ornamental; use them raw in salads or fried as an appetizer. Once the flowers are gone, the tree is covered with green heart-shaped leaves that turn a pretty yellow in the fall. After the leaves fall, a graceful silhouette is left to adorn the winter landscape. The redbud fruit is a dry, flat pod about 2 to 3 inches long and ½ inch wide. Redbuds are native to southern Michigan and can thrive throughout the state with proper selection, siting and care.

When, Where, and How to Plant
Redbuds respond best to spring planting, which allows them to start establishing before winter. Grow redbuds in a protected location. They do best in full sun to part shade in moist, well-drained soil. Plant the tree with the root flare at or slightly above the soil line. Follow the planting directions in the chapter introduction.

Growing Tips
Growing a hardier strain of redbuds in a protected location will increase longevity and reduce maintenance needs. Water plants thoroughly whenever the top 4 to 6 inches of soil are crumbly and moist. Mulch the soil to keep the roots cool and moist. Wait a year to fertilize new plantings. Avoid excess amounts and fast-release, high-nitrogen fertilizers. This can diminish flowering and winter hardiness.

Regional Advice and Care
Prune young trees to establish a strong framework. Established trees need minimal pruning. Remove winter-damaged and wayward branches. Prune in late winter or early spring when the wounds will close quickly and reduce the risk of disease. Winter injury is the biggest problem with these trees. Proper selection, siting, and care will help with this and reduce the risk of insect and disease. Verticillium wilt can be a problem. Remove infected branches, disinfecting your tools between cuts. Do not replace verticillium wilt-killed trees with susceptible plants.

Companion Planting and Design
Redbuds often grow wider than tall, so give them plenty of room to show off their attractive form. They are often used as specimen plants, along a woodland edge, or in a naturalized setting. Their strong, horizontal branching and flower display make them a good addition to a Japanese garden.

Try These
Redbuds are available as single or multi-stemmed plants. Increase your success by purchasing a northern grown Redbud. Those gardening in the Upper Peninsula may want to consider the Minnesota Strain, which was propagated from plants in the Minnesota Landscape Arboretum and introduced in 1992. These small trees have dark pink to purple flowers in early May.

Serviceberry

Amelanchier species

Botanical Pronunciation
am-el-AN-keer

Other Name Juneberry

Bloom Period and Seasonal Color
Spring blooms in white; fall foliage in yellow, orange, and red

Mature Height × Spread
Up to 40 feet × 30 feet

Our native serviceberry is among my favorite small trees. It provides four seasons of interest. The white flowers open in spring followed by the fruit. They start out pink and then turn purple-black and resemble a blueberry. Don't worry about a mess; the birds will clean up the fruit before it hits the ground. I have robins lined up on my fence every June waiting for the fruit to ripen. And I've been told the cedar waxwings also love the fruit. Next comes the colorful fall display when the leaves turn a brilliant yellow, orange, or red. The smooth gray bark provides winter interest. Serviceberries are edible and have a nutty blueberry flavor. The only trick is beating the birds to the fruit.

When, Where, and How to Plant

Plant balled-and-burlapped trees as soon as possible after purchase. Plant container-grown plants throughout the growing season. Serviceberries take time to establish after transplanting. Grow serviceberries in moist, well-drained soil. Dig a shallow planting hole the same depth as, and three to five times wider than, the root system. Plant the tree with the root flare at or slightly above the soil line. Remove the container, twine, and metal baskets, and cut away the burlap. Fill the hole with existing soil, water to settle the soil, and mulch. See the chapter introduction for more details.

Growing Tips

Serviceberries often take time to adjust to a new location. Be patient because the tree puts down roots before growing taller. Water established trees thoroughly whenever the top 4 to 6 inches of soil

are crumbly and moist. Mulch the soil to conserve moisture, eliminate grass competition, and keep the roots cool. Wait a year to fertilize new plantings. Properly mulched and watered trees need minimal fertilizer.

Regional Advice and Care

Serviceberries don't have serious insect or disease problems. Prune young trees to establish a strong framework. Mature trees need minimal pruning. I prefer late winter or early spring pruning; the wounds close quickly, reducing the risk of pest problems.

Companion Planting and Design

Serviceberries are native to woodland edges, stream banks, fence rows, and hillsides. This adaptability helps them tolerate a wide range of landscape conditions. Use the shrub forms of serviceberry in groupings, as screens, or as an unsheared hedge. The small trees make good specimen plants near water features, in planting beds, or small landscapes. Larger trees can provide shade and ornamental value in larger settings.

Try These

Apple serviceberry, *Amelanchier* × *grandiflora*, is slow growing, tolerates partial shade. 'Princess Diana' has an abundance of white flowers, large fruit, and excellent red fall color. *Amelanchier alnifolia* 'Obelisk' is tall and narrow (15 × 4 feet) making it a great choice for small space or hedges. Downy serviceberry, *Amelanchier arborea*, is an upright, small tree. This slow grower tolerates drier soil.

Spruce

Picea species

Botanical Pronunciation
py-SEE-ah

Bloom Period and Seasonal Color
Evergreen needles

Mature Height × Spread
Up to 60 feet × 30 feet

Spruce trees start out and end up about the same shape; they're just bigger. These large trees provide a strong, pyramidal silhouette in the garden. Remember, these trees will get huge. Too many gardeners have planted a cute little spruce by their front entrance only to have it consume the whole yard. The most popular spruce for the home landscape is probably the Colorado blue spruce, *Picea pungens f. glauca*. It can reach a height of 60 feet and is hardy throughout our region. It will tolerate dry soil and urban conditions. Its stiff, pyramidal shape and blue needles make it hard to blend with the rest of the landscape. Several diseases can diminish its beauty over time. Consider proper siting and care or make another choice.

When, Where, and How to Plant
Plant balled-and-burlapped trees in the spring as soon as possible after purchasing. Plant container-grown trees by October 1 for greater chances of winter survival. Grow in moist, well-drained soil. Consult the chapter introduction for planting tips.

Growing Tips
Water established trees whenever the top 4 to 6 inches of soil are moist and crumbly. Mulch to conserve moisture and to suppress weeds (don't bother with grass under the trees). Wait a year to fertilize new plantings. Properly watered and mulched spruce need minimal fertilization.

Regional Advice and Care
Spruce need very little pruning. Touch-up pruning can be done in the spring before growth begins.

Make cuts on branch tips above a healthy bud. You do not have to prune off the lower branches of these trees. Limbing them up is for the gardener's benefit, not the plant's. Spruce growing in optimum conditions are less susceptible to damage from disease. Mites can be a problem in hot dry weather. Spray infested plants once a week with a strong blast of water from the garden hose to keep these pests under control. Colorado blue spruce is susceptible to cytospora canker, rhizosphaera needle blight, spruce needle drop, and spruce galls. The first two diseases can greatly disfigure trees. Remove infested branches, disinfecting tools between cuts. Consider hiring a certified arborist for proper diagnosis and treatment. Galls don't harm an established tree's overall health.

Companion Planting and Design
These large trees provide a strong, pyramidal silhouette in the garden. Use them as screens, windbreaks, and specimens. Dwarf cultivars are suitable for smaller landscapes and for use in perennial and rock gardens.

Try These
Serbian spruce, *Picea omorika*, has a narrow pyramidal shape and grows to 50 feet tall. Its pendulous branches make a graceful statement in the landscape. White spruce, *Picea glauca*, is native and hardy throughout our region and needs moist soil. Black Hills spruce is shorter, 20 feet, and slower growing. Bird's nest spruce, *Picea abies* 'Nidiformis', is a low growing spreader. Dwarf Alberta spruce, *Picea glauca* 'Conica', needs protection from winter wind and sun to prevent browning.

Turkish Filbert

Corylus colurna

Botanical Pronunciation
KOR-ih-lus koe-LER-nuh

Other Name Turkish hazel

Bloom Period and Seasonal Color
Long narrow catkins in spring, with mostly yellow-green fall color

Mature Height × Spread
Up to 50 feet × 25 feet

Consider being a trendsetter and adding a Turkish filbert to your landscape. This underutilized tree has good year-round interest and is tolerant of difficult growing conditions. The strong pyramidal shaped gives it a stately feel in any landscape. The light brown, exfoliating bark exposes a colorful orange inner bark. The limbs are somewhat corky, adding to this tree's winter appeal. In spring, long narrow catkins sway from the branches signaling the end to winter. Their drought tolerance and pest resistance means good-looking foliage all summer long. The fall color is variable but usually a yellow-green. In fall, mature trees will develop fruit. The filbert (hazelnut) is surrounded by a bristly covering. These are edible, but the squirrels usually get to them first.

When, Where, and How to Plant
These trees are a bit slow to establish. Plant balled-and-burlapped or container-grown trees in spring or early summer. This gives the plant time to put down roots before winter. Grow Turkish filberts in full sun with well-drained soils. These tough trees can tolerate urban conditions, drought, poor soils, and high pH. Plant the tree with its root flare at or slightly above the soil line. Follow the planting directions in the chapter introduction.

Growing Tips
Make sure to provide adequate water to the tree in the first few years after planting. Water thoroughly whenever the top few inches of soil are moist and crumbly. Mulch the soil to conserve moisture, suppress weeds, and eliminate the frustration of trying to grow grass. Established trees can tolerate drier soil conditions. Wait one year to fertilize new plantings according to soil test results or using a low-nitrogen slow-release fertilizer. Properly managed trees need minimal fertilization.

Regional Advice and Care
This is a fairly disease- and pest-free tree. It thrives in hot summers and cold winters. Train young trees to maintain central leader and to develop a strong framework. Prune in late winter so wounds will close quickly. This dense tree makes it hard to grow grass. Consider mulching or using shade tolerant groundcovers instead.

Companion Planting and Design
Use this stately tree as a focal point, between the sidewalk and curb, or for shading your house, patio, or deck. Its strong pyramidal shape makes it a good substitute for the acid-loving pin oak or less drought tolerant littleleaf linden.

Try These
Turkish filbert may be difficult to find. Check with your local specialty nursery. Or consider some of its relatives. 'Purple Haze' filbert has maroon-purple foliage all season grows fast to 8 to 10 feet. Harry Lauder's walking stick, *Corylus avellana* 'Contorta'; grows 8 to 10 feet tall. The contorted stems and twisted leaves give this plant interesting texture and form in the landscape. It is often used as a focal point near an entryway or in a mixed border.

Yellowwood

Cladrastis kentukea

Botanical Pronunciation
kluh-DRASS-tiss ken-TUCK-ee-uh

Bloom Period and Seasonal Color
White flowers in May to June and yellow fall color

Mature Height × Spread
30 to 50 feet × 40 to 55 feet

The graceful yellowwood is guaranteed to stand out in any landscape in or out of bloom. The smooth gray bark resembles a beech, providing an attractive framework year-round. The leaves emerge a bright yellowish green, changing to bright yellow for the summer. The fall color is a beautiful yellow to golden. Ten- to 16-inch-long, pendulous clusters of fragrant white flowers cover mature plants in late spring or early summer. They resemble wisteria flowers that you and the bees will enjoy. Trees may only bloom heavily every other or every third year, but the floral display is worth the wait. Dried brown pea pods appear in fall and persist adding winter interest. The yellow heartwood inspired this plants common name.

When, Where, and How to Plant

This urban-tolerant tree is native to rich well-drained limestone soils in river valleys, slopes, and along ridges of southeastern United States. Grow it in full sun for best flowering and fall color, though it will tolerate partial shade. Select a sheltered location protected from winter wind and sun with good drainage. This tree is pH adaptable tolerating high pH as well as acidic soils. Plant small balled-and-burlapped or container-grown trees. See the chapter introduction for planting instructions.

Growing Tips

Water new plantings thoroughly and often enough to keep the rootball and surrounding soil slightly moist. Established trees can tolerate dry soil. Water thoroughly whenever the top 4 to 6 inches are crumbly and moist. Mulch the soil surrounding the trees with a 2- to 3-inch layer of shredded bark or woodchips. Wait a year to fertilize new plantings. Properly sited established trees need little if any fertilizer. Proper pruning, starting early, is critical to establish a strong framework for longevity. Remove branches with narrow crotch angles (angle between trunk and branch) to create a framework of branches with wide crotch angles. You can prune in early summer to avoid the mess this heavy bleeder makes when pruned in winter or spring.

Regional Advice and Care

This tree has flowered reliably at the Minnesota Landscape Arboretum, and I stumbled upon a memorable specimen while touring gardens with the Perennial Plant Association (PPA) in Minneapolis. A student pulled me aside to identify a tree. The beech-like bark, delicate branching, and bright green leaves grabbed her attention. We were late getting back to the bus and the perennials enthusiasts gave us a hard time for looking at a tree, instead of perennials. But any who knew this tree understood our fascination.

Companion Planting and Design

Yellowwood make a nice shade tree for smaller yards or an ornamental specimen in any size landscape. Those with large yard can plant in groupings.

Try These

'Perkins Pink' ('Rosea') has fragrant pink flowers.

VINES
FOR MICHIGAN

Expand your garden space, screen a poor view, or create a bit of privacy with vines. These plant don't need much—just a little soil and a wall, fence, or other vertical support. Select vines that will tolerate the growing conditions, fit your design, serve your needs, and climb on the type of support provided.

Vines attach themselves to structures in different ways. Some, like American bittersweet and clematis, have twining stems and work well on chain-link fences, arbors, and trellises. Don't grow twining vines up tree trunks. They can encircle the trunk and kill the tree. Other vines have holdfasts. Boston ivy, climbing hydrangea, and other clinging vines have stick-tight tendrils, aerial rootlets, or adhesive pads for attaching to masonry or wood structures. Grow these vines on brick or stonewalls and on wooden trellises, arbors, or pergolas. Do not grow these vines on wood-sided homes. They can damage the siding and must be removed every time your home needs painting or repair.

Climbing rose 'Iceberg' with lobelia.

Supporting Your Vines

Use your imagination when selecting a support structure suitable for the vines you have chosen. I have seen twining vines climb up mailbox posts, lampposts, and downspouts. Some gardeners use attractive antique grates, doorframes, or discarded play structures. Others attach a section of plastic or wire mesh to a wall or fence to give the twining vines something to attach to. It also makes maintenance much easier. You can carefully remove the support from the wall, lay it on the ground, and make needed repairs to the fence or wall. When the work is complete, reattach the support, vine and all, to the structure.

No matter what type of support you select, make sure it is well anchored. Vine-covered structures can act like a sail and take off in a strong wind. The structure also must be strong enough to support the weight of the vine. Bittersweet, trumpet vine, and wisteria can become quite massive and heavy. These plants will need a strong, well-anchored structure for support.

Once the support is in place, it's time to select the best vine for the landscape design and maintenance. Rampant growers like Boston ivy may not be as showy as clematis, but they can quickly cover an ugly wall or hide a bad view. They will need regular pruning to keep them in line. Honeysuckle vines are beautiful flowering plants that need very little yearly pruning, but they may need occasional aphid control.

For added interest, mix several vines together on one support structure. Combine an annual with a perennial

Make sure that the structure you provide for vines, such as this *Lonicera* × *heckrottii*, is sturdy enough to support them.

vine the first few years. The annual vine will provide quick cover and beauty while the perennial vine gets established. You can do the same with two perennial vines. Use two different species or varieties for double the impact or to extend the bloom time. Select vines that are equally aggressive, or the stronger plant will engulf the weaker one, giving you a single-plant display.

Vines can also be used as groundcovers. Allow them to crawl unrestrained through the garden to create attractive and unexpected plant combinations. Monitor and prune vines to make sure they don't overrun or choke out their neighbors.

Getting Started

Get your vines off to a good growing start. Carefully slide the plant out of the pot, or better yet, cut the pot away at planting to minimize root disturbance. Simply remove the bottom of the container. Set it in a planting hole that is the same depth and at least two to three times wider than the rootball. Slice down the side of the pot and peel it away, leaving the rootball intact. Loosen any circling roots, fill the hole with the existing soil, and water. Pruning and training techniques vary. See the care information under each vine for specific directions. Now go outside and take a look around your landscape. I bet you can find a little vertical space just begging for a vine.

American Bittersweet

Celastrus scandens

Botanical Pronunciation
sell-ASS-trus scan-DENS

Bloom Period and Seasonal Color
May to June blooms in yellow-white; fall foliage in yellow

Mature Length 20 to 30 feet

American bittersweet is the perfect vine for large, tough places. It is a fast-growing plant that will quickly cover a fence or trellis and mask a bad view. This ornamental native can add year-round interest. Bittersweet's yellow fall color can be effective, and the decorative fruit can be used in dried arrangements. Birds enjoy feeding on the seeds throughout the winter. You will need at least one male for every five females for fruit. Although bittersweet is a vigorous plant, it is illegal to collect fruit from these native plants growing on public property. Ask permission of private property owners before collecting fruit from their plants. Beware the Oriental bittersweet, *Celastrus orbiculatus*, which looks very similar to American bittersweet but should not be planted as it is invasive.

When, Where, and How to Plant
Plant bare-root plants in early spring before growth begins. Plant container-grown plants anytime during the growing season. Bittersweet thrives and fruits best in full sun and well-drained soil. But consider planting in less-than-ideal soil to limit its growth. You will need at least one male for every five female plants to have fruit. You can only tell the sex of the plants by the flowers; check the label for that. Many nurseries include both a male and female plant in the same pot. Plant bare-root bittersweet with the crown even with the soil surface where the roots join the stem and keep soil moist. Gently loosen potbound roots of container-grown plants prior to planting. Place the plant in a hole as deep as the rootball and at least two to three times wider.

Growing Tips
Water established plants thoroughly whenever the top few inches of soil starts to dry. If bittersweet receives lots of moisture and fertilizer, it will grow bigger and faster with lots of leaves but no fruit. Practice benign neglect to keep them under control.

Regional Advice and Care
Train new growth to a support after planting. Bittersweet needs regular pruning. Prune in the late winter or early spring before growth begins. Prune dead, damaged, or out-of-place stems back to where they join another stem. Long side shoots can be pruned back to within three or four buds of the main stem. Just prune enough to control growth; overpruning can lead to excessive growth and poor fruit production.

Companion Planting and Design
Train bittersweet on to a large pergola or arbor, allow it to crawl over a rock pile, or use it to cover a fence. Just remember it grows quickly and needs a strong support and regular pruning to keep it under control. Keep it away from more timid plants that can easily be overrun by this aggressive grower.

Try These
'American Revolution' is self-fertile, meaning you only need one plant to have fruit. No more looking under the petals or trying to guess if the male or female plant died and needs replacing.

Arctic Beauty Kiwi

Actinidia kolomikta 'Arctic Beauty'

Botanical Pronunciation
ak-tin-ID-ee-ah koe-lo-MIK-tah

Bloom Period and Seasonal Color
White flowers mid-May through June; colorful foliage spring through summer, yellow fall color

Mature Length 15 to 20 feet

This vine is a hardy and ornamental relative of the edible kiwi you may have purchased in the grocery store. The emerging heart-shaped leaves start out purple and then turn green with a white and pink blotch. In fall, the leaves turn yellow before dropping to the ground. The attractive foliage makes a nice seasonal screen, vertical accent, or backdrop for other plants. I have seen this twining vine trained on tall posts, trellises, and arbors. A close look in late May and early June will reveal small fragrant flowers. If you have both male and female plants, you will be rewarded with sweet edible kiwis the size of grapes. Just the right size for popping in your mouth as you work in the garden.

When, Where, and How to Plant
Plant container-grown plants anytime during the growing season. Spring through early summer allows plants time to establish before winter. 'Arctic Beauty' kiwi will have the best foliage color in partially shaded locations; foliage tends to bleach out in full sun and fade in heavy shade. Grow in a protected spot with moist, well-drained soils for best results. You will need at least one male for every five female plants for fruit (the plant's gender should be on the label). Gently loosen potbound roots prior to planting. Place the plant in a hole that is as deep as the rootball and at least two to three times wider.

Growing Tips
Water established plants thoroughly when the top 4 to 6 inches are moist but crumbly. Avoid excess nitrogen fertilizer, which inhibits flowering, fruiting, and good foliage color.

Regional Advice and Care
Hardiness is its biggest problem. Those on the northern limits of hardiness may consider using this in a somewhat sheltered location. Increase survival rates by providing winter protection the first year or two after planting. Wrap new plantings with burlap or surround them with hardware cloth sunk in the ground and filled with evergreen boughs or straw. Prune new plantings back to a strong bud about 12 to 16 inches above the ground. Train five to seven strong shoots onto the support. Next spring, prune stout side shoots by one-third and weak branches back to one to two buds. Prune established plants back by one-third or one-half in early spring before growth begins. Occasionally remove old stems to ground level to promote new growth at the base.

Companion Planting and Design
Train 'Arctic Beauty' kiwi on a trellis or other structure. It creates a colorful screen to mask bad views or a nice backdrop to any garden. Use plantings with white and pink flowers nearby to maximize the impact of the multicolored foliage.

Try These
Tara vine, *Actinidia arguta*, is less ornamental but produces more fruit. The green leaves will quickly cover the support. Select the less ornamental self-fruitful cultivar 'Issai' to eliminate the need for male and female plants.

Boston Ivy

Parthenocissus tricuspidata

Botanical Pronunciation
par-then-oh-SIS-us tri-kuss-pih-DAY-tah

Other Name Japanese creeper

Bloom Period and Seasonal Color
Insignificant bloom; red fall color

Mature Length 50 to 60 feet

You are probably looking at Boston ivy when you see a vine-covered cottage or an old university building in our region. Though not a true ivy, this tough, fast-growing plant gives you the same look. It is an excellent vine for covering large areas quickly. It attaches itself to structures and plants with holdfast tipped tendrils. Boston ivy is one of the first plants to brighten up the fall landscape with its brilliant red fall color. The blue, grape-like fruit is apparent after the leaves drop. Don't eat them; leave them for the birds. A close relative is the native Virginia creeper, *Parthenocissus quinquefolia*. It has five-part leaves, grape-like fruits, and good fall color. Both provide food and shelter for the birds.

When, Where, and How to Plant

Plant container-grown Boston ivy anytime during the growing season. This tough plant will tolerate most difficult growing conditions. Grow it in full sun to full shade. Boston ivy prefers well-drained soil but can take just about any type of soil. It can survive pollution, road salt, and wind. Dig a planting hole the same depth as the rootball and two to three times wider. Plant container-grown Boston ivy at the same level it was growing in the pot. Gently loosen potbound roots. Water thoroughly and mulch.

Growing Tips

Established plants are drought tolerant. Water thoroughly whenever the top few inches of soil start to dry. Minimal fertilizer is needed for this grower. Excess nitrogen can result in even more rampant growth and poor fall color. Watch for and remove seedlings as the birds spread seeds around yours and your neighbor's landscapes.

Regional Advice and Care

Pruning is the only regular maintenance established plants need. They can grow as much as 6 to 10 feet in a year. Prune vines away from windows, eaves, and gutters. Remove stems that are no longer attached to the structure. Older overgrown plants can be renovated. Prune them back to 3 feet. Boston ivy is difficult to remove from buildings and other structures. Prune the vines off the structure and rub the holdfasts off the with leather glove-clad hands. Or you can wait until they eventually dry up and fall off, but that will take quite a while.

Companion Planting and Design

This fast-growing plant can be trained on stone and brick buildings, walls, or other structures. It attaches with suction cup–like pads and needs no additional support.

Try These

The Boston ivy cultivar 'Veitchii' is less aggressive and finer textured. The leaves are purple when young, green for the summer, and red in fall. This cultivar is a better choice than the species for most landscape situations. 'Fenway Park' was discovered near its namesake. The leaves emerge yellow, turn green, and then red in fall. 'Star Showers'® Virginia creeper is less aggressive and has white speckled variegation on the leaves.

Clematis

Clematis species

Botanical Pronunciation
KLEM-ah-tis

Bloom Period and Seasonal Color
Summer blooms in white, purple, pink, or red

Mature Length 5 to 18 feet

Most gardeners can't resist clematis once they have seen it in full bloom. This small plant provides lots of late spring, summer, or fall color, even in very small spaces. The old saying, "Clematis like their face in the sun and their feet in the shade" is true. Grow in a sunny location with the roots mulched or shaded by a groundcover. Small dormant plants are a common sight in the garden center in early spring. They are often sold with their roots packed in peat moss–filled plastic bags. These plants often break dormancy and begin to grow on the shelves of garden centers. Plant the growing clematis in containers and grow it indoors or outside in a cold frame until after the danger of frost has passed.

When, Where, and How to Plant
Plant container-grown clematis in the spring and early summer. Plant dormant clematis outdoors as soon as the soil is workable. Grow clematis in moist, well-drained, alkaline soil. Do not add lime unless directed by your soil test. Clematis plants often come with a stake. This can be cumbersome and may even damage the plant. Remove the stake and plant at the same level it was growing in the container or in the nursery. Pinch off the growing tips of newly planted clematis. Carefully attach the young stems to the trellis or support.

Growing Tips
Mulch the soil around the clematis after planting to keep the roots cool and moist. Avoid piling mulch over the stems. Keep the soil moist, but not wet, throughout the growing season.

Regional Advice and Care
Clematis is fairly pest free. Moving struggling plants to a new location, even a few feet, often helps. Yellow clematis leaves are common in early spring. Once the soil warms, the plants will green up and start to flourish. Avoid injuring stems with rough handling and tools. These wounds create entryways for stem wilt disease. Infested stems turn black and wilt. Prune and destroy infected stems to ground level in fall. The early spring blooming clematis bloom on old wood and are pruned after flowering. These are generally not hardy in our area. Most gardeners prune heavily each year to maintain a small flowering plant. Prune summer and fall bloomers during the dormant season. I prefer late winter. Prune stems above a set of healthy buds 6 to 12 inches above the soil.

Companion Planting and Design
Use clematis to brighten up any vertical space. Train the twining vines on trellises, mailboxes, and lampposts. Plant several clematis varieties on the same trellis or add a rose for double the bloom.

Try These
Clematis viticella 'Betty Corning' is my favorite. It produces blue, downward-facing blooms through most of the summer. Sweet autumn clematis, *Clematis terniflora*, provides fragrant white fall flowers on an easy-care, fast-growing plant.

Climbing Hydrangea

Hydrangea anomala petiolaris

Botanical Pronunciation
hy-DRAIN-jah an-NOM-al-a pet-ee-oh-LAY-riss

Bloom Period and Seasonal Color
June or early July blooms in white

Mature Length 60 to 80 feet

Climbing hydrangea is a great four-season vine. The beautiful, fragrant, white flowers appear in mid-June to early July. These flowers last for two weeks or more, but seed heads persist all season. The plant does not grow flat against its support, which adds texture, depth, and interesting shadows to the landscape. The leaves may turn yellow or drop off green in fall, exposing this hydrangea's beautiful bark. The cinnamon brown peeling bark adds interest all winter. Be patient as it does take several years to get established and start flowering. I grew mine in a container for several years. It bloomed beautifully, but I had trouble finding help sinking the large pot in the ground for winter protection. Now it adorns the north side of my home.

When, Where, and How to Plant
Climbing hydrangea is usually container grown. Plant in spring as it is slow to recover from transplanting. Grow it in partial or shaded locations. It prefers moist, well-drained soil and may suffer from scorch (brown leaf edges) if grown in full sun or dry soil. Plant climbing hydrangeas at the same level they were growing in the container. Handle with care. To minimize root disturbance when transplanting, first cut off the bottom of the container. Place the plant in a hole that is the same depth and at least two to three times as wide as the rootball. Slice and peel the side of the pot, leaving the rootball intact. Fill the hole with the existing soil, and water.

Growing Tips
The first few years climbing hydrangeas may barely grow. By the third or fourth year, the roots are established and the plant seems to take off. Mulch and keep the soil moist, but not wet, throughout the growing season. Avoid high-nitrogen fertilizers that can inhibit bloom.

Regional Advice and Care
Remove wayward branches in the summer right after flowering. Prune the stems back to a healthy bud. Avoid severe pruning; it can decrease flowering for several years. Tie young shoots to a support; they will climb on their own once aerial roots form. Established plants need minimal pruning.

Companion Planting and Design
Train this plant on a brick or stonewall, a fence, or an arbor using a sturdy support. Or allow it to creep over the ground. It combines nicely with hosta, ginger, and other shade tolerant plants. A container planting of this vine is a good way to include this beauty in your landscape when limited by a lack of planting space or cold temperatures. Sink the pot in the ground for winter or move into an unheated garage and provide added insulation. Water whenever the soil is thawed and dry.

Try These
'Miranda' is a relatively new introduction. The dark green leaves have a yellow to creamy white margin. I have seen this growing in several botanical gardens in our area.

Climbing Rose

Rosa × hybrida

Botanical Pronunciation ROE-sah

Other Name Ramblers

Bloom Period and Seasonal Color
Once or repeat blooming in summer; various flower colors including red, pink, salmon, yellow, and white

Mature Length 6 to 20 feet

The climbing rose is a jack-of-all-trades in Mother Nature's garden. Use climbing roses as vertical accents, flowering specimens, and screens. Or let them grow up and over an arbor to create a colorful and fragrant welcome for your guests. The possibilities are endless. Climbing roses are grouped into two major categories. The ramblers are big, fast-growing, hardy roses. Rambling roses are an old variety, a kind everyone's grandmother seemed to grow. They bloom profusely early in the season and require very little care and no winter protection. Rambling rose flowers are small and grow in clusters. New disease-resistant and repeat-blooming hybrids are being introduced. The large-flowered climbing roses grow slower. Climbers come from a variety of sources including mutations of hybrid tea, grandiflora, and multiflora roses.

When, Where, and How to Plant
Plant bare-root and container-grown climbing roses early in the season. Climbers, like all roses, grow best in full sun and moist, well-drained soil. Plant near a fence, trellis, or arbor that is large and sturdy enough to handle the size and weight of the mature plant. Grafted climbers should be planted with the graft union 2 inches below the soil surface. Non-grafted climbers can be planted at the same level as they were grown in the nursery.

Growing Tips
Train and attach climbers to their support. Loosely tie the stems to the support with twine. Keep the training simple if plants must be moved for winter protection.

Regional Advice and Care
Only prune dead and damaged wood during the first few years and do not cut plants back for winter protection. Each spring, remove only dead stems back to ground level. After blooming you can remove one-third of the older canes. Single bloomers can be pruned back by two-thirds of their size. Trim side branches by two-thirds if desired. After temperatures hover near the freezing mark for about a week, its time to protect non-hardy climbers. Roses in sheltered locations may survive with soil mounded over the graft and a burlap wrap filled with evergreen boughs or straw. Or use the "Minnesota tip" method. Remove the climber from its support. Tie canes together and bend or tip the roses over, lay them on the ground and secure in place. Cover the entire plant with soil. Once the soil covering freezes, mulch with straw, or evergreen branches.

Companion Planting and Design
Use roses as a backdrop for perennial gardens, as a fragrant screen, or to cover an arbor. Mix with sweet autumn or summer blooming clematis for added color and texture.

Try These
'William Baffin', a large shrub rose that can be trained as a climber, is a low-maintenance repeat bloomer with deep pink flowers and good pest resistance that needs no winter protection. 'Ramblin Red', hardy to Zone 3, has deep red flowers. 'New Dawn' is hardy, disease resistant, and has survived unprotected in Zone 4.

Dutchman's Pipe

Aristolochia macrophylla

Botanical Pronunciation
ah-ris-toe-LOH-kee-uh mak-roh-FIL-uh

Bloom Period and Seasonal Color
Late May or early June pipe-shaped blooms

Mature Length 15 to 30 feet

Dutchman's pipe is an old fashioned favorite worthy of a second look. This vine has long been used to screen a porch or climb a trellis. The large heart-shaped leaves form a dense screen and shade. A look under the leaves in late May or early June reveals the source of its common name. Small pipe-shaped flowers provide a hidden treasure for children and visitors to uncover. I was lucky enough to witness an outstanding bloom on a Dutchman's pipe at Boerner Botanical Gardens a few springs ago. And just a few years prior, the pipevine swallowtails blew in on the spring winds. I witnessed them lay their eggs and their prickly black larvae soon appeared to feast on the abundant leaves.

When, Where, and How to Plant
Grow this Michigan and eastern U.S. native in full to part sun and moist well-drained soil. Plants may be difficult to find at your local garden center. If so, check with specialty nurseries or online. You may start plants from seed. They need three months of cold treatment to germinate. So plant seeds outdoors in fall or store in a refrigerator for winter. Check the label on the seed packet for more specific directions. Or ask a fellow gardener to share a piece of their plant. Divide in spring, layer, or take cuttings in midsummer. Plant container grown dutchman's pipes in a hole the same depth as and 2 to 3 times wider than the rootball. Fill with soil and water. Mulch to keep roots cool and moist.

Growing Tips
This twining vine is easy to grow and will quickly fill its support. Train strongest shoots to support and prune out any weak or damaged stems back to the base. Prune in late winter or early spring before growth begins to control its size. Once established these plants will tolerate severe pruning. Cut back long side shoots back to the second or third bud from the main stem.

Regional Advice and Care
This plant tolerates pollution and urban conditions. Water during dry periods as they prefer moist soil. There are no serious pest problems. The pipevine swallowtail is a rare occurrence in our area. And when warm winds bring them here there is no need to worry. The large amount of foliage ensures they are not detrimental to the health of an established plant.

Companion Plants and Design
Use as a backdrop for other shade plants. Mine is trained up my fence behind a collection of baneberry, ferns, and hosta. Or use it to screen a bad view or create privacy in your outdoor living space.

Try These
Adventuresome and indoor gardeners may want to try calico vine, *Aristolochia litteralis*, that is hardy in Zones 9 to 12. Grow this in a container outdoors for summer and winter it indoors in a sunroom or a greenhouse.

Hyacinth Bean

Lablab purpureus

Botanical Pronunciation
LAB-lab per-per-EE-us

Bloom Period and Seasonal Color
Summer through fall with rosy purple flowers
and purple fruit

Mature Length 10 to 20 feet

No, it isn't a typo or a joke on you. The botanical name and the plant are both quite eye-catching. This annual twining vine is the fancy relative of our bean plant. The dark green, heart-shaped leaves with purple veins are held on reddish stems. The fragrant, rosy purple flowers are followed by dark purple beans. The plant will be covered with both flowers and fruit from summer through frost. Grown here as an ornamental, this is an important food crop in Africa and India, but special preparation is required to make them safe. New to many gardeners, this old-fashioned favorite has been grown in the United States for many years. Thomas Jefferson apparently had it growing in his home in Monticello in the early 1800s.

When, Where, and How to Plant
Start seeds indoors four to six weeks before the last spring frost for early summer bloom. Plant in 3- to 4-inch clean containers or biodegradable pots filled with sterile potting mix. Keep the soil warm, 65 to 70 degrees Fahrenheit, and moist. Or wait until the danger of frost has passed and sow the seeds 1 inch deep directly outdoors. If using transplants, remove the stake (if one was included) prior to planting to avoid damaging the vine. Slide the plant out of the container and loosen any potbound roots before planting. Grow hyacinth beans in full sun and moist, well-drained garden soil.

Growing Tips
Keep the soil moist during sprouting and the seedling stage of growth. Water established plants thoroughly whenever the top few inches of soil are crumbly and moist. Fertilize according to soil test recommendations or with a low-nitrogen slow-release fertilizer. Watch for volunteer seedlings in next year's garden.

Regional Advice and Care
This low-maintenance vine will provide lots of color summer through frost. Tie young plants to a trellis, fence, or other support. Once it makes contact, it will climb up the structure with minimal guidance. Only remove ripe fruit if production slows. Hyacinth beans are edible but contain a toxin. Improperly prepared or overindulging can make you sick. North Carolina State recommends thoroughly boiling the seeds and pods, changing the water several times before eating. I think I'll stick to Kentucky wonder pole beans and just enjoy the hyacinth bean's colorful show.

Companion Planting and Design
Show off the flowers and fruit by training your vine on a white picket fence or other light colored structure. The herb gardener at Boerner Botanical Gardens grew these on several teepee type structures marching down the center of a bed. The beans were surrounded by parsley, purple alyssum, santolina, and other green, silver, and purple flowers and herbs.

Try These
'Ruby Moon' has pink to violet and lavender flowers and deep violet fruit. Check the Internet and garden catalogues if you have trouble finding seeds or transplants at your local garden center.

Honeysuckle Vine

Lonicera species

Botanical Pronunciation
lon-ISS-er-ah

Bloom Period and Seasonal Color
June through October blooms in orange, pink, or red

Mature Length 12 feet

Here's a vine suited to most gardens. The non-invasive honeysuckle vines include goldflame *(Lonicera × heckrottii),* Dropmore Scarlet *(Lonicera × brownii* 'Dropmore Scarlet', and trumpet honeysuckle *(Lonicera sempervirens),* which is native to much of eastern United States. These fast-growing twining vines with attractive foliage produce colorful flowers from spring through summer. Single plants can be trained on an arbor, creating lots of color in a small yard. Larger plantings can be used to mask a chain-link fence or create a fence full of blossoms. Plant it in an area where you can enjoy the fragrant flowers and hummingbirds that come to visit. Grow it in full sun and partial shade with moist well-drained soils. Avoid growing the invasive Japanese honeysuckles *(Lonicera japonica).*

When, Where, and How to Plant
Container-grown vines can be planted anytime during the growing season but do best if planted in spring. This plant thrives in moist, well-drained soil. Minimize root disturbance especially on late-season plantings by cutting away the pot at transplant time. Cut off the bottom of the container. Set it in a planting hole that is the same depth and at least two to three times wider than the rootball. Slice the side of the pot and peel it away, leaving the rootball intact. Loosen any potbound roots and fill the hole with existing soil and water.

Growing Tips
Mulch and keep the soil moist, but not wet, throughout the growing season. Avoid excess nitrogen that encourages leaf growth and discourages flowering.

Regional Advice and Care
Prune damaged shoots at planting time. Tie young shoots to a support. They will soon attach to the structure on their own. Trumpet honeysuckle is a low-maintenance vine but may have problems with aphids and mildew. The plants will survive, but an infestation can ruin many of the blossoms. Heavy rains and lady beetles, green lacewings, praying mantis, and other natural predators may keep this pest in check. If not, start with a strong blast of water or insecticidal soap to reduce the aphid population without harming the beneficial insects that feed upon them. Powdery mildew can be a problem, especially on vines grown in the shade. Thinning will help improve air circulation and reduce disease problems. Established plants can tolerate this disease. Mask the diseased foliage with nearby plantings. Prune overgrown plants to fit the available space. Trim them to where the branches join, or above a healthy bud. Prune older stems back to ground level. Renovate older plantings by pruning stems back to 2 feet above the ground.

Companion Planting and Design
Use it on a fence, arbor, or other upright structure. It works well in wildlife and cottage gardens.

Try These
Woodbine honeysuckle, *Lonicera periclymenum,* tend to be more resistant to mildew. The cultivar 'Jubilee' has bright yellow flowers. *Lonicera* × 'Mandarin' has pale orange flowers.

Morning Glory

Ipomoea purpurea

Botanical Pronunciation
eye-poe-MEE-ah pur-pur-EE-ah

Bloom Period and Seasonal Color
Summer blooms in purple, blue, pink, red, and white

Mature Length 8 to 10 feet

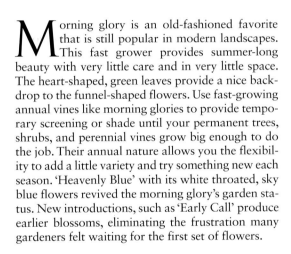

Morning glory is an old-fashioned favorite that is still popular in modern landscapes. This fast grower provides summer-long beauty with very little care and in very little space. The heart-shaped, green leaves provide a nice backdrop to the funnel-shaped flowers. Use fast-growing annual vines like morning glories to provide temporary screening or shade until your permanent trees, shrubs, and perennial vines grow big enough to do the job. Their annual nature allows you the flexibility to add a little variety and try something new each season. 'Heavenly Blue' with its white throated, sky blue flowers revived the morning glory's garden status. New introductions, such as 'Early Call' produce earlier blossoms, eliminating the frustration many gardeners felt waiting for the first set of flowers.

When, Where, and How to Plant

Start seeds indoors, four to six weeks prior to the last spring frost. Nick the seed or soak it in warm water for twenty-four hours before planting. The seeds need moist, warm temperatures, 70 to 85 degrees Fahrenheit, to germinate in five to seven days. Plant hardened-off transplants outdoors after the last spring frost. Space transplants 12 inches apart. Or seed directly outdoors after all danger of frost is past. Grow morning glories in full sun with well-drained soil. Plant seeds 6 inches apart and 1 inch deep. Thin 3-inch-tall plants to 12 inches apart. Morning glory will reseed; remove unwanted seedlings.

Growing Tips

Each flower opens in the morning and lasts only one day. But it is replaced the next day with new blossoms. Once a vine starts flowering, it will remain in bloom all season. The less care morning glories receive, the better their bloom. Excess water and fertilizer result in lots of leaves, but no flowers.

Regional Advice and Care

Guide young plants onto a support until they take off on their own. All parts of morning glory are toxic.

Companion Planting and Design

Grow morning glory vines in areas you will see early in the day since the flowers tend to close in the low light of afternoon and on cloudy days. Try growing them on small trellises in large containers. They make great vertical accents and mix well with other plants. Mix morning glories with perennial vines to provide quick cover and bloom while the perennials are getting established. Or use them with established vines to extend or double your flowering effect.

Try These

'Minibar' rose cultivar brightens up the landscape with its pink flowers and ivy shaped variegated foliage. Moonflower, *Ipomoea alba*, has white flowers that open at dusk. Start them indoors for earlier bloom in the garden. Star glory, *Ipomoea quamoclit*, and cardinal climber, *Ipomoea × multifida*, have attractive deeply lobed foliage and red, funnel-shaped flowers. Spanish flag, *Ipomoea lobata* (formerly *Mina lobata*), is shade tolerant with narrow tubular flowers that start scarlet and mature to yellow and orange.

Trumpet Vine

Campsis radicans

Botanical Pronunciation
KAMP-sis RAD-ih-kanz

Other Name Trumpet creeper

Bloom Period and Seasonal Color
July blooms in orange and yellow

Mature Length 40 feet or more

Trumpet vine's beautiful flowers and its hummingbird appeal make it a good addition to any landscape. The vine produces clusters of large, orange, trumpet-shaped flowers often featured in artwork, on book covers, and with articles on hummingbirds and nectar plants. Trumpet vines are excellent choices for large, difficult locations. These rampant growers will overtake anything in their path. Its aggressive nature means you will need to get out the pruners every year. They also spread underground developing suckers near and even quite a distance from the parent plant. Use a sharp shovel to prune out the suckers at ground level. But once the suckers are removed and the pruning is finished, so is the yearly maintenance for the trumpet vine. Just sit back, relax, and enjoy the show.

When, Where, and How to Plant
Plant bare-root trumpet vines in early spring before growth begins. Plant container-grown plants anytime during the growing season. Grow them in full sun with well-drained moist to dry soil. The vines tolerate most growing situations, including drought and exposure to deicing salt. Gently loosen pot-bound roots. Plant trumpet vines at the same depth they were growing previously. Water thoroughly and mulch to keep roots cool and moist. Train new growth to the support. Once aerial rootlets form, it will attach itself. The vines will also twine around structures and plants in its way.

Growing Tips
It may take several years for your plant to bloom. Excessive shade and nitrogen can prevent flowering.

Trumpet vines are luxury feeders, consuming all available nutrients. This results in lots of leaves and stems but no flowers. Avoid high-nitrogen fertilizers around trumpet vines.

Regional Advice and Care
Trumpet vines are slow to leaf out and may suffer winter injury. This is not a problem since they grow so fast. You may need to provide additional help to keep this fast-growing plant attached to its support structure. Yearly pruning is necessary to keep vines under control. The best time to prune is late winter through early spring. Prune young plants to fit the support structure. This will be the plant's basic framework and your basis for future pruning. Cut back the side shoots on established plants each year. Prune back to within three or four buds of the main framework. Remove overcrowded shoots as needed.

Companion Planting and Design
Trumpet vines need strong structures for support. They are great on fences in the landscape or on more unusual supports. One family let a trumpet vine wind around their children's old play structure. The vine had the support it needed, and the family got to keep their memories neatly tucked away under this plant. A bakery near me has trained its trumpet vine into a small tree.

Try These
Add a bit of variety with the yellow flowered cultivar 'Flava', apricot orange flowered 'Madame Galen', and 'Balboa Sunset's' velvety red and orange flowers.

Wisteria

Wisteria species

Botanical Pronunciation
wis-TEER-ee-ah

Bloom Period and Seasonal Color
Late spring or early summer blooms in purple
to violet

Mature Length 30 feet

Wisteria is the classic beauty of flowering vines. Unfortunately, the pictures in books look much better than the plants growing in our northern landscapes. Japanese and Chinese wisteria vines are sold as hardy to Zones 4 or 5. The plants will survive but seldom flower in our region. Kentucky wisteria, *Wisteria macrostachya*, is a better choice. It's not quite as dramatic, but it is more reliable and still an impressive sight in bloom. Kentucky wisteria produces beautiful 12-inch purple flowers in the summer after the leaves emerge. The American Medical Association (AMA) reports that all parts of this plant are toxic. Some older gardening books talk about how the Chinese harvested, steamed, and ate the mature blossoms of Chinese wisteria. I'm going with the AMA on this one.

When, Where, and How to Plant
Plant container-grown wisteria in spring in full sun to light shade and in moist, well-drained soil. Plant container-grown wisteria at the same level it was growing in the container. Handle wisteria with care to reduce transplant shock. Cut off the bottom of the container. Place the plant in a hole that is the same depth and at least two to three times as wide as the rootball. Slice the side of the pot and peel it away, leaving the rootball intact. Loosen any circling roots, then fill the hole with soil and water.

Growing Tips
Mulch and keep the soil moist, but not wet, throughout the growing season. Avoid Japanese and Chinese wisterias. Though their long flowers are impressive, the flower buds are usually killed by our cold winters. Every few years, after a mild winter, you may see one of their breathtaking flower displays, but most years you have large plants with nothing but leaves. The Kentucky wisteria is plant- and flowerbud-hardy to Zone 4, with reports of plants surviving and even blooming in Zone 3. Avoid overfertilizing.

Regional Advice and Care
Pruning is the only real maintenance needed. Prune Kentucky wisteria in late winter before growth begins. At planting, cut the main stem back to 30–36 inches. Spend the next few years developing a strong framework to cover the support. Lightly prune established plants after flowering as needed. Yearly pruning will help control growth. Avoid overpruning that can stimulate excess vegetative growth and discourage flowering. Wisteria may not bloom for the first seven years.

Companion Planting and Design
Espalier wisteria vines on a wall or grow them on a pergola. You can develop a tree-form wisteria by training the main stem to a stake. The tree takes shape after several years of pruning back the main stem and side shoots. Prune yearly to maintain size and shape. Use sturdy supports. These fast growers can cause weak structures to collapse.

Try These
Grow Kentucky wisteria for most reliable bloom. 'Blue Moon' is a fast blooming variety that is hardy and blooms up to three times a season.

MICHIGAN
FROST MAP

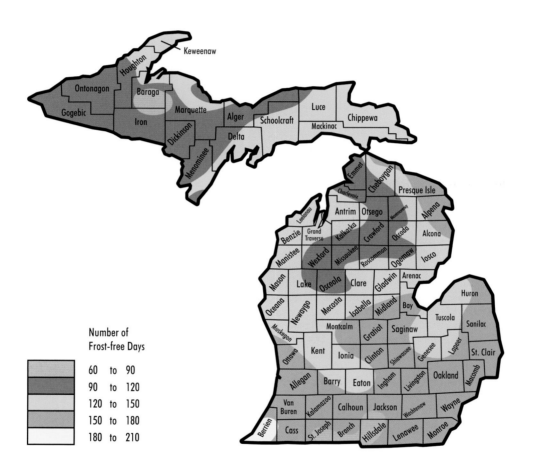

Number of
Frost-free Days

60 to 90
90 to 120
120 to 150
150 to 180
180 to 210

GARDENING WITH NATIVE PLANTS

Michigan is renowned for its distinctive natural landscape and abundance of natural areas. Our shorelines, lakes, prairies, forests, and wetlands draw visitors from all over the world. Residents enjoy heading up to the lake or woods to vacation, reinvigorating their senses and souls when the pace of daily life gets overwhelming.

These days, though, what used to be rural and remote in Michigan is rapidly becoming developed. Woodlands and fields are being dug up for housing developments. County roads, once lined with gray dogwood and Michigan holly, are now lined with a numbing number of discount and convenience stores. Population growth and development sprawl mean that Michigan's natural areas are disappearing, and the trend is unlikely to diminish in coming years.

What does that mean to gardeners? For many of us, it means changing the way we think about the spaces we maintain.

Bring the Natural World Closer

Early settlers built gardens to exclude and control the wildness of the natural world. Today, more people are using native plants to bring the natural world closer and to take an active role in preserving biodiversity for future generations. Native plants are those that originated in our region before European settlers arrived and have adapted to continue growing here.

Some people may be intimidated by the prospect of growing native plants. They may be unfamiliar with the plants themselves, compared to mainstream perennials. They may worry that the natives won't be attractive or, if introduced, will do too well, dominating the plantings and the character of their gardens.

The native plants selected for this book, which are designated with the symbol Ⓝ, can be easily integrated into your existing garden. You can plant just one, or just a few, or design an entire landscape. A good start is to consider a native tree when choosing one for your lawn or street. Or choose a native shrub for use as a privacy screen. In a perennial garden, native and non-native perennials and grasses can flourish when grown side by side. You don't have to switch entirely to natives, although some gardeners may choose to do that. Others will start new beds featuring native plants. Once you introduce more native plants, you'll notice and appreciate nature's seasonal rhythms in your own garden.

Reasons to Go Native

Here are a few more reasons to garden with native plants:

- Many natives require less supplemental water. Some native plants have deep roots. They have evolved to survive in this region without extra moisture—although, during drought, gardeners may choose to provide water to keep them healthy and attractive.
- Natives need no supplemental chemicals. Given the right site, soil, and light, native plants will thrive without additional fertilizers or pesticides.
- Once established, natives generally require less routine maintenance. In most cases, chores like deadheading and pruning, as well as extensive soil preparation, are unnecessary. Cleanup can be limited to an early-spring gathering of old foliage or errant branches that need cutting back to maintain size or shape.
- Natives provide a habitat for wildlife. Birds, butterflies, other insects, and mammals that occur naturally in our region will use native plants for food and shelter. Especially in urban and suburban areas, landscapes incorporating native plants create a welcome green oasis for wildlife.
- A community or grouping of native plants can absorb storm water runoff and even help filter pollutants from the water and soil. This can ease the burden on sewer systems and reduce what goes into nearby lakes and rivers.
- Natives are usually, although not always, less invasive. That means they won't get out of control like exotics like vinca, Norway maple, or purple loosestrife, which can outcompete and crowd out native plants. Certainly there are exceptions: pokeweed comes to mind, for its ability to spread from seed. However, since the pokeweed's berries are a favorite with migrating birds, it's a valued plant among birding enthusiasts.

It comes down to making choices. By planting natives, you can help preserve Michigan's diverse natural heritage.

Working with Nature

Gardening with natives is sometimes called natural landscaping. Perhaps the most important guideline to making it work is to select plants that fit the site, rather than trying to adapt the site to fit a particular plant's requirements. Work with nature. Don't fight it. Coaxing plants to survive where they would not, except for extraordinary measures, is a waste of time when there are so many plants to choose from. Plants sited incorrectly become stressed and are more prone to disease and insect problems.

After planting, mulch native plants to conserve water in the soil. As the leaves decompose, they return nutrients to the soil, which nourishes the plants. Allow leaves that fall in the autumn to remain. It's all part of the natural cycle.

With an eye on design, some prairie or meadow gardens of native plants may look weedy to people accustomed to manicured lawns and gardens. To offset this, many gardeners who use native plants include a strip of grass that can be mowed around the perimeter. They may also incorporate some plants with bright flowers. These elements may reassure worried neighbors that the yard is, in fact, a designed and kept area.

Check local ordinances, too. Some communities take a relaxed approach to the enforcement of weed ordinances that can thwart gardeners who want to turn portions of their yards into havens for native perennial plantings. If that is a concern to you, plant native trees and shrubs, which look no more or less weedy than non-native woody plants.

For inspiration on gardening with native plants, walk through a Michigan woodland in May, when trilliums carpet the forest floor. Admire the tenacity of dune plants that survive the intense heat and light of a July afternoon along Lake Michigan. Look carefully at the places where native plants grow, and observe the related plants that form.

Protecting Native Plants

When purchasing native plants, be sure they have been propagated and grown in nurseries rather than taken from the wild, or that they have been rescued with the owner's permission from land slated for development. This protects the supply of native plants, some of which are on state or federal lists of threatened or endangered species. Patronize nurseries that specialize in native plants.

The inspiration of nature is all around us. Bring to it your own style of gardening. Even in the midst of a city, growing native plants is a way to reintroduce nature.

As people become more accustomed to seeing and appreciating native plants, they will be more inclined to consider the ways that the soil, climate, plants, wildlife, and the gardeners' fates are intertwined.

TREE PLANTING DIAGRAM

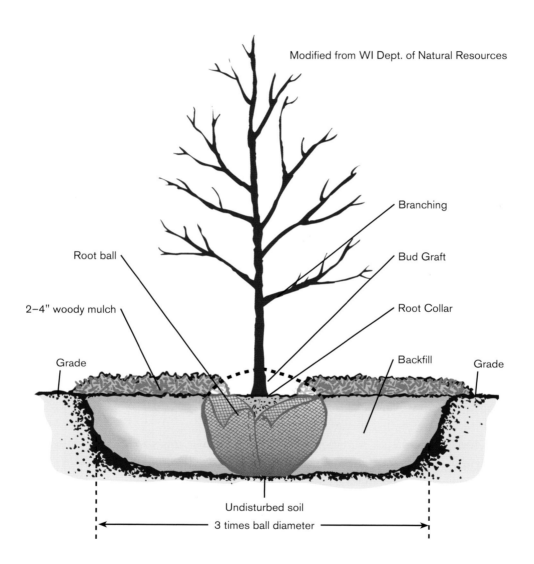

Modified from WI Dept. of Natural Resources

Branching

Bud Graft

Root Collar

Root ball

2–4" woody mulch

Backfill

Grade

Grade

Undisturbed soil

3 times ball diameter

Diggers Hotline

Diggers Hotline is a free utility-locating service. They will mark the location of any underground utilities in the planting area. Give them three working days to complete the task. This is important for your safety and pocketbook. Digging into a utility line can be expensive and even deadly. Call 811 or go online at www.call811.com/.

GLOSSARY

Acid soil: soil with a pH less than 7.0. Acid soil is sometimes called "sour soil" by gardeners. Most plants prefer a slightly acid soil between 6 and 7 where most essential nutrients are available.

Alkaline soil: soil with a pH greater than 7.0, usually formed from limestone bedrock. Alkaline soil is often referred to as sweet soil.

Annual: a plant that completes its entire life cycle in one season. It germinates, grows, flowers, sets seed, and dies within one year.

Balled and burlapped: describes a large tree whose roots have been wrapped tightly in protective burlap and twine after it is dug. It is wrapped in this manner to protect it for shipping, sales, and transplanting.

Bare-root: trees, shrubs, and perennials that have been grown in soil, dug, and have had the soil removed prior to sales or shipping. Mail-order plants are often shipped bare-root with the roots packed in peat moss, sawdust, or similar material and wrapped in plastic.

Barrier plant: a plant that has thorns or impenetrable growth habit and is used to block foot traffic or other access to an area in the landscape.

Beneficial insects: insects or their larvae that prey on pest organisms and their eggs. They may be flying insects such as ladybugs, parasitic wasps, praying mantids, and soldier bugs; or soil dwellers such as predatory nematodes, spiders, and ants.

Berm: a low, artificial hill created in a landscape to elevate a portion of the landscape for functional and aesthetic reasons such as added interest, screening, and improved drainage.

Bract: a modified leaf resembling a flower petal, located just below the true flower. Often it is more colorful and visible than the actual flower, as in poinsettia.

Bud union: the place where the top of a plant was grafted to the rootstock; a term frequently used with roses.

Canopy: the total overhead area of a tree, including the branches and leaves.

Cold hardiness: the ability of a perennial plant (including trees, shrubs, and vines) to survive the minimum winter temperature in a particular area.

Complete fertilizer: powdered, liquid, or granular fertilizer with a balanced proportion of the three key nutrients—nitrogen (N), phosphorus (P), and potassium (K).

Composite: an inflorescence (cluster of flowers) also referred to as a head container petal and disk-like flowers. They are often daisylike with a flat (disk-like flowers) center and petal-like flowers surrounding the outside.

Compost: decomposed organic matter added to the soil to improve its drainage and ability to retain moisture.

Corm: a modified bulb-like stem. It is swollen, short, solid, and located underground. Crocus and gladiolus are two such plants.

Crown: (a) the point where the stems and roots meet. Located at, or just below the soil surface. (b) the top part of the tree.

Cultivar: a CULTIvated VARiety. A unique form of a plant that has been identified as special or superior and has been selected for propagation and sale.

Deadhead: to remove faded flowers from plants to improve their appearance, prevent seed production, and stimulate further flowering.

Deciduous plants: trees and shrubs that lose their leaves in the fall.

Desiccation: drying out of foliage, usually due to drought or wind.

Division: splitting apart perennial plants to create several smaller rooted segments. The practice is useful for controlling a plant's size and for acquiring more plants.

Dormancy: the period, usually the winter, when perennial plants temporarily cease active growth and rest. (The verb form is "dormant.")

Established: the point at which a newly planted tree, shrub, or flower has recovered from transplant shock and begins to grow. Often indicated by the production of new leaves or stems.

Evergreen: perennial plants that do not lose their foliage annually with the onset of winter. Needled or broadleaf foliage will persist and continues to function on a plant through one or more winters, aging and dropping unnoticed in cycles of one, two, three, or more.

Foliar: of or about foliage—usually refers to the practice of spraying foliage with fertilizer or pesticide for absorption by the leaves.

Floret: a small individual flower, usually one of many forming an inflorescence considered the blossom.

Germinate: to sprout. Germination is a fertile seed's first stage of development.

Graft (union): the point on the stem of a woody plant where a stem or bud of a desirable plant is placed onto a hardier root system. Roses, apples, and some ornamental trees are commonly grafted.

Hardscape: the permanent, structural, non-plant part of a landscape; such as walls, sheds, pools, patios, arbors, and walkways.

Herbaceous: plants having fleshy or soft stems that die back with frost; the opposite of woody.

Hybrid: a plant produced by crossing two different varieties, species or genera. Usually indicated with a × in the name such as Acer × fremanii.

Inflorescence: a cluster of flowers occurring at the tip of a stem. This includes such arrangements as umbels (Queen Anne's lace), composite or head (daisy), spike (salvia), raceme (snapdragon) and panicle (coral bells).

Mulch: a layer of material used to cover bare soil to conserve moisture, discourage weeds, moderate soil temperature, and prevent erosion and soil compaction. It may be inorganic (gravel, fabric) or organic (wood chips, bark, pine needles, chopped leaves).

Naturalize: (a) to plant seeds, bulbs, or plants in a random, informal pattern as they would appear in their natural habitat; (b) to adapt to and spread throughout natural areas and appear as if native to that location (a tendency of some non-native plants).

Nectar: the sweet fluid produced by glands on flowers that attract pollinators such as hummingbirds and honeybees for whom it is a source of energy.

Organic material, organic matter: any material or debris that is derived from plants.

Peat moss: organic matter from peat sedges (United States) or sphagnum mosses (Canada) often used to improve soil drainage and water holding abilities.

Perennial: a flowering plant that lives over two or more seasons. Many die back with frost, but their roots survive the winter and generate new shoots in the spring.

pH: a measurement of the relative acidity (low pH) or alkalinity (high pH) of soil or water based on a scale of 1 to 14, with 7 being neutral. Individual plants require soil to be within a certain range so that nutrients can dissolve in moisture and be available to them.

Pinch: to remove tender stems and/or leaves by pressing them between thumb and forefinger. This pruning technique encourages branching, compactness, and flowering in plants.

Pollen: the yellow, powdery grains in the center of a flower. A plant's male sex cells, they are transferred to the female plant parts by means of wind, bees, or other animal pollinators to fertilize them and create seeds.

Raceme: an arrangement of single stalked flowers along an elongated, unbranched stem.

Rhizome: a swollen energy-storing stem structure, similar to a bulb, that lies horizontally in the soil. Roots emerge from its lower surface and stems emerge from a growing point at or near its tip, as in bearded Iris.

Rootbound (or potbound): the condition of a plant that has been confined in a container too long, its roots are forced to wrap around themselves and even swell out of the container. Successful transplanting or repotting requires untangling and trimming away some of the matted roots.

Root flare: the transition at the base of a tree trunk where the bark tissue begins to differentiate and roots begin to form just before entering the soil. This area should not be covered with soil when planting a tree.

Self-seeding: the tendency of some plants to sow their seeds freely around the yard. It creates many seedlings the following season that may or may not be welcome.

Semievergreen: tending to be evergreen in a mild climate but deciduous in a harsher one.

Shearing: the pruning technique whereby plant stems and branches are cut uniformly with long-bladed pruning shears (hedge shears) or powered hedge trimmers. It is used when creating and maintaining hedges and topiary.

Slow-acting (slow-release) fertilizer: fertilizer that is water insoluble and releases its nutrients when acted on by soil temperature, moisture, and/or related microbial activity. Typically granular, it may be organic or synthetic.

Succulent growth: the sometimes undesirable production of fleshy, water-storing leaves or stems that results from overfertilization.

Sucker: a new growing shoot. Underground plant roots produce suckers to form new stems and spread by means of these suckering roots to form large plantings, or colonies. Some plants produce root suckers or branch suckers as a result of pruning or wounding.

Tuber: a thickened portion of underground stem used for energy storage and reproduction. Irish potato is a tuber.

Tuberous root: a swollen root with one point of growth where stem joins the root. Sweet potatoes and dahlias grow from tuberous roots.

Variegated: having various colors or color patterns. The term usually refers to plant foliage that is streaked, edged, blotched, or mottled with a contrasting color, often green with yellow, cream, or white.

White grubs: fat, off-white, worm-like larvae of Japanese and other beetles. They live in the soil and feed on plant (especially grass) roots until summer when they emerge as beetles to feed on plant foliage.

Wings: (*a*) the corky tissue that forms edges along the twigs of some woody plants such as winged euonymus; (*b*) the flat, dried extension of tissue on some seeds, such as maple, that catch the wind and help them disseminate.

BIBLIOGRAPHY

Brickell, Christopher, and Judith D. Zuk, ed. *The American Horticultural Society: A-Z Encyclopedia of Garden Plants.* DK Publishing, Inc., New York, NY, 1997.

Brickell, Christopher, and David Joyce. *The American Horticultural Society: Pruning and Training.* DK Publishing, Inc., New York, NY, 1996.

Browne, Jim, William Radler, and Nelson Sterner, ed. *Rose Gardening.* Pantheon Books, New York, 1995.

Coombes, Allen J. *Dictionary of Plant Names.* Timber Press, Portland, OR, 1993.

Curtis, John T. *The Vegetation of Wisconsin.* The University of Wisconsin Press, 1978.

Dirr, Michael A. *Manual of Woody Landscape Plants, 4th edition.* Stipes Publishing Co., Urbana, IL, 1990.

DiSabato-Aust, Tracy. *The Well-Tended Perennial Garden.* Timber Press, Portland, Oregon, 1998.

Fell, Derek. *Annuals.* HP Books, Los Angeles, CA, 1983.

Martin, Laura. *The Folklore of Trees and Shrubs.* The Globe Pequot Press, Chester, Connecticut, 1992.

Reilly, Ann. *Park's Success with Seeds.* Geo. W. Park Seed Co., Inc., Greenwood, South Carolina, 1978.

Schneider, Donald. *Park's Success with Bulbs.* Geo. W. Park Seed Co., Inc., Greenwood, South Carolina, 1981.

Still, Steven M. *Manual of Herbaceous Plants, 4th Edition.* Stipes Publishing Company, Urbana, IL, 1994.

Wisconsin Department of Natural Resources. *Wisconsin's Champion Trees.* 1998.

Wyman, Donald. *Wyman's Gardening Encyclopedia.* Macmillan Publishing Co., Inc., New York, 1977.

INDEX

PHOTO CREDITS

Bill Adams: pp. 41

Liz Ball: pp. 24, 69, 80, 123, 182, 212

Cathy Barash: pp. 107

Mike Dirr: pp. 205, 209

Tom Eltzroth: pp. 9, 23, 25, 26, 27, 29, 31, 33, 35, 36, 37, 38, 40, 42, 43, 44, 49, 50, 52, 55, 57, 58, 61, 64, 65, 70, 71, 72, 74, 78, 83, 87, 88, 91, 92, 96, 99, 103, 108, 111, 114, 115, 119, 120, 125, 128, 130, 134, 136, 138, 139, 143, 145, 146, 147, 149, 158, 159, 162, 168, 173, 177, 179, 184, 185, 192, 193, 198, 203, 210, 217

Katie Elzer-Peters: pp. 59

Flower Fields: pp. 75

Pam Harper: pp. 160, 199

Dave MacKenzie: pp. 73

Melinda Myers: pp. 17, 28, 45, 53, 54, 62, 68, 76, 77, 81, 82, 84, 94, 95, 97, 100, 101, 109, 112, 113, 117, 121, 126, 131, 132, 133, 140, 141, 142, 148, 150, 151, 153, 154, 155, 156, 161, 163, 164, 166, 167, 169, 170, 171, 174, 176, 178, 180, 183, 187, 188, 190, 191, 194, 195, 196, 197, 201, 202, 213, 214

National Garden Bureau: pp. 46

Jerry Pavia: pp. 6, 10, 13, 15, 18, 22, 30, 32, 34, 39, 47, 48, 51, 56, 60, 66, 67, 79, 85, 93, 98, 102, 104, 105, 106, 118, 122, 124, 127, 129, 135, 137, 144, 152, 157, 165, 172, 175, 181, 189, 200, 206, 207, 215, 216, 218, 219

Ralph Snodsmith: pp. 63, 116

Andre Viette: pp. 110, 211

Mike Wendt: pp. 186, 204

David Winger: pp. 208

MEET
MELINDA MYERS

Nationally known gardening expert, TV and radio host, author, and columnist Melinda Myers has more than thirty years of horticulture experience. She has written more than twenty gardening books, including *Can't Miss Small Space Gardening*, *The Garden Book for Wisconsin*, *Minnesota Gardener's Guide*, *Month-by-Month Gardening in Wisconsin*, the *Perfect Lawn* Midwest series, as well as the upcoming *Midwest Gardener's Handbook* and *Michigan Getting Started Garden Guide*.

In addition to authoring books, Myers hosts the nationally syndicated "Melinda's Garden Moment" segments that air on over 115 TV and radio stations throughout the United States. She is also the instructor for *The Great Course How to Grow* DVD series. Myers is a columnist and contributing editor for *Birds & Blooms* magazine and writes the twice monthly "Gardeners' Questions" newspaper column. She also has a column in *Gardening How-to* magazine and *Wisconsin Gardening* magazine. Melinda hosted *The Plant Doctor* radio program for over twenty years as well as seven seasons of *Great Lakes Gardener* on PBS. She has written articles for *Better Homes and Gardens* and *Fine Gardening* magazines, and was a columnist and contributing editor for *Backyard Living* magazine. Melinda has a master's degree in horticulture, is a certified arborist, and was a horticulture instructor with tenure. Melinda Myers's many accomplishments include starting the Master Gardener program in Milwaukee County and winning two Garden Media Awards (a Garden Globe Award for radio talent and a Quill and Trowel Award for her television work), both from the Garden Writers Association. She has also won the American Horticultural Society's B.Y. Morrison Communication Award for effective and inspirational communication. Melinda was the first woman inducted into the Wisconsin Green Industry Federation Hall of Fame.

Visit with Melinda at her website www.melindamyers.com.